D1085516

PHYSICAL ACTIVITY IN HUMAN EXPERIENCE

Interdisciplinary Perspectives

Sponsored by the Canadian Fitness and Lifestyle Research Institute
With the Support of Health Canada

James E. Curtis
University of Waterloo

Storm J. Russell
Canadian Fitness and Lifestyle Research Institute

HUMAN KINETICS

Library of Congress Cataloging-in-Publication Data

Physical activity in human experience : interdisciplinary perspectives
/ James E. Curtis, Storm J. Russell, editors ; sponsored by Canadian
Fitness and Lifestyle Research Institute.
     p.   cm.
  Includes index.
  ISBN 0-87322-765-4
  1. Physical education and training. 2. Physical education and
training--Social aspects. 3. Physical education and training-
-Psychological aspects. 4. Physical education and training-
-Political aspects. I. Curtis, James, E. II. Russell, Storm J.,
1952- . III. Canadian Fitness & Lifestyle Research Institute.
GV342.P43   1997
796--dc20   96-8065
                                   CIP

ISBN: 0-87322-765-4

Acquisitions Editor: Richard D. Frey; **Developmental Editor**: Marni Basic; **Assistant
Editors**: Susan Moore, John Wentworth, Erin Cler; **Editorial Assistant**: Amy Carnes;
Copyeditor: Mike Ryder; **Proofreader**: Karen Bojda; **Indexer**: Theresa Schaefer; **Graphic
Artist**: Sandra Meier; **Text Designer**: Robert Reuther; **Cover Designer**: Stuart Cartwright;
Illustrator: Studio 2-D; **Printer**: Braun-Brumfield, Inc.

Printed in the United States of America   10 9 8 7 6 5 4 3 2 1

Human Kinetics
Web site: http://www.humankinetics.com/

United States: Human Kinetics, P.O. Box 5076, Champaign, IL 61825-5076
1-800-747-4457
e-mail: humank@hkusa.com

Canada: Human Kinetics, Box 24040, Windsor, ON N8Y 4Y9
1-800-465-7301 (in Canada only)
e-mail: humank@hkcanada.com

Europe: Human Kinetics, P.O. Box IW14, Leeds LS16 6TR, United Kingdom
(44) 1132 781708
e-mail: humank@hkeurope.com

Australia: Human Kinetics, 57A Price Avenue, Lower Mitcham, South Australia 5062
(08) 277 1555
e-mail: humank@hkaustralia.com

New Zealand: Human Kinetics, P.O. Box 105-231, Auckland 1
(09) 523 3462
e-mail: humank@hknewz.com

CONTENTS

FOREWORD

Most social movements begin as small stirrings in people's day-to-day lives. As a fitness leader and trainer of fitness professionals, I first noticed such stirrings in relation to physical activity during the mid-1970s, when both leaders and participants in fitness programs began to question whether their programs were meeting Canadians' needs. At a practical level, their questions were based on emerging trends.

- New findings confirmed the benefits of low-intensity physical activity, supporting activity choices such as gardening, folk dancing, and walking as legitimate forms of exercise.
- The growing self-help movement encouraged Canadians to think about physical activity in a positive, holistic context, that is, with respect to mental, emotional, and spiritual health.
- A rise in consumer confidence encouraged people to demand partnerships with experts in health and fitness rather than accept subservient relationships. Canadians wanted to develop their own prescriptions for fitness based on their personal life situations and preferences rather than relying on fitness professionals for direction.
- Middle-aged baby boomers began to look for lifelong physical activity options that were both beneficial and enjoyable.

These trends had a significant impact on people's perceptions of physical activity. The initial promise had been clear: If you exercised vigorously for 20 to 30 minutes, a minimum of three times a week, you would become fit, your health would improve, and you would feel better, look better, and have more energy. Although millions of Canadians and Americans accepted the truth of that basic promise and experienced its benefits, the reality of their day-to-day lives throughout the late '70s and '80s began to demand a more flexible and inclusive approach with less emphasis on mechanical measurement of heart rates and exercise. They wanted physical activity to be an integral part of their lifestyles and work settings.

The stirrings in the field of fitness were part of a much larger evolution in people's perceptions of the world. The Western values of rational science and consumerism, which had dominated the '50s and '60s, were giving way to a holistic and participatory worldview that embraced environmental consciousness, community participation, sport and health for all, feminism, and individual empowerment. The concept of active living was a natural outgrowth of that evolution.

An important sign of the emergence of this concept appeared at the Canadian Summit on Fitness, initiated by Fitness Canada in 1986, when meeting participants adopted a broader meaning of fitness as an individual's state of *total* well-being—physical, mental, emotional, spiritual, and social. This helped establish the need for a new perspective on physical activity. As the Assistant Deputy Minister for Fitness and Amateur Sport in Canada commented in 1992,[1]

> A very clear message and recommendation came out of the 1986 Canadian Summit on Fitness—the message that fundamental change was required in our traditional view of fitness. Delegates to this important conference pointed out that the exclusive focus on cardiovascular endurance, flexibility, and muscular strength was extremely limiting. They reminded us that fitness was not just physiological fitness, but total fitness—physical, mental, social, and spiritual. They also tied fitness to daily living patterns and expressed a need for a more inclusive approach to promoting physical activity. And they recommended that individuals, industry and social institutions work together to ensure that physical activity and optimal well-being could become an integral part of life in this country—a Canadian cultural trademark.

The summit conference initiated a developmental process that involved a conceptual paper, contributed by the Canadian fitness community, that would capture the spirit of people's thinking. As one of the draftees of the paper, I was impressed by the collaborative energy that went into the process: Regional representatives provided extensive input; position papers were developed and discussed; a national workshop explored the concept of active living; and an international conference contributed to its understanding and evolution. In 1991, Fitness Canada published the results of these reflections in a conceptual overview of active living.

This working document described active living as a way of life in which physical activity is valued and integrated into daily life—a description which emerged from the search for a concept that could embrace all the dimensions of physical activity and be both experiential and dynamic. The description[2] emphasized the following three principles:

Active living is individual. There is no single best way to live actively. People are active for many reasons—play, work achievement, health, creative and cultural expression, contemplation, personal development, and social interaction. While experts can provide information and guidance in support of specific actions, the participant, not an outside expert, is in the best position to decide how to live actively and also to judge the worth of the activity.

Active living is social. People live in complex societies; social institutions and cultural traditions play a central role in how physical activities are conducted and experienced. Therefore, living actively is not simply a matter of personal preference. To integrate active living into Canadian society there is a need for systems, processes, and institutions that are responsive to the changing needs, aspirations, and values of Canadians.

Active living is inclusive. Active living takes many forms and involves a wide range of experiences, thus providing ways for people to express who they are as individuals or as groups. Physical activity should be accessible to all Canadians, regardless of ability, age, gender, race, ethnicity, religion, socioeconomic status, education level, or geographic environment.

Six years after the first Summit on Fitness, delegates at the 1992 Fall Forum integrated the notion of active living into a vision for the movement. This vision describes active living as

a visible and important expression of Canadian culture, wherein:

- all Canadians have access to equitable opportunities for active living, appropriate to their age, gender, language, heritage, ability, and socioeconomic status;

- a broad range of physical activity choices are available to meet individual needs and preferences;

- active living plays an important role in personal development and lifelong learning;

- all partners are committed to providing a safe, supportive, and sustainable environment for active living; and

- active living spans all facets of daily life including work, education, family life, and leisure.[3]

Within this forum, the active living movement began to take more substantive shape. Fitness Canada had already confirmed the need for comprehensive, reflective work to explore the many dimensions of active living and delve into the implications of its promotion and integration for individuals and groups in Canadian culture. This book provides another essential piece in the ongoing process of understanding this larger perspective on physical activity.

Because active living is a relatively new concept, it will take time to demystify the idea, explore it thoughtfully, develop a knowledge base, and discover ways to make it both practical and attainable. Each of the contributors to this book has accepted part of this challenge—their chapters explore the implications of a broad conceptual approach to physical activity and, as such, are essential building blocks in the conceptual development of active living.

Being involved as a writer, leader, and trainer in the physical activity field over the past 25 years has meant being part of this evolution in thought—a stimulating and rewarding experience. It is important for all of us involved to acknowledge, support, and strengthen the small stirrings that began so many years ago and have developed into such a strong movement. The emergence of the active living concept was an important turning point. This volume is another significant event—the first comprehensive look at active living by an interdisciplinary group of academics—a "must read" for all those interested in deepening their understanding of this concept. It is worth wondering where this evolutionary movement will lead us over the next 25 years.

Dorothy Strachan
Ottawa, Canada

Notes

[1]Lyle Makosky (1994). "The Active Living Concept", Toward Active Living. Proceedings of the International Conference on Physical Activity, Fitness, and Health. H. Arthur Quinney, Lise Gauvin, A.E. Wall (Eds.). Champaign, IL: Human Kinetics. p. 272, adapted.

[2]Active Living: A Conceptual Overview. Ottawa: Government of Canada, Fitness and Amateur Sport. 199, p. 10, 11, adapted.

[3]Unpublished report of the Active Living Assembly, October 29-31, 1993, Fern Resort, Orillia.

PREFACE

The idea for this book grew out of discussions that originated in North America in the mid-1980s. Around that time, questions began to emerge about the way in which we were promoting physical activity and fitness in the general population. Research in the social sciences had shown that approximately 50 percent of participants in a typical supervised exercise program dropped out within 6 to 12 months.[1] The work of Blair and others in the biological sciences had contradicted the prevalent, relatively narrow "exercise prescription" for protection against cardiovascular disease—that is, 20 minutes of vigorous aerobic activity at least three times a week to obtain cardiovascular health benefits—by demonstrating that regular, *moderate* exercise indeed had measurable health benefits.[2] The psychological and other benefits of regular physical activity were becoming increasingly apparent, again broadening both the scope and area for research and debate.

Findings such as these prompted policy makers and researchers to reconsider and reevaluate current approaches to understanding and promoting physical activity. Government-supported intervention strategies, such as "Active Living" in Canada, "Exercise Lite" in the United States, and "Life—Be In It" in Australia, emerged and seemingly "legitimized" popular participation in a far broader range of both moderate and vigorous physical activities. Meetings such as the first International Conference on Exercise, Fitness and Health held in Toronto in 1988 and the later International Conference on Physical Activity, Fitness and Health, also held in Toronto in 1992, were convened, and issues related to "dose-response," exercise adherence, measurement of activity, and appropriate operational definitions for terms like physical activity, active living, and exercise became subjects for frequent and sometimes vigorous debate. The rapidly growing body of research on physical activity provoked considerable discussion, which spilled across disciplines and involved researchers and practitioners alike.

While this discussion continues within each of the various disciplines comprising the physical activity sciences, few attempts have been made to date to examine specifically human physical activity from a broader, holistic, interdisciplinary perspective, as embodied by concepts like active living. Yet it seems that we are indeed moving irrevocably and justifiably toward a broader conception of human physical activity as being associated in multiple, complex ways with an equally broad range of outcomes and variables. In this scenario, increased interaction and critical discussion between scholars in the various subfields and disciplines of the physical activity sciences becomes crucial.

A central aim of this volume, then, is to foster a critical, informed, cross-disciplinary discussion of the implications of a broader approach to the study of physical activity. We believe strongly that there is a need for a comprehensive, critical, interdisciplinary examination of the implications of a broader holistic approach for research in physical activity, as well as for practice and ongoing policy development in health and physical activity.

To address these issues, we invited prominent researchers and scholars from the wide range of disciplines comprising the physical activity sciences to contribute their thoughts, knowledge, and insights on active living and physical activity. Together, they have delivered, in no short measure, a unique, substantial contribution to the field of the physical activity sciences, one which addresses far-ranging issues related to the biological aspects of active living; the phenomenological experience of human activity and personal growth; the social psychology of physical activity; sociological, historical, and cultural perspectives on active living; economic approaches to the study of physical activity; and the interaction between active living and the environment.

For my colleague and co-editor Jim Curtis and me, developing the volume has been both rewarding and refreshing. The opportunity to work together with these scholars has enriched our understanding and provided new insights and directions. We have realized once again the need to encourage close links between researchers, scholars, administrators, and professionals working in all areas of the expanding and diverse field of physical activity science. We reiterate the importance and unique contribution of an interdisciplinary and holistic study of physical activity and active living. Finally, we propose that we need to take stock periodically, to move beyond the disciplinary boundaries that define and at times constrain our greater understanding of physical activity in human experience. We need to turn our collective efforts to integrating research and knowledge, so that when we examine each part of the picture we do not lose sight of the whole. The contributors to this volume have directed their attention to this important task, and it is the product of their efforts that we can now read and appreciate.

Storm J. Russell

Notes

[1]Dishman, R.K. (Ed.). (1988). *Exercise adherence: Its impact on public health.* Champaign, IL: Human Kinetics.

[2]Blair, S.N., Wells, C.L., Weathers, R.D., & Paffenbarger, R. (1994). Chronic disease: The physical activity and dose-response controversy. In R.K. Dishman (Ed.), *Advances in exercise adherence.* Champaign, IL: Human Kinetics.

ACKNOWLEDGMENTS

We want to express our sincere appreciation to the seven scholars whose work appears in this volume. This is largely their book, and they deserve our admiration and praise for providing us with seven important research perspectives—or windows—through which to observe the physical activity of human beings. Taken together, these perspectives provide the essentials necessary for a sound understanding of physical activity.

We are also indebted to numerous other individuals who provided us with valuable assistance of various types. The following scholars from a number of fields gave the authors helpful comments on their draft chapters, initially prepared for a workshop held in Ottawa: Morris Barer (University of British Columbia), Rob Beamish (Queen's University), Stephen Birch (McMaster University), Jay Coakley (University of Colorado), Peter Donnelly (McMaster University), Lise Gauvin (Concordia University), Geoffrey Godbey (Pennsylvania State University), Gaston Godin (Laval University), Steven Hardy (University of New Hampshire), John Kelly (University of Illinois), Robert Malina (Michigan State University), Stephen McCool (University of Montana), Klaus Meier (University of Western Ontario), James Skinner (Indiana University), and Geoffrey Wall (University of Waterloo).

Hart Cantelon (Queen's University), Léo-Paul Bordeleau (University of Ottawa), and Barry McPherson (Wilfrid Laurier University) also provided valuable input at the Ottawa workshop. Professors Cantelon and Bordeleau's contributions to the workshop will be published in a special series of Scientific and Technical Reports produced annually by the Canadian Fitness and Lifestyle Research Institute. Professor McPherson's observations are included in the closing remarks at the end of this volume.

Christine Cameron, at the Canadian Fitness and Lifestyle Research Institute (CFLRI), very ably prepared the manuscript for the volume, handled correspondence, arranged meetings for the authors, and generally provided help whenever it was needed. She deserves our special thanks. At Human Kinetics, Richard Frey gave strong support to the project, and Marni Basic gave valuable assistance in moving the manuscript through the editorial and production stages.

Finally, we gratefully acknowledge the financial support of the CFLRI and Health Canada. In particular, we thank Cora Lynn Craig,

CFLRI president, and Art Quinney, past chair of the CFLRI Board, for their commitment and valuable input throughout all stages of the project's development. Special thanks also to the staff of Fitness Canada for their keen interest in the volume.

INTRODUCTION

Storm J. Russell
and James E. Curtis

In recent years, increasingly urgent calls have been made by practitioners and policy makers for research and theory that links and explains the multitude of findings emerging from the various disciplines and subdisciplines of the physical activity sciences. In particular, the need for valid models and information to assist in the development of effective health policy is becoming a priority for governments now struggling to cope financially and politically with rapidly rising health care costs. The positive role of physical activity in relation to population health is well-documented, and accordingly, as national health bills continue to escalate, governments are turning more of their attention to examining those factors which promote active living and healthy lifestyles among the general population. In turn, pressure has increased on academic communities to produce holistic, interdisciplinary approaches to active living, which explain the precedents, outcomes, and correlates of physical activity and provide direction to governments in formulating an integrated set of effective health and social policies.

In North America, recognition of this need for integrated, holistic models of human physical activity has led the Canadian government to sponsor and host the International Conference on Exercise, Fitness and Health, the associated Consensus Symposium in 1988, and the International Conference and Consensus Symposium on Physical Activity, Fitness and Health, held in Toronto in 1992. Similarly, in the United States, the President's Council on Physical Activity and Sport, the U.S. Centers for Disease Control, and the American College of Sports Medicine recently brought together a group of leading researchers to review the scientific evidence and formulate policy recommendations related to physical activity and individual and public health.

Consultation among national governments, national organizations, and the academic community on the topic of physical activity and population health has resulted in the emergence of such concepts as "Active Living" in Canada, "Exercise Lite" in the United States, and "Life—Be In It" in Australia, to name a few. Such notions differ substantially from earlier approaches to thinking about physical activity (e.g., as it relates to cardiovascular "fitness") and extol a far wider range of physical, psychological, social, and (more recently) environmental benefits known to be associated with a physically active life. These newer concepts also share many similarities with the popular "Sport-for-All" movement, which has grown steadily in Europe and the United Kingdom since the 1950s. Many of these notions also have a sociopolitical dimension, emphasizing mass participation, inclusion, and the democratization of sport and physical activity.

The trend toward integrated models and holistic thinking evident in current national health strategies and policies pertaining to physical activity and active living, however, is not reflected in any significant degree in the halls of our universities or our research laboratories. On one hand, there has been a virtual explosion of research and theory in the physical activity sciences over the past three decades, and our knowledge of many aspects of physical activity has expanded exponentially in recent years. Yet, at the same time—perhaps necessarily, given the sheer volume of available information—there has been an increasing specialization within the various subfields and disciplines that comprise the physical activity sciences. Our research efforts and thinking have been characterized by a certain disciplinary linearity; research problems tend to be defined narrowly and remain very specific to a particular discipline. Broad, interdisciplinary studies and conceptual approaches are rare and present considerable challenges to scholars and researchers who venture beyond the relative comfort of their own disciplinary boundaries.

This book attempts to fill the need for a critical, interdisciplinary discussion of physical activity in human experience. It presents the results of a project in which seven scholars who have studied human physical activity intensively within different research disciplines were assembled to prepare and present papers on the insights on activity arrived at in their fields. These papers form chapters 1 through 7 of this book.

Each of the contributors was given two objectives: (1) to provide a comprehensive overview of the state of knowledge on human physical activity in their field and (2) to show how the knowledge concerning physical activity developed in the field helps contribute to a broad, multifield, interdisciplinary conception of physical activity. As the reader will discover, the authors have delivered in strong measure on both tasks, providing a veritable feast of information and interesting interpretations of physical activity while crossing disciplinary boundaries to form a holistic view of physical activity for the individual and society.

Each chapter is preceded by a section entitled "In Perspective," in which the authors comment on the progress of their research and thinking over the course of their careers and offer thoughts and observations on the development of the field as a whole. These statements highlight major research trends in the authors' fields. They also provide rare insights into the way researchers' ideas develop and change over time in response to the broader academic milieu and as a function of personal experience. As such, these pieces provide a personal and philosophical context for each author's contribution to a broader interdisciplinary study of physical activity and active living.

The contributors are eminent scholars from seven disciplines: (1) biology and physical science, (2) psychology, (3) social psychology, (4) social history and cultural studies, (5) sociology, (6) economics, and (7) environmental studies.

In general, the physical and biological sciences study physical activity in terms of physical and biological processes and analyze the biological antecedents and consequences of physical activity. Professor Claude Bouchard's chapter, based on this type of research, looks particularly at the outcomes of physical activity and relationships among physical activity, fitness, and health. For example, some of his own research has shown that there are marked individual differences in responses to physical activity and in the fitness and health yields of activity, and that these phenomena appear to be rooted in genetic factors. However, like all other contributors to this volume, Bouchard finds that he cannot limit himself to strictly physical or biological variables for a thorough, expansive explanation of the phenomena of physical activity. His wide-ranging analysis asks us to consider issues in human evolution: how physical activity, active living, health, and fitness are "structured" by the social institutions of work and leisure; and how social policy measures and researchers' theories of physical activity can affect the fitness and health of the population.

In the second chapter, Professor Mihaly Csikszentmihalyi explores some of the same issues addressed by Bouchard, among many others, from the perspective of psychology. This approach involves focusing on the individual—his or her activity and cognitions, perceptions, and feelings. Csikszentmihalyi suggests that we label some of the cognitive, perceptual, and affective aspects of activity as "spiritual." He further argues that one major consequence of the psychological approach is that we should understand most activity to be, above all, *voluntary* or volitional, and we must explore the consequences of this defining

characteristic of activity. Another implication of the psychological perspective is that we should view the person's activity patterns as only
partially "physical," at least as far as our common understanding of that
term goes. Activity is always much more—cognitive, perceptual, and
emotional. Csikszentmihalyi presents findings on the proportionate
place of "physical activity" among all of the activities of people's
everyday lives. He also spells out the positive psychological consequences for the individual of particular forms of activity high in "complexity." Further, he emphasizes that activity affects both the individual
and society. He comes to the conclusion that, for both individuals and
societies, "we are what we do and become what we have done."

Professor Leonard Wankel's chapter pursues relevant social psychological literature. This approach focuses on the interaction of the individual and his or her surrounding social environment. This, of course,
is not unlike Csikszentmihalyi's approach, but Wankel emphasizes two
quite different types of research: (1) studies on the social situations and
individual characteristics that best predict people's becoming and stay-
ing involved in physical activity, and (2) studies of the various psychological outcomes of physical activity. This material, too, leads to the
conclusion that, for any full understanding of the phenomena of active
living, a narrowly conceived view of "physical activity" is inadequate;
also relevant are physical processes, psychological processes, social
situations, and more.

Chapters 4 through 6 focus even more intently on physical activity
and active living in the broader social and cultural context. Professor
Nancy Theberge's chapter explores research from the sociological approach. This perspective deals with the ways social groups and society
are organized and how some aspects of the society or group affect other
aspects. As Theberge shows, the central issues for research and theory
when this approach is applied to the study of active living are (1) the
social categories of people who most get involved in physical activity
and sports, and those who do not; (2) exclusionary practices in sport,
applied to women and other social groups; (3) sport as an arena of
resistance, and empowerment, for disadvantaged groups; (4) popular
views on "the body," and the consequences for people's involvement in
physical activity; (5) the respective roles of the state (government and
related institutions), capital, and the media in structuring the way sport
and physical activity are organized in society; and (6) "commodification"
and "consumerism" in the areas of physical activity and fitness.

The economic approach is akin to the sociological approach in that
social relationships are emphasized, but this time a central issue is the
cost-benefit relationship. The economic approach can also be quite
individualistic and incorporate social psychology, with a focus on the

choices of individual consumers who think in terms of costs and benefits. For example, the choices of individuals to pursue or forego physical activity opportunities, and how costs and benefits vary for different choices, are of concern to the economist studying physical activity. The chapter by Professor Louise Russell illustrates this approach. She also emphasizes that an analog of an individual's cost-benefit comparisons can be pursued by groups or organizations—say government bodies. The study of this process is called *cost-effectiveness analysis*. For example, the analyses might involve "benefits" expressed as recreational activities provided, cases of illness avoided, or years of lives saved. Government policy makers and politicians are the decision makers—the "consumers" or "choosers." Russell details how cost-effectiveness analyses of programs promoting physical activity may be undertaken using life expectancy rates as a measure of "effects." A detailed analysis of the effects of jogging activity shows the utility of cost-effectiveness analysis. Russell also discusses some of the challenges associated with examining economic impacts in the context of a broader definition of physical activity and active living.

Professor Rick Gruneau's chapter discusses physical activity from the perspective of social history and cultural studies. This approach focuses on the fact that all societies have cultures—shared beliefs, values, and norms—that shape patterns of behavior in society. People are the creators of culture, and culture, in turn, influences people's shared perceptions and actions. This perspective holds, further, that culture changes over time and, in the process, changes the organization of the society. This approach is not unlike the broad psychological approach used by Csikszentmihalyi, who describes how people shape their social environment and vice versa. Nor is it unlike the sociological approach of Theberge, wherein developments in the economy, the state, and media are linked to the perception of fitness. However, Gruneau's approach squarely emphasizes the historical sweep of culture, including reasons for cultural changes and the way they shape perceptions of activity. Gruneau demonstrates how ideals of active living and the body have changed quite markedly over the centuries. He discusses theory and evidence on how current conceptions of activity and the body are deeply rooted in ideological aspects of Protestantism, industrial capitalism, and the development of the modern state. Among other things, he argues that the most significant cultural aspect of the current century for understanding approaches to physical activity is the "marketing of the body" to a consumer society.

The final chapter is Professor Thomas Burton's review of theory and research from the environmental approach. His emphasis is upon the reciprocal relationships between the physical environment and people's beliefs and activities. When Burton applies this approach to the phenomena of physical activities, he finds three broad areas of research to be especially illuminating: (1) studies of people's environmental attitudes; (2) work on the impact of recreational activities on the environment; and (3) work on approaches to management of the environment for recreational activity. In the process, we also learn much about approaches to "sustainable living" and the relevant roles of physical activity and the locations for recreational activity.

Whether taken separately or as a group, the seven chapters reinforce the idea that a multifield, interdisciplinary approach to physical activity yields a much more thorough and solid understanding of physical activity than does a narrow approach based only on one or two fields or disciplines. The chapters show that human physical activity implies much more than simply biological or physical considerations, or simply psychological, sociological, cultural, economic, or environmental considerations. The book argues that we are best informed if we adopt a broad, *holistic* approach to physical activity. Such an approach spans the seven traditional fields of study listed above, including insights from each of them, and features interdisciplinary research.

In preparing this volume, we chose what are generally agreed to be central fields for a comprehensive understanding of physical activity. However, we could easily have gone beyond the seven major disciplines in our pursuit of material on physical activity. Practical considerations, including keeping the length of the book within reasonable limits, demanded that we omit representation from other research fields. In particular, we have not included chapters which focus specifically on chemistry, sociobiology, health studies, and philosophy. Nevertheless, the contents of the book are of broad scope and, indeed, one can readily identify instances where various authors draw on one of these other areas for material.

We hope that readers of this book—whether you are students, experienced researchers, practitioners, or policy makers—come away with a clearer perspective on the scope and possibilities of a holistic study of physical activity, and that its contents contribute to the ongoing development of their own current and future work. We also trust that readers will enjoy the feast of information and thought-provoking discussion contained in the following chapters as much as we have enjoyed bringing it together.

In Perspective

BIOLOGICAL ASPECTS OF THE ACTIVE LIVING CONCEPT

Claude Bouchard

My research career began in the mid-1960s with an interest in exercise and growth and the development of children and adolescents. In the early 1970s, the focus of my work shifted to the effects of regular exercise on the cardiovascular system and performance capacity. My current interest in the causes of the individual differences in response to regular exercise can be traced to our laboratory's recent move to the spacious facilities in the Pavillon de L'Education Physique et des Sports on the campus of Laval University.

At that time, a series of studies based on the comparisons of trained versus sedentary persons of both genders, along with several other studies in which sedentary people were brought to the laboratory to train for weeks or months, were instrumental in my future career orientation. I became convinced that biological individuality in the response to regular exercise and in the benefits that can be derived therefrom was of the utmost importance. Needless to say, these studies were also relevant to the field of high-performance sport and detecting the performance potential of talented individuals. I also began to suspect that these individual differences were related to genetic variation. In the mid-1970s, having decided that I should learn more about human genetics as a source of human variation, I enrolled in a program of biological anthropology, which included human adaptability and population genetics as fields of study, at the University of Texas in Austin. There I had the opportunity to interact over a period of three years with human geneticists, molecular biologists, population geneticists, behavior geneticists, physical anthropologists, exercise scientists, and biochemists and to consult every day with my close friend and advisor, Robert M. Malina. I became more convinced than ever that I was on the right track. The major hurdle left was to translate these ideas into research projects and fundable grant applications.

In the late 1970s before it became possible to contemplate the study of genetic variation of complex human phenotypes at the DNA level, I developed a twin study design which required that identical twins be exposed to an intervention program so that the between-genotype and the within-genotype components of the variance in response could be quantified. We established a panel of families in order to investigate the genetic epidemiologic features of physical activity, fitness, body composition, and common risk-factor phenotypes. We learned a lot from these studies. Then the possibilities offered by the DNA technology changed dramatically: It became possible to establish stable cell lines for each individual of a cohort, to bank DNA, to identify specific sites of variation in a gene or in noncoding regions of the genome, to amplify a DNA fragment from one copy to a million and more, to type people for the number of repeated sequences or copies of DNA motives at a large number of sites distributed among the various chromosomes, and to employ a large and rapidly growing number of probes to assist in the detection of variation in candidate genes (presumed relevant to the response to regular exercise) and other anonymous markers.

These technologies and other molecular biology tools, along with the advances in genetic epidemiology and informatics applied to genetic issues, make it possible to identify the genes determining the response to regular exercise for a variety of health and performance-related phenotypes and to define precisely the DNA sequence variants responsible for these manifestations of biological individuality. These are exciting times. We now have the tools to understand why we are not all equally prone to certain common disease, to benefit from a low-fat diet, or to reduce the risk of morbidity or premature death through a physically active lifestyle. The task will not be easy; we are dealing with highly complex biological phenotypes that are influenced by a number of behaviors and social and environmental factors. But we have no choice—we need to understand better the fundamental biological mechanisms linking genes to lifestyle and to health.

I have had the privilege of being closely associated with my friends and colleagues Barry McPherson, Norm Gledhill, Art Salmon, Roy Shephard, Art Quinney, Tom Stephens, and the late John Sutton in the development of two international consensus conferences designed to examine the relationships between regular physical activity and health. These conferences and the publications derived from them have revealed that, even though heterogeneity in benefits from a physically active lifestyle is commonly observed, we are still ignorant about the causes of these individual differences. We hope that by the time of the third consensus meeting convened by Canadian scientists and clinicians we will be in a position to be more specific about the role of biological inheritance and DNA polymorphism with respect to health-related phenotypes and perhaps the process of improving health-related fitness.

Chapter 1

BIOLOGICAL ASPECTS OF THE ACTIVE LIVING CONCEPT

Claude Bouchard

Physical activity has been a major force in the evolution of Homo sapiens. Hunting, gathering, escaping, and fighting were essential actions for the survival of our ancestors. They had to throw, lift, carry, climb, walk, run, and perform all kinds of basic motor skills throughout their lives. They would not have reached reproductive age if they had poor endurance, lacked speed and power, and were clumsy. In other words, survival and reproductive success over tens of thousands of years required physical prowess. Darwinian fitness was closely associated with physical fitness in the early ages of our species. However, the reproductive capacity of modern-day humans is much less dependent upon the level of physical activity and ability than it used to be (Malina, 1991).

Physical activity has been ubiquitous throughout the ages of Man. Even though its specific manifestations change with time, physical activity remains embedded in religious rituals, warfare, games, occupations, personal chores, dance and other forms of artistic expression, and the exploration of unknown territories to the present century. This phenomenon in the evolution of humankind is highlighted in this chapter.

Homo sapiens has attempted for millennia to reduce the amount of muscular work and physical activity required in daily life. The war on manual labor has been a remarkable success. Thus, the amount of energy expended by individuals to ensure sustained food supply, decent housing under a variety of climatic conditions, safe and rapid transportation, personal and collective security, and diversified and abundant leisure activities has decreased. The decline in the amount of physical activity has been so dramatic that a variety of health problems, nurtured by a sedentary mode of life, are thought to have increased in the present century. These health problems were collectively referred to as "hypokinetic diseases" more than 30 years ago (Krauss & Raab, 1961). The present chapter addresses the issue of the relationships that exist among physical activity, sedentarism, fitness, and health.

As our primary interest lies in the biological aspects of active living, we will examine physical activity in terms of energy requirements and metabolic demands rather than from a behavioral perspective. Fitness will be discussed in a physical and physiological context rather than a psychological, social, or spiritual one (although these various dimensions of so-called total fitness are obviously interrelated). Health will be defined in a broad context but discussed mainly in terms of longevity, duration of life free from disease, risk factors, and morbidity. Finally, this chapter will discuss the limitations of the active living approach from the biological sciences point of view, as well as its implications for conceptual models and research in the physical activity sciences and biomedical sciences in general.

HOMO SAPIENS IN ACTION

Although debate persists about the time frame and circumstances of the emergence of Homo sapiens, those who accept the basic principles of Darwinian evolutionary theory commonly acknowledge that the emergence of Man was intimately related to progressive molecular changes in genes affecting brain functions of closely related nonhuman primates. The evolution of the brain led to not only greater brain capacity, progressive mastering of language, and more refined intelligence, but also growing control over an expanded movement repertoire. Drawing on the research of paleontologists, anatomists, archeologists, and, more recently, molecular biologists, the main events of the evolution of our species are here briefly outlined, with an emphasis on those that have implications for the physical activity domain.

The most important events in the evolutionary changes leading to modern Homo sapiens occurred within the last 10 million years. The exact details of these molecular events are still a matter of debate; however, the most important and critical episodes are faithfully registered within the human genome. Over millions of years, molecular alterations in the DNA of the germ cells of our primate ancestors led to small creatures, clearly hominid in appearance, which are collectively referred to as Australopithecus. Several species of Australopithecus were found in large numbers on the African continent 3 to 4 million years ago. They generally reached a stature of about 1.5 meters, with a brain size approximately 40 percent of that of modern Homo sapiens. About 2.5 million years ago, Homo habilis, a more closely related ancestor of Homo sapiens, was present in the fossil record, followed about 1 million years later by Homo erectus. Archeological research in several areas of the planet have yielded numerous independent proofs for the presence of an ancestor of modern Homo sapiens about 200,000 years ago, and it has become clear that modern Homo sapiens was present in many parts of our world about 50,000 years ago.

During this long journey, under the influence of selective advantages resulting from alterations in the DNA of the gametes of some members of closely related nonhuman primates, Homo sapiens emerged through small, successive steps. It is difficult to establish the role played by motor ability and physical performance capacity in the evolutionary history of our species. Fossil records and molecular biology will probably never allow us to define these contributions in a precise manner. Comparative studies of DNA sequences and proteins indicate that biological differences between Homo sapiens and the most closely related nonhuman primates, such as chimpanzees and gorillas, are generally of the order of 5 percent and less. However, these relatively small molecular differences carry major functional and behavioral implications. Thus, humans have optimized several advantageous traits, such as upright position, bipedal locomotion, well-articulated thumbs for better hand prehension, vertical head position facilitating visual scanning, and refined language capacity, to name but a few. All of these characteristics had enormous selective advantages in the hostile environments prevailing during the human evolutionary journey. They conferred an improved capacity to walk and run, and to grasp, catch, and throw; and they also meant a greater performance potential in activities requiring precision, speed, strength, and endurance.

The emergence and spread of Homo sapiens probably involved conditions which required a high level of habitual physical activity, especially relative to today's standard. Further, performance capacity and motor skill must have played a major role in survival. One can easily imagine that the best performers succeeded in the quest for food and as defenders against animal predators and in times of conflict. The males among this elite may have contributed more genes to following generations than other males by imposing their wills on the fertile clanswomen. Likewise, fitness and performance capacities played an important role in the success of females, who were called upon to gather food, firewood, and other necessities while caring for the children. It seems clear that physical activity and performance capacity were important features during the evolutionary history of our species, conferring mating advantages to the carriers of the genes associated with these traits.

With the advent of communities, agriculture, and animal domestication, muscular work remained important. Strength, endurance, and skill became associated with economic success. Our ancestors learned to use various metals; the wheel was conceived; and tools of all kinds appeared to ease the burden of hunting, agriculture, and various domestic chores. Soon, some people began to have more leisure time. Indeed, archeological records have provided us with ample evidence of leisure activities in communities living 5,000 to 8,000 years ago in several parts of the world. Among these leisure activities, physical activities were quite popular: Iconographs and artifacts in the world's museums show evidence of foot races, throws, wrestling, dances, and hunting.

About three millennia ago, physical activities were popular in part because people believed that they influenced normal development and health. Elite performers were deified. In ancient Greece, the antique Olympic Games commenced around 776 BC and were intimately associated with the civilization of the time. For a while, physical activities flourished in a large segment of the human population. Abusive practices and wars changed this proclivity, and people were soon less interested in being active than in cheering gladiators and warriors, as they did in the Coliseum of ancient Rome. With the decline of the Roman Empire, the major Games almost disappeared.

During the next millennium, men and women remained interested in physical activities. Various types of games, tournaments, dances, and hunting expeditions captured the attention of the nobles and the wealthy. For most, however, physical activity meant long, hard work in order to subsist and satisfy a demanding master. Living conditions obviously had improved, but muscular work remained absolutely essential for the survival of most people. Numerous wars, well-documented in the annals of history, also tested the fitness levels and performance capacities of the soldiers and of the people caught between rival factions.

The Renaissance period, with its taste for beauty and knowledge, changed the world. Physical activities remained quite popular among both the prosperous and the poor. Games evolved, but remained largely influenced by preoccupations with war and hunting. Large tournaments became regular occurrences on the aristocrats' agenda. Dances were also highly popular with the nobility. Peasants continued working hard, but they also enjoyed wrestling matches, horse racing, archery competitions, and dances. All along, efforts to reduce physical exertion at work and when performing all kinds of chores went unabated. Jean Jacques Rousseau introduced proposals to revive the education of children that were quite compatible with the teachings of those who thought that physical activity should be part of the educational system. Sport soon appeared on the scene.

The struggle to free human beings from labor was a constant feature of this journey. It made very impressive gains around the period of the Industrial Revolution and, even more, in the present century, aided by the technological progress achieved in industrialized countries. Lately, however, the alarm bell was activated to propose that the reduction in the amount of physical work may have gone too far. The benefits of a physically active lifestyle have been compared with those of an inactive mode of life, and while all the evidence is not in, it seems that human beings are better off when they maintain a physically active lifestyle. This is certainly one of the most striking paradoxes emanating from the evolutionary and historical journey of Homo sapiens.

PHYSICAL ACTIVITY, FITNESS, AND HEALTH

There is no doubt that the relationships among physical activity, fitness, and health are highly complex. One way to make these relationships clear is to demonstrate the hierarchical relations among the major elements. Figure 1.1 is the result of such an attempt. It was produced for the 1988 International Consensus Conference on Physical Activity, Fitness and Health, held in Toronto (Bouchard, Shephard, Stephens, Sutton, & McPherson, 1990), and has been modified for the 1992 Consensus Symposium on the same topic (Bouchard & Shephard, 1993). The model defines the causal relationships among the various components, as well as the feedback loops and the endogenous and exogenous affectors.

The model specifies that habitual physical activity can influence fitness, which in turn may modify the level of habitual physical activity of the individual. For instance, the fittest individuals tend to be the most

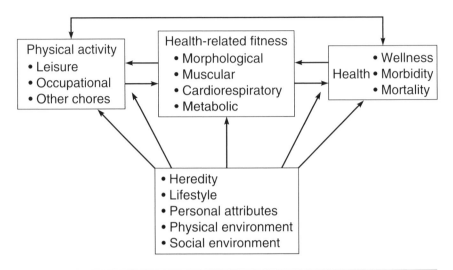

Figure 1.1 A model describing the complex relationships among physical activity, health-related fitness, and health status. Reprinted, by permission, from C. Bouchard and R.J. Shephard, 1993, Physical activity, fitness and health: A model and key concepts. In *Proceedings of the international consensus symposium on physical activity, fitness and health,* edited by C. Bouchard, R.J. Shephard, and T. Stephens (Champaign, IL: Human Kinetics), 78.

active and, with increasing fitness, people tend to become more active. The model also specifies that fitness is related to health in a reciprocal manner—that is, fitness not only influences health, but health status also influences both habitual physical activity and fitness. In reality, the relationships among the level of habitual physical activity, fitness, and health are more complex. Other factors are associated with individual differences in health status. Likewise, levels of fitness are not determined entirely by an individual's level of habitual physical activity. Other lifestyle components, the physical and social environment, personal attributes, and genetic characteristics also affect the major components of the basic model and their interrelationships.

PHYSICAL ACTIVITY

In the context of the model, physical activity comprises any body movement produced by the skeletal muscles that results in an increase in energy expenditure. We are particularly interested in leisure time physical activity, such as physically active leisure, exercise, sport, a variety of outdoor activities, and occupational work and other chores; that is, all activities that affect total daily energy expenditure.

Energy expenditure reflects the total metabolic processes and metabolic fuel oxidized to sustain life and to meet the demands imposed upon the organism. The most important elements of daily energy expenditure are the basal and resting metabolic rates, the energy expended for physical activity, and the thermic effect of food.

Basal and resting metabolism account for the largest proportion of the total daily energy expenditure, about 65 to 70 percent in sedentary people. The basal and resting metabolic rates are primarily determined by the fat-free mass of the individual (which is mainly skeletal muscle), and by the brain, liver, heart, and kidney metabolism. Basal metabolic rate per unit of fat-free body mass is highest in infancy, declines during growth (with a temporary small increase at puberty), remains quite stable for several decades, and then shows a slight decrease with advancing age. The thermic response to food is the energy expended above the resting metabolic rate following the ingestion of food. The thermogenic potential of proteins and carbohydrates is higher than that of dietary fat. On average, the thermic response to a meal over several hours reaches about 8 to 10 percent of the energy content of the food ingested.

Physical activity is the most variable component of total daily energy expenditure. Depending on the fitness of the individual, a 5- to 20-fold increase of resting metabolic rate can be sustained for a few minutes. Total daily energy expenditure is highly variable among human beings, with a range of about 5 to 6 MJ expended by sedentary old or sick persons, to as much as 30 to 40 MJ by highly active endurance athletes (Bouchard & Shephard, 1993).

Leisure Physical Activity

The average adult has about three to four hours of leisure or discretionary time per day, after completing work, commuting, domestic chores, and personal hygiene. However, there is considerable variation depending in part upon individual circumstances (Bouchard & Shephard, 1993). Leisure physical activity is an activity that leads to a significant increase in total daily energy expenditure. The element of personal choice is inherent in the definition. Activity is selected on the basis of personal needs and interests. In some instances, the motivation will be an improvement of health and/or physical fitness, but there are many other possible motivations (Kenyon, 1968; Dishman, 1990), including aesthetic (pursuit of a graceful body or an appreciation of the beauty of movement); ascetic (the setting of a personal physical challenge); the thrills of fast movement and physical danger; chance and competition; social contacts; fun; mental arousal; relaxation and détente; and perhaps even an addiction to endogenous opioids (Bouchard & Shephard, 1993).

Exercise. *Exercise* is a form of leisure physical activity that is usually performed on a repeated basis over an extended period of time (exercise training) with a specific external objective, such as the improvement of fitness, physical performance, or health. Occasionally, the optimal regimen is carefully prescribed for the individual by a physician or an exercise specialist (American College of Sports Medicine, 1990). The participant is advised to conform to the recommended mode, intensity, frequency, and duration of such activity.

The mode of exercise covers not only the type of activity to be performed (for instance, speed walking, jogging, or swimming), but also the temporal pattern of activity that is recommended (i.e., continuous or intermittent activity), with a detailed specification of the duration of exercise and rest periods in the case of intermittent activity. The issues of intensity, frequency, and duration of exercise are therefore of considerable importance to prescription and activity assessment.

The intensity of exercise can be expressed in either absolute or relative terms. The absolute intensity (for example, 20 kJ/minute) is frequently used when classifying participants in occupational and epidemiological studies. Alternatively, absolute data may be expressed as a multiple of the basal metabolic rate, or METS (Table 1.1). A third option is to express relative intensity as a percentage of the individual's maximal aerobic power output, maximal oxygen intake, or maximal heart rate. Intensity is the most difficult factor to control because it is relative to each person's maximal capacity, which varies greatly among individuals and for the same person with changes in age, fitness, and health.

The frequency of activity is normally reported as the number of sessions undertaken in a typical week. Frequency may vary with season and other factors. The duration of an individual exercise session is usually reported in minutes or in hours. Mode, intensity, frequency, and duration of activities are all critical determinants of the amount of energy expended over a given period of time.

Sport. *Sport* is defined as a form of physical activity that involves competition. The term may also embrace activities in a predominantly recreational context, with little or no competition.

Occupational Work

In the past, occupational work and the demands of transportation accounted for a major fraction of total daily energy expenditure. Heavy

Table 1.1
A Characterization of the Intensity of Leisure Activity

Categorization	Relative intensity (% $\dot{V}O_2$max)	Absolute intensity in METS			
		Young	*Middle-aged*	*Old*	*Very old*
Rest	<10	1.0	1.0	1.0	1.0
Light	<35	<4.5	<3.5	<2.5	<1.5
Fairly light	<50	<6.5	<5.0	<3.5	<2.0
Moderate	<70	<9.0	<7.0	<5.0	<2.8
Heavy	>70	>9.0	>7.0	>5.0	>2.8
Maximal	100	13.0	10.0	7.0	4.0

Reprinted, by permission, from C. Bouchard, R.J. Shephard, and T. Stephens et al., 1990, Exercise, fitness and health: The consensus statement. In *Exercise, fitness and health: A consensus of current knowledge*, edited by C. Bouchard et al. (Champaign, IL: Human Kinetics), 6.

work was typically sustained for about 40 hours per week over many years. Today, in the Western world, occupational categories with a high energy demand are not very numerous. Nonetheless, people from the lowest socioeconomic strata are often involved in jobs requiring the largest daily energy expenditure.

Other Chores

In developed societies, automation has progressively reduced the energy demands associated with the operation of a household. Most necessary domestic chores now fall into the "light" category. The one possible exception is the care of dependents. Both playing with young children and the nursing of elderly relatives can involve higher levels of energy expenditure.

Physical activity is almost universally accepted as relevant to health. However, many unanswered questions remain, and several issues are only partially resolved. For instance, we still do not know enough about the optimal combination of mode, intensity, frequency, and duration of activity with respect to health and wellness or specific health objectives. The cumulative impact of many years of participation remains to be elucidated. The interactions between regular physical activity and other lifestyle components, such as nutrition, sleeping habits, smoking, and alcohol consumption, are largely unknown. We are even more ignorant about individual differences in the sensitivity to an active mode of life in terms of health outcomes.

Habitual Physical Activity

The concept of habitual physical activity has been present in the exercise and epidemiology literature for decades. By definition, it encompasses information on leisure physical activity, exercise, sports, occupational work, and other chores to assess the overall level of regular engagement in physical activity. This is not easily achieved, however, because of methodological difficulties in assessing the pattern of activity over defined periods of time. Nonetheless, the concept of habitual physical activity as an integrator of the amount of energy expended for activity is very useful.

Habitual physical activity is commonly assessed through interviews, questionnaires, diaries, mechanical devices such as pedometers, accelerometers, and other instruments, or continuous heart rate recordings over hours or days (Tremblay & Bouchard, 1987). More recently, stable isotopes have been used to estimate the total amount of carbon dioxide produced by terminal oxidation of substrates in the human body over periods ranging from 7 to 14 days and to compute the total energy expenditure for the period of time. This procedure is known as the doubly labeled water method, and it has been validated in humans against metabolic chamber measurements of energy expenditure by indirect calorimetry (Schoeller et al., 1986).

HEALTH-RELATED FITNESS

There is no universally agreed upon definition of fitness and its components. In the present context, we are particularly interested in what is now referred to as health-related fitness, that is, the physical and physiological components of fitness that have a direct impact on health status. The World Health Organization (1968) defined fitness as "the ability to perform muscular work satisfactorily." The definition is relevant to health but also to muscular performance and occupational tasks, and therefore is not sufficiently specific for our purpose.

Health-related fitness refers to the favorable influence of habitual physical activity on health status. It is the state of physical and physiological characteristics that defines the risk levels for the premature development of diseases or morbid conditions presenting a relationship with a sedentary mode of life. Important determinants of health-related fitness include such factors as body mass for height, body composition, subcutaneous fat distribution, abdominal visceral fat, bone density, strength and endurance of the abdominal and dorsolumbar musculature, heart and lung functions, blood pressure, maximal aerobic power and tolerance to submaximal exercise, glucose and insulin metabolism, blood lipid and lipoprotein profile, and the ratio of lipid to carbohydrate oxidized in a variety of situations. A favorable profile for these various factors presents a clear advantage in terms of health outcomes as assessed by morbidity and mortality statistics.

In contrast, performance-related fitness refers to those components of fitness that are necessary for optimal work or sport performance (Gledhill, 1990; Pate & Shephard, 1989). It is defined in terms of ability in athletic competition, performance tests, or occupational work. Performance-related fitness depends heavily upon motor skills, cardiorespiratory power and capacity, muscular strength, power or endurance, body size, body composition, motivation, and nutritional status.

The numerous components of health-related fitness are determined by several variables, including the individual's pattern and level of habitual activity, diet, and heredity. There are various ways of defining and classifying these components, and one such proposition is summarized in Table 1.2 (Bouchard & Shephard, 1993). It includes morphological, muscular, motor, cardiorespiratory, and metabolic fitness components, each of which is briefly highlighted below.

Morphological Component

The weight for height relationship is commonly expressed as the body mass index (BMI) (body mass in kg divided by height in m^2). High and very low BMI values are both related to a higher all-cause mortality rate (Van Itallie & Abraham, 1985; Waaler, 1983). Excessive weight for height is also associated with a greater likelihood of impaired glucose tolerance, hyperinsulinemia, hypertension, hypertriglyceridemia, and dyslipoproteinemia (Stamler, 1979; Glueck et al., 1980; National Research Council, 1989). BMIs in the range of 20 to 25 are considered desirable among young adults (Health and Welfare Canada, 1989). Desirable values tend to shift slightly upward (26 and 27) with age (Andres, 1985), although this remains a controversial issue.

Body fat content is the source of the higher risk of morbidity and mortality associated with a high BMI. However, there is no epidemiological study that has assessed the relationship between total body fat content and health outcomes. Nonetheless, small-scale laboratory studies indicate that the percentage of body fat and fat mass are significantly

Table 1.2

Components and Factors of Physical and Physiological Fitness

Morphological component
  Body mass for height
  Body composition
  Subcutaneous fat distribution
  Abdominal visceral fat
  Bone density
  Flexibility
Muscular component
  Strength and power
  Endurance
Motor component
  Speed
  Agility
  Balance
  Coordination

Cardiorespiratory component
  Submaximal exercise capacity
  Maximal aerobic power
  Heart functions
  Lung functions
  Blood pressure
Metabolic component
  Glucose tolerance
  Insulin sensitivity
  Blood lipids and lipoproteins
  Ratio of lipid to carbohydrate
    oxidation

Reprinted, by permission, from C. Bouchard and R.J. Shephard, 1993, Physical activity, fitness and health: A model and key concepts. In *Proceedings of the international consensus symposium on physical activity, fitness and health,* edited by C. Bouchard, R.J. Shephard, and T. Stephens (Champaign, IL: Human Kinetics), 81.

correlated with blood lipid, lipoprotein, and insulin levels as well as with blood pressure (Després et al., 1988; Krotkiewski, Björntorp, Sjöström, & Smith, 1983).

The topography of adipose tissue is considered as an important indicator of enhanced risk for cardiovascular disease morbidity and mortality and for noninsulin dependent diabetes mellitus (Bouchard, Bray, & Van Hubbard, 1990). A male profile of regional fat distribution (or preponderance of fat on the trunk) is associated with insulin resistance and elevated blood insulin level (Kissebah & Peiris, 1989; Kalkhoff, Hartz, Rupley, Kissebah, & Kelber, 1983; Evans, Hoffman, Kalkhoff, & Kissebah, 1984), a more atherogenic plasma lipid and lipoprotein profile (Kissebah et al., 1982; Després, Moorjani, et al., 1990) and a higher blood pressure (Kalkhoff et al., 1983; Després et al., 1988). Upper body fat is also associated with a higher mortality rate in both genders (Lapidus et al., 1984; Larsson et al., 1984). Studies in which fat on the trunk was assessed by skinfolds or by computerized tomography have indicated that both metabolic alterations and increased cardiovascular mortality rates were associated with the profile of subcutaneous fat distribution (Ducimetière & Richard, 1989; Ducimetière, Richard, & Cambien, 1986; Higgins, Kannel, Garrison, Pinsky, & Stokes, 1988; Després, Moorjani, et al., 1990).

In addition to the effects of truncal-abdominal subcutaneous fat on the risk profile, abdominal visceral fat exerts a profound influence on insulin and lipoprotein metabolism (Kissebah, Freedman, & Peiris, 1989; Fujioka, Matsuzawa, Tokunaga, & Tarui, 1987; Després, Moorjani, et al., 1990). Within the abdominal visceral depot, it is thought that fat depots draining into the portal circulation exert the most devastating effects on hepatic glucose, lipid, and insulin metabolism (Björntorp, 1990). The amount of abdominal visceral fat can be assessed only by computerized tomography or other medical imaging techniques. In summary, it is useful to distinguish a minimum of three morphological factors: percent fat, truncal-abdominal subcutaneous fat, and abdominal visceral fat (Bouchard, 1991). A fourth trait, lower-body fat (a female type of fat deposition) apparently has only limited metabolic implications.

As osteoporosis reaches epidemic levels among the senior citizens of developed countries of the Western Hemisphere, it is of great importance to understand the associations between habitual physical activity, fitness, and bone density. Bone mass is maximal in the third or fourth decade of life, followed by a progressive decrease which may progress to clinical osteoporosis and an increased susceptibility to bone fracture. Risk factors for osteoporosis include inherited susceptibility, a decrease in estrogen levels, a calcium-deficient diet, and a low level of habitual physical activity, among others. Currently available data support the notion that some types of physical activity may exert beneficial effects on bone mineral content and bone strength (Tipton & Vailas, 1990; Oakes & Parker, 1990; Smith, Smith, & Gilligan, 1990).

Another factor of some importance in the morphological component of fitness is flexibility, generally defined as the range of motion at a joint. Flexibility is specific for a given joint and is determined by a variety of factors, including the bony and cartilagenous surfaces and the soft tissues around the articulation. It can be improved by specific exercises designed to increase the range of motion at that particular joint. It has been suggested that maintaining normal joint flexibility may help prevent some manifestations of upper- and lower-back pain and osteoarthritis.

Muscular Component

Muscular fitness is an important component of health-related physical and physiological fitness. Three factors are of particular interest: muscular strength, muscular power, and muscular endurance. All three factors can be improved in both genders at all ages given an appropriate regimen of exercise. Habitual activity does not appear to alter the slope of the aging curve, but the physically active person begins with a higher level of function and may thus experience less health impairment at a later age (Shephard, 1987).

The progressive loss of lean tissue and muscular fitness with aging leads to a situation where desired activities such as lifting a load from the floor, carrying groceries, or raising oneself from a chair become difficult or impossible (Shephard, 1987). A person with a reasonable level of muscular fitness should have a greater resistance to fatigue. It has been suggested that muscular fitness is helpful in the prevention of upper-back and lower-back pain, which are rather common in industrialized societies. Maintaining a reasonable level of muscular fitness through regular physical activity may also be important for normal hormonal and substrate metabolism, particularly for the sensitivity of the skeletal muscle tissue to insulin (Exercise and NIDDM, 1990).

Motor Component

Motor fitness is of particular importance during growth, when the child explores his or her movement potential and develops basic motor skills. Speed of movement, agility, balance, and motor coordination are major facets of the motor component of fitness. Motor fitness contributes only marginally to health-related physical and physiological fitness in young and middle-aged adults. However, it has important implications for elderly people. It must be noted that the more-skilled people in various ages and socioeconomic classes tend to be the most active.

Cardiorespiratory Component

The cardiorespiratory component of physical and physiological fitness has traditionally been viewed as the most important from a health perspective. Cardiorespiratory fitness encompasses many factors, the most relevant of which are listed in Table 1.2.

Submaximal exercise capacity, or endurance performance, can be defined as the tolerance to low or moderate intensity power outputs for prolonged periods of time. It is determined primarily by the oxygen delivery system, but is also affected by the peripheral utilization of oxygen to regenerate adenosine triphosphate (ATP) substrate mobilization and utilization, thermoregulatory mechanisms, and other physiological and metabolic factors. A person with a poor submaximal exercise capacity will experience fatigue sooner and may have problems undertaking the normal activities of daily life. Maximal aerobic power or maximal oxygen intake decreases by about 10 percent per decade throughout adult life (Shephard, 1987). The elderly individual becomes adversely affected by this decrease, as some of the tasks of normal daily life require an increasingly larger fraction of the maximal aerobic power.

Cardiac function is assessed by a variety of indicators, including the cardiovascular response to exercise. The heart rate for a given power output (adjusted for body mass), the exercise stroke volume and cardiac output, the exercise electrocardiogram and vectocardiogram, and various imaging techniques that assess myocardium perfusion are among such indicators. Pulmonary function may be assessed by measuring static and dynamic lung volumes. In most circumstances, the cardiorespiratory fitness of a healthy adult is limited by cardiac rather than by respiratory function. Nevertheless, it is ultimately better to have larger pulmonary volumes and higher flow rates for several reasons, including the ability to draw on them to accommodate the hazards of exposure to cigarette smoke, industrial dusts, and other air pollutants (Bouchard & Shephard, 1993).

Blood pressure is of particular importance, because hypertension is associated with an increased risk of death from ischemic heart disease, cardiac failure, cerebrovascular accident, rupture of other major blood vessels, and renal failure. Regular physical activity and an improved fitness level may have positive influences on both hypotensive or hypertensive states (Holmgren, 1967; Hagberg, 1990). In addition to resting measurements of blood pressure, further information can be derived from the blood pressure response to exercise.

Metabolic Component

Metabolic fitness is a new and evolving concept. One definition of this component of health-related fitness suggests that it could result from normal hormonal actions, especially for insulin, catecholamines, and other hormones involved in substrate metabolism, from normal lipid-lipoprotein metabolism, and from being a high lipid oxidizer. The relations among glucose, insulin, lipoprotein metabolism, and habitual physical activity will be addressed later in this chapter. The ratio of lipid to carbohydrate oxidized under standardized conditions at rest or during steady-state exercise is an important indicator of metabolic efficiency. For instance, the respiratory quotient measured over a 24-hour period in a metabolic chamber is significantly and positively correlated with the amount of fat and weight gained over a period of about two years (Zurlo et al., 1990). Oxidizing more lipids than carbohydrates in a variety of conditions seems to be a desirable metabolic characteristic from a fitness and weight control point of view.

EFFECTS OF PHYSICAL ACTIVITY ON HEALTH OUTCOMES

An assessment of the holistic approach evident in concepts such as active living requires an understanding of the effects of regular physical activity, across a spectrum of risk factors for the common causes of death, on various morbid conditions and mortality rates. This section reviews the evidence of the influence of regular physical activity on selected health outcomes. It also summarizes the role of physical activity during growth and aging.

A word of caution is warranted. Obviously, we still have far to go before we reach a complete understanding of all the effects of regular physical activity or persistent sedentarism. Thus, at present, an evaluation of the benefits and risks of regular physical activity or of an inactive lifestyle can be based only on partial evidence. Moreover, the small body of knowledge accumulated to date, although quite impressive by some standards, pertains only to mean effects seen in limited samples of a population and does not even begin to address seriously the issue of individual differences in host susceptibility to benefits and risks. It is important for everyone involved in the areas of physical activity, fitness, and health to be neither overly optimistic about the role of regular physical activity on health outcomes nor unduly pessimistic about the consequences of a sedentary mode of life. Neither zealousness nor skepticism can replace solid scientific evidence. Further progress in this field, as in any other areas pertaining to the health and well-being of humans, depends on long-term, excellent programs of basic and clinical research. There is no reasonable and credible alternative.

Energy Balance, Body Composition, and Regional Fat Distribution

In theory, one can easily accept the notion that the augmented energy expenditure associated with regular physical activity should have a favorable impact on energy balance. In practice, however, it is very difficult to demonstrate in free-living individuals. Variations in body energy content over time can provide an indication as to whether the person is generally in positive or negative energy balance. Figure 1.2 schematically illustrates the major determinants of energy balance and their interactions. The determinants can be grouped into three categories: energy intake, energy expenditure, and nutrient partitioning. All three classes of affectors are very difficult to measure with precision in

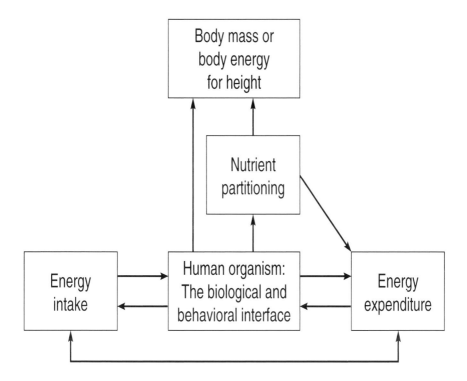

Figure 1.2   A model of the major determinants of body energy content or body fat. Reprinted, by permission, from C. Bouchard, 1991, "Heredity and the path to overweight and obesity," *Medicine and Science in Sports and Exercise* 23: 285-291.

free-living individuals. Typically, the technical error (standard deviation of repeated measurements) of these determinants reaches about 10 percent of the mean value. In addition, energy intake and energy expenditure fluctuate naturally from day to day. For instance, the standard deviation of energy intake assessed over a large number of days for a given person reaches about 1,000 kJ per day. Since physical activity accounts for only about 20 percent of the daily energy expended, a slight increase in habitual physical activity is not likely to dramatically alter the total amount of energy expended or thus energy balance. Moreover, the increase in level of activity may be accompanied by a corresponding increase in energy intake. Both factors are likely to obscure the effects of a slight increase in regular physical activity on energy balance and body energy content.

A more substantial energy expenditure as a result of a higher level of habitual physical activity is likely to have a greater influence on energy balance and body energy content (Thompson, Jarvie, Lahey, & Cureton,

1982; Tremblay, Després, & Bouchard, 1985; Bouchard, Després, & Tremblay, 1993). From a practical point of view, daily physical activity leading to an extra energy expenditure of approximately 800 to 1,000 kJ, or about 5.5 to 7.0 MJ, per week should be sufficient to generate a significant energy deficit. There is clear experimental evidence that an energy deficit of that magnitude sustained for several months causes a substantial loss of body energy content (Bouchard et al., 1990, 1992). Interestingly, when a negative balance of that magnitude is generated by regular physical activity instead of reduced caloric intake, the weight loss is almost entirely accounted for by the loss of body fat (Tremblay et al., 1985; Bouchard et al., 1990). In contrast, when the negative energy balance is caused by lowering energy intake, one loses a significant amount of lean tissues, sometimes as much as 50 percent of the total weight loss (Tremblay et al., 1985).

It seems that a sustained negative balance as a result of a higher level of habitual physical activity is more characterisitic of men than women (Després et al., 1984; Krotkiewski, 1983, 1985; Tremblay, Després, Leblanc, & Bouchard, 1984). The most important reason for such a gender difference appears to be the acute increase in energy intake in response to exercise in women, a phenomenon which is not seen in men (Tremblay, Després, & Bouchard, 1988). These observations on men and women are also seen in male and female rodents exposed to regular exercise. Another potential gender difference in response to regular physical activity associated with a sustained negative energy balance state concerns the site of fat mobilization. Thus, upper-body fat and abdominal fat are apparently mobilized to a greater extent in men than in women (Després, Tremblay, & Bouchard, 1989). This is not a trivial issue given the metabolic impact of abdominal and upper-body fat (Bouchard et al., 1990) and the fact that the loss of abdominal and upper-body fat is well-correlated with the improvement in glucose and lipid metabolism observed with regular aerobic exercise (Després et al., 1991).

Bone Density

With advancing age, bone mineral content decreases and the risk of bone fracture increases. Imbalance between the bone metabolic pathways leading to greater bone resorption than bone formation progressively leads to osteoporosis, a state of weakened bony structures resulting from bone loss. Preventing osteoporosis requires high bone density and bone strength. Even though the etiology of osteoporosis has not been fully defined, it is commonly recognized to be multifactorial. Understanding the factors leading to an osteoporotic condition is of great importance, as there are more than 1 million osteoporotic fractures per year in the United States alone (Smith & Gilligan, 1989).

Major risk factors for the loss of bone density include being a woman; having Caucasian ancestry; total bone mass at skeletal maturity; and, in adulthood, advancing age, estrogen deficiency, inadequate dietary calcium intake, dietary calcium malabsorption, smoking, alcohol consumption, undetermined genetic factors, weightlessness, and sedentary lifestyle (Aloia, 1989; Seeman & Allen, 1989; Smith & Gilligan, 1989). The prevention of osteoporosis with advancing age is currently based primarily on dietary calcium supplementation, regular physical activity, and estrogen replacement therapy for postmenopausal women (Smith & Gilligan, 1989).

Several lines of evidence support the contention that regular physical activity is conducive to bone mineral mass and bone strength, but there are also equivocal results (Smith et al., 1990). A dramatic bone loss in the spine of almost 1 percent per week is observed as a consequence of bed rest and weightlessness. On the other hand, athletes generally have a higher bone mineral content than age- and gender-matched sedentary persons. Intervention studies with populations of elderly men or women indicate that bone loss can be prevented and, under certain conditions, bone mass may increase. Research suggests that the skeleton should be moderately overloaded by the mechanical forces generated by physical activity. The emphasis should be on the body regions most at risk for bone fracture (Smith & Gilligan, 1990).

Blood Pressure

Hypertension is a major public health problem. Elevated diastolic or systolic blood pressure is associated with a greater risk of developing congestive heart failure, coronary heart disease, stroke, kidney failure, and intermittent peripheral claudication in men and women. The risk for these diseases is nearly doubled when blood pressure is greater than 140/90 mmHg and increases at least threefold when pressure values of 160/95 and higher are reached. The prevalence of hypertension is higher in men prior to age 65, but is greater in women 65 years and older (National Heart, Lung, and Blood Institute Report, 1991). Approximately 4 to 5 million Canadians are afflicted by elevated blood pressure.

Hypertension is a heterogeneous condition, and individuals with high blood pressure are also heterogeneous in their responses to preventive and therapeutic measures. Obesity, and the hyperinsulinemic state often associated with obesity, particularly android obesity, are important risk factors for hypertension. High alcohol and salt intake may cause hypertension in a large segment of the population. Losing weight and reducing alcohol and salt intake may reduce elevated blood pressure

in many cases. Essential hypertension is the result of functional disturbances in blood volume, cardiac output, total peripheral resistance, and
regulation of kidney functions. Any perturbation in the regulatory
mechanisms of these functions and systems may chronically elevate
blood pressure. Without considering all of the details of the biology of
hypertension, one can intuit that regular physical activity may reduce
blood pressure in some individuals.

Many epidemiological studies have reported an inverse relationship between level of habitual physical activity and resting blood
pressure (Hagberg, 1989, 1990; Paffenbarger, Jung, Leung, & Hyde,
1991). Intervention studies have shown that regular physical activity in essential hypertensives can reduce systolic and diastolic blood
pressures by approximately 10 mmHg (Hagberg, 1990), a result
which is of clinical significance. This favorable effect is not seen in all
cases, and physical activity is not generally sufficient to normalize
blood pressure. At present, the data suggest that regular endurance
exercise at an intensity of 40 to 60 percent $\dot{V}O_2$max is sufficient to
induce these effects (Hagberg, 1990). The same beneficial influences
of regular physical activity on blood pressure are also observed in
elderly subjects (Hagberg, 1989). On the other hand, regular physical activity is not likely to have a major impact on the blood pressure
of normotensive subjects. However, as suggested by large-scale
epidemiological studies, a reasonable level of habitual physical
activity may protect against the increase in blood pressure commonly seen with age in Western societies (National Heart, Lung, and
Blood Institute Report, 1991).

Blood Lipids and Lipoprotein

The effects of regular physical activity or a sedentary lifestyle on blood
lipids and lipoproteins have been intensely investigated during the past
decade. The surge in scientific and clinical research was motivated by
the observation that the lipid and lipoprotein profile is one of the
strongest predictors of coronary heart disease and other atherosclerotic
diseases. It is now generally recognized that regular physical activity
has favorable effects on several aspects of lipid metabolism (Wood &
Stefanick, 1990) and may also be helpful in the nonpharmacological
treatment of some dyslipoproteinemias (Hanefeld, 1991). Cross-sectional
comparisons of athletes or very active individuals with age- and gender-
matched sedentary persons have consistently found substantial differences in plasma lipids and lipoprotein profile in favor of the active
people. Although exercise intervention studies have supported these
findings, the magnitude of the changes in blood and lipoproteins with

regular physical activity is smaller than suggested by cross-sectional comparisons.

Briefly, regular physical activity lowers plasma triglycerides in subjects with initially high levels but has little impact on those with normal levels. On the average, regular physical activity increases HDL cholesterol, particularly HDL_2 cholesterol, and may also increase apolipoprotein A-I, the main apoprotein of HDL molecules. Occasionally, especially in hypercholesterolemic individuals, regular physical activity is associated with decreases in total cholesterol, VLDL cholesterol, and LDL cholesterol. Several ratios of plasma lipids and lipoproteins are commonly used to assess the overall risk of atherogenic diseases, and all are favorably influenced by regular physical activity. Thus, the ratio of total cholesterol to HDL cholesterol, the ratio of HDL_2 cholesterol to HDL_3 cholesterol, and the ratio of apolipoprotein A-I to apolipoprotein B are greater in highly active subjects than in sedentary ones and are increased by regular exercise interventions. Typical differences between highly active (i.e., long-distance runners) and sedentary middle-aged men are illustrated in Table 1.3.

In other words, low-plasma triglycerides, total cholesterol and LDL cholesterol, and high-plasma HDL cholesterol are generally recognized as characteristics associated with a low risk of atherosclerotic diseases, particularly coronary heart disease. Regular physical activity is thought to alter lipid transport in the direction of this favorable profile (Haskell, 1986; Wood & Stefanick, 1990). Moreover, the lipid profile may be favorably altered with exercise at a lower intensity than has generally been thought to be required (Sopko et al., 1983; Hardman, Hudson, Jones, & Norgan, 1989; Leon, Conrad, Hunninghake, & Serfass, 1979; Tucker & Friedman, 1990).

The mechanisms by which these plasma lipid and lipoprotein changes occur with regular physical activity are only partially understood. Two key enzymes of lipoprotein metabolism appear to be favorably influenced: Lipoprotein lipase activity is increased, while hepatic lipase activity is decreased with regular physical activity (Haskell, 1986; Wood & Stefanick, 1990; Després et al., 1991). The increase in lipoprotein lipase activity, the key enzyme in the conversion of VLDL to HDL (associated with regular exercise), may be related to the augmentation of the HDL cholesterol level. On the other hand, hepatic lipase is thought to affect many aspects of lipoprotein metabolism, one of which is involved in the conversion of HDL_2 to HDL_3. The reduction in hepatic lipase activity observed with regular exercise may be one of the mechanisms favoring the high levels of HDL_2 cholesterol observed in active individuals. Another mechanism that should be considered is the role of regular physical activity on insulin metabolism, as activity tends to increase

Table 1.3

Comparison of Lipids, Lipoproteins, Lipoprotein Lipase,
and Hepatic Lipase Measurements in Cross-Sectional Samples
of Long-Distance Runners and Sedentary Men

	Runners (M ± SD)	Sedentary men (M ± SD)	Significance (P)
Age (yr)	46.9 ± 7.5	45.7 ± 6.1	0.81
BMI (kg/m²)	22.6 ± 2.0	25.1 ± 3.3	0.006
Lipids and lipoproteins			
Plasma total cholesterol (mg/dl)	190.9 ± 36.6	217.0 ± 31.1	0.02
Plasma total triglycerides (mg/dl)	70.8 ± 35.0	123.0 ± 59.3	0.001
Plasma HDL cholesterol (mg/dl)	64.9 ± 12.5	49.6 ± 8.7	0.0001
Plasma LDL cholesterol (mg/dl)	147.0 ± 27.5	161.1 ± 30.7	0.004
Serum LDL mass of S 0-7 (mg/dl)	138.4 ± 45.3	227.6 ± 67.9	0.0001
Serum LDL mass of S 7-12 (mg/dl)	136.7 ± 39.8	134.2 ± 43.8	0.85
Plasma VLDL cholesterol (mg/dl)	9.1 ± 8.3	20.4 ± 11.7	0.001
Postheparin lipase activity			
Lipoprotein lipase (mEq fatty acid/ml/h)	5.0 ± 1.8	3.6 ± 1.2	0.04
Hepatic lipase (mEq fatty acid/ml/h)	4.1 ± 2.1	6.5 ± 2.6	0.02

Sample sizes are 12 runners and 64 nonrunners (sedentary men) for all lipid and lipoprotein variables, and 12 runners and 16 nonrunners (sedentary men) for lipoprotein and hepatic lipase measurements.

Reprinted, by permission, from P.T. Williams et al., 1986, "Lipoprotein subfractions of runners and sedentary men," *Metabolism* 35: 45-52.

insulin sensitivity and reduce plasma insulin levels—a phenomenon that may influence the lipid-lipoprotein profile (see next section).

The preceding summary presents an ostensibly optimistic picture of the net effects of regular physical activity on blood lipids and lipoproteins. Several complications must be considered before the specific influences of regular physical activity can be fully appreciated. For instance, some of the changes observed in lipoprotein metabolism in exercise intervention studies may be related to changes in body mass and body composition. Cross-sectional comparisons of active versus inactive individuals may likewise be affected by group differences in body composition. Other confounding factors that may contribute in cross-sectional or longitudinal study designs include amount of upper-body fat, amount of abdominal visceral fat, smoking, dietary cholesterol, dietary fat, and alcohol consumption.

Glucose and Insulin Metabolism

Impairment in oxidative or nonoxidative glucose disposal rate in the presence of insulin reflects an insulin-resistant state in peripheral tissues, particularly skeletal muscle. A diminished insulin-mediated inhibition of hepatic glucose output occurs when the liver becomes resistant to the action of insulin. Both phenomena are associated to various degrees with the advent of abnormal glucose tolerance, leading to compensatory higher insulin secretion and hyperinsulinemia. These are characteristic features of the etiology of noninsulin dependent diabetes mellitus (NIDDM), which develops primarily in adult men and women who are obese (about 85 percent of NIDDM cases) and have an android profile of fat distribution. Diabetes is a strong risk factor not only for coronary heart disease, but also for peripheral vascular disease, nephropathy, retinopathy, and other conditions.

Regular physical activity is believed to have beneficial effects on glucose and insulin metabolism in nondiabetic and NIDDM subjects. One apparent consequence of regular exercise is an improvement in the sensitivity of liver, skeletal muscle, and adipose tissues to insulin action (Rodnick, Haskell, Swislocki, Foley, & Reaven, 1987). Among the manifestations of the phenomenon are a decrease in the basal level of plasma glucose in hyperglycemic subjects, a decrease in fasting insulin levels, a reduction of the insulin response to a glucose load, and an increase in the glucose disposal rate assessed under various conditions during euglycemic-hyperinsulinemic clamp procedures (Exercise and NIDDM, 1990; Vranic & Wasserman, 1990). Several epidemiological studies suggest that regular physical activity may also play a significant role in maintaining normoglycemia and insulin sensitivity in nondiabetic persons.

Regular physical activity improves glycemic control, the response to training generally being better in those with an initially impaired glucose tolerance (Exercise and NIDDM, 1990). Plasma insulin levels decrease with regular exercise (Leon et al., 1979; Tremblay et al., 1990), with hyperinsulinemic patients responding best (Exercise and NIDDM, 1990). Such changes are seen with programs of walking (Leon et al., 1979) and other low-intensity, long-duration exercise sessions that do not necessarily cause an increase in maximal oxygen intake (Oshida, Yamanonchi, Hazamizu, & Sato, 1989; Tremblay et al., 1990). It is not fully established whether the insulin-lowering effect of regular physical activity and the apparent improvement of an insulin-resistant state result from an acute or a persistent increase in the insulin sensitivity of skeletal muscle and other peripheral tissues, a reduction in insulin secretion, an increased rate of hepatic removal of insulin, or a combination of these mechanisms.

The specific contribution of physical activity versus those of dietary changes and weight loss that are generally observed with adherence to a regimen of regular physical activity has not been clearly delineated (Exercise and NIDDM, 1990). An important issue is whether the improvements generally seen in glucose and insulin metabolism are lasting effects of the previous exercise episode or result from long-term adaptations and fitness increments. Despite these limitations in current knowledge, it is widely recognized that regular physical activity is beneficial to NIDDM patients who are prone to atherosclerotic diseases (Exercise and NIDDM, 1990; Vranic & Wasserman, 1990) by normalizing triglyceride and lipoprotein levels (Lampman & Schteingart, 1991).

However, the most compelling evidence for a useful role of regular physical activity has to do with the prevention of NIDDM. Three large prospective studies have been reported concerning the relations between regular exercise and the incidence of NIDDM in adult men or women (Helmrich, Ragland, Leung, & Paffenbarger, 1991; Manson et al., 1991, 1992). They unanimously concluded that active people were less likely to become diabetic with age, the reduction in risk reaching about 20 percent and even more with the heavy exercisers. The protective effects of regular exercise were strongest in the obese individuals and others who were more at risk for the development of NIDDM.

Vascular Diseases

There is some evidence indicating that regular physical activity may be beneficial in the prevention and treatment of three main types of vascular diseases: peripheral vascular disease, coronary heart disease, and stroke. Progressive atherogenic obstruction of peripheral blood vessels is not a rare phenomenon—about 10 percent of the adult population suffers from peripheral claudication. Regular physical activity may indeed be a method of choice in the prevention of the clinical symptoms associated with claudication and also in the treatment of the early stages of the disease (Ernst, 1987). The mechanisms by which these benefits are brought about with regular physical activity are still a matter of debate.

In the case of stroke, the evidence is somewhat tenuous. Some epidemiological evidence suggests that the risk of cerebrovascular accidents is less in active individuals (Kohl, LaPorte, & Blair, 1988). It is not clear, however, if the reduced risk can be accounted for by conventional risk factors, such as high blood pressure or obesity. One cannot rule out the possibility that regular exercise may have a favorable influence on cerebral blood vessels and blood flow, clot formation, fibrinolytic activity (Bourey & Santoro, 1988), and other important aspects of the brain circulation.

Several epidemiological studies, dating back to the 1953 study of Morris, Heady, Raffle, Roberts, and Parks, have shown that high levels of energy expenditure on the job were related to a lower rate of coronary episodes and to less severe and less often fatal heart attacks (Paffenbarger, Hyde, & Wing, 1990). Similar trends have been reported for leisure time physical activity. Those active in sports or other physical activities during their leisure time have a lower rate of ischemic heart disease and fatal heart attacks. The effect is graded; that is, the risk decreases progressively with the increase in the level of habitual physical activity. The same trend is observed for both sports and other physical activities. The volume of activity necessary to induce some of these apparent benefits is not overwhelmingly high, as the risk diminishes almost linearly with weekly energy expenditure due to physical activity ranging from about 500 to 3,000 kcal (Paffenbarger et al., 1990). In other words, a low level of habitual physical activity will have only a small effect, but higher levels will reduce the risk significantly. If 2,000 kcal per week is taken as the threshold between low and high levels of activity, the more active subjects of the 16,936 members of the Harvard Alumni Study had a 28 percent lower risk of death from any cause during a 16-year follow-up period (Paffenbarger et al., 1990).

Some evidence suggests that the level of cardiopulmonary fitness, as assessed variously from cycle ergometer or treadmill tests, is also negatively related with all-cause mortality rates and death rates from coronary heart disease (Paffenbarger et al., 1990). Similar relationships have been observed in men and women (Blair et al., 1989). For both level of habitual physical activity and level of fitness, the effects on mortality are significant and graded even after adjustment for a variety of common risk factors, such as body mass index, blood pressure, smoking, blood cholesterol, and parental history.

An extensive review of 43 studies that provided sufficient data to calculate a relative risk for the occurrence of coronary heart disease at different levels of physical activity was published in 1987 by Powell, Thompson, Caspersen, and Kendrick. They concluded that an inverse association between physical activity and incidence of coronary heart disease was consistently observed, particularly in the better designed studies. They also reported that the association was appropriately sequenced, biologically graded, and coherent with existing knowledge. Several other investigators have since confirmed this inverse relationship in various populations. A recent meta-analysis of studies dealing with physical activity in the prevention of coronary heart disease concluded that the overall relative risk of experiencing a coronary episode was about 1.9 for sedentary persons compared with active ones (Berlin & Colditz, 1990). There is also suggestive evidence to the effect that regular physical activity may help prevent new infarctions in post-myocardial patients (O'Connor et al., 1989; Oldridge, Guyatt, Fischer, & Rimm, 1988).

Some mechanisms that may account for the potential influences of regular physical activity on the proneness to ischemic heart disease have been reviewed by Leon (1991) and Morris and Froelicher (1991). These include attenuation of other risk factors, antithrombotic effects, increased myocardial vascularity and function, and better cardiac electrical stability. The intensity and volume of physical activity needed to bring about these beneficial effects is an important issue. Many have reported that a moderate volume of physical activity was sufficient (Blair et al., 1989; Leon, 1991; Shaper & Wannamethee, 1991), while others found that the effect was graded (Paffenbarger, Hyde, & Wing, 1990). This deserves further research because of its potentially enormous impact on the health of the citizenry; coronary heart disease is still the number one cause of mortality in North America.

If physical inactivity is an important risk factor for ischemic heart disease, it is interesting then to compare it to other known risk factors. A major U.S. study has estimated that the association between physical inactivity and coronary heart disease was similar to that for hypercholesterolemia, hypertension, and cigarette smoking (Pooling Project Research Group, 1978). As shown in Figure 1.3, hypertension and high cholesterol levels are seen in about 10 percent of the U.S. adult population. Twenty percent of these adults are smokers, but almost 60 percent are classified as inactive. Hence, the population-based attributable risk analysis would indicate that because physical inactivity is so prevalent, it constitutes a more important risk factor than the other three combined (U.S. Department of Health and Human Services, 1987).

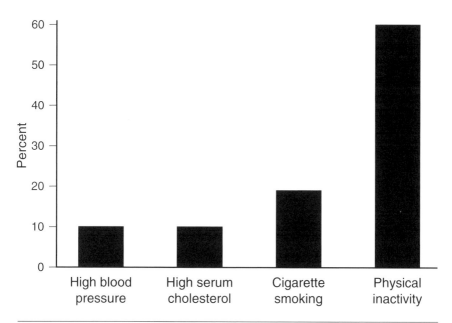

Figure 1.3 Estimated percentage of population having selected risk factors for coronary heart disease. Based on U.S. adult data from 1980-1987.

Other Biological Influences

Other influences of regular physical activity on the human body may also contribute significantly to the prevention of various disorders or to the rehabilitation from several debilitating conditions. Although they cannot be reviewed exhaustively in this chapter, it is appropriate to mention a few. Some of the evidence can be found in Bouchard et al. (1990).

- Physical activity may exert favorable influences on some aspects of the immune system and the immune response.
- It is also thought that it may be a useful adjunct in the treatment of joint flexibility, osteoarthritic problems, and back pain.
- Regular physical activity and specific exercise have a place in the management of patients with chronic airflow obstruction.
- Persons with bladder control deficiencies can, in some cases, benefit from a program of adapted exercises (Bø et al., 1990).
- A growing body of knowledge suggests that regular physical activity may have favorable influences on the gastrointestinal tract

and may even offer some protection against colon cancer (Kohl, LaPorte, & Blair, 1988; Shephard, 1990).

• Some data also point to a favorable effect of physical activity on the risk of breast cancer.

• There is growing interest in the topic of benefits versus risks of regular physical activity, particularly intensive training, on the reproductive functions of men and women. One universal observation is that there are considerable individual differences in the susceptibility to reproductive dysfunction as a result of training. Vigorous physical activity may induce menstrual dysfunction, ranging from subtle changes to more serious disturbances (Henley & Vaitukaitis, 1988). Reduction of training intensity and volume is often sufficient to alleviate the problem. There is evidence that disruption also occurs in men, but it is still unclear whether it results in clinically manifest reproductive dysfunction (Cumming, Wheeler, & McColl, 1989). It is commonly recognized that the disturbances in reproductive functions induced by physical activity in both men and women are reversible with cessation of the activity regimen.

• Regular physical activity is also believed to affect the pregnant mother and her fetus. Research to date seems to indicate that it neither significantly benefits nor seriously harms them; however, caution is warranted as there are concerns that strenuous physical activity may be associated with premature birth and low birth weight (Warren, 1991). Thus, it seems prudent to recommend a conservative approach and to advise low-intensity exercise in moderate amounts, particularly for previously untrained pregnant women.

Growth and Development

As the Canada Fitness Survey (1983) demonstrated, most children are physically active. However, participation in physical activity decreases around puberty, and more so in girls than in boys. We know surprisingly little about the benefits of regular physical activity from birth to maturity and the effects of a sedentary lifestyle during the growing years. Most of the evidence comes from correlational studies or from cross-sectional observations, which have limited value in assessing the specific role of regular activity or sedentarism on children and adolescents. The few longitudinal studies that have incorporated the potential role of physical activity on growth and maturation have generally reported no differences on gross phenotypes such as height, weight, skeletal maturation, sexual maturation, and others.

Briefly, depending on the circumstances of the activity regimen, physically active children and youth exhibit no difference in stature or level of maturation, a higher bone density and fat-free mass but a lower body fat content, a greater skeletal muscle mass with larger muscle fibers, an increase in muscular strength and endurance, and a higher $\dot{V}O_2$max with an augmented performance capacity compared to inactive children (Malina & Bouchard, 1991). However, all these adaptive responses to an active lifestyle are apparently transient and are progressively reduced if the growing person shifts to a more sedentary mode of life. There are perhaps more permanent adaptations, but if so they have not been identified. There is one exception: The motor skills learned and mastered during growth are largely retained during adult life.

Another line of evidence is the relationship between level of activity during growth and risk factors for various diseases. Physical activity offers little protection against chronic diseases during growth, with perhaps the exception of childhood obesity (Simons-Morton, Parcel, O'Hara, Blair, & Pate, 1988). This topic has been reviewed from the point of view of the common risk factors for NIDDM and cardiovascular diseases, and the results are rather disappointing (Montoye, 1986; Després, Bouchard, & Malina, 1990). The exception is the obese child who is often hypertriglyceridemic and hyperinsulinemic, with elevated blood pressure and low HDL cholesterol level. He or she may greatly benefit by becoming more active, both in terms of weight control and improved metabolic profile.

Aging

Universally, age brings a progressive decrease in the functional capacity of systems, organs, tissues, and cells of the body. No individual is known to have escaped its manifestations. It commences soon after biological maturity has been attained. In most people, the first perceived signs of aging become apparent at around 40 years of age, although there are wide individual differences. The effects of aging become more visible in years 55 to 60. Beyond 60, it is often difficult to distinguish aging from the symptoms of abnormal processes associated with the onset of diseases that may or may not have a relationship with advancing age. After 65, a growing proportion of men and women experience some forms of disability, with the result that they become less autonomous (Shephard, 1987). Actually, more than 50 percent of people over 65 years of age have some type of chronic pain, chronic degenerative disease, or reduction of personal autonomy; this proportion increases with advancing age. This has considerable social and economic implications when seen in light of increased average life expectancy. If projections are approximately correct, about 15 percent of the population will be 65 years and older by the turn of the century and, shortly thereafter, almost 5 percent will attain 85 years of age and older (Spirduso, 1989).

Such observations have led to the emergence of the important concept of disability-free or healthy aging. The concept recognizes that duration of life is not the same as aging without impairment or disability and enjoying personal autonomy. An important conclusion from the available research is that, while women live on average six to eight years longer than men, life expectancy free from disability is almost identical for both genders (Blanchet, 1990). It stands at about 60 years in both men and women. The central question then becomes, can active living make a difference in terms of disability-free aging and personal autonomy? Obviously, the answer to this question cannot be a simple yes or no. It is also not presently possible to develop a detailed answer. Moreover, the data are insufficient or nonexistent to address many aspects of this question. We will therefore outline only key points that can be addressed with some confidence.

It is a reasonable proposition that regular physical activity, in contrast to a sedentary lifestyle, can reduce the occurrence of morbid conditions. Indeed, active living may be associated with a decreased risk for obesity, hypertension, NIDDM, peripheral vascular disease, coronary heart disease, osteoporosis, and perhaps other disorders. However, it is unlikely that all of the known benefits of regular physical activity can be induced in 60-, 70-, or 80-year-olds if they were totally inactive prior to these years. In addition, it should be kept in mind that, based on current knowledge of the role of genetic differences in the response to nutrition, exercise, smoking, alcohol, and other factors, the benefits of regular physical activity on the susceptibility to various morbid conditions will vary from individual to individual and may range from none to much.

One of the most important biological benefits associated with an active mode of life is its influences on physical working capacity and muscular fitness. The capacity of the cardiovascular, respiratory, and muscular systems to undertake and sustain a power output level that is about four to five times the equivalent of the resting metabolic rate is essential to remain independent as a person. The decrease in the maximal oxygen transport capacity with age in normal sedentary individuals of both genders is quite dramatic, as shown in Figure 1.4. The phenomenon is illustrated in terms of multiples of the resting metabolic rate (METS). Regular physical activity cannot prevent the age-associated decline in the performance capacity of the human body, as assessed by the maximal number of METS. However, the physically active person can reach a higher performance level than the inactive person. The

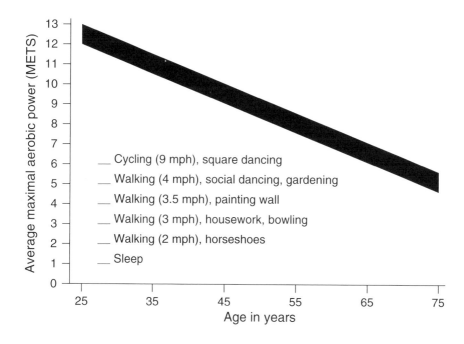

Figure 1.4 Average decrease in maximal aerobic performance capacity with age. Performance is expressed in terms of multiples of the resting metabolic rate (METS) adjusted for body mass differences. The upper boundary of the curve represents the mean value for men, while the lower boundary is the mean value for women.

difference between active and inactive individuals is particularly important beyond retirement age, when it may affect the level of autonomy. Thus, one recommendation could be to emphasize volume and intensity of regular physical activity sufficient to prevent a decrement of aerobic performance capacity below the equivalent of five to six METS. The same rationale applies for muscular fitness. In this case, senior citizens with higher levels of muscular strength and muscular endurance have a better chance of accomplishing the physical tasks required for independence.

Longevity

Is there evidence to the effect that regular physical activity increases life expectancy? In other words, the likelihood that regular physical activity increases, on the average, the duration of a disability-free life appears to be reasonably good, but does it increase the overall duration of life or prevent premature death? Convincing data on these questions are difficult to generate, but some suggest that regular physical activity may indeed exert such favorable influences.

Two studies are of particular interest. The first is a Finnish study of 636 men, 45 to 64 years of age, followed for 20 years. This group experienced a total of 287 deaths, and 39 percent of the cohort were classified as being highly physically active (Pekkanen et al., 1987). Of the men who died, the active subjects lived 2.1 years longer than the inactive men after adjustment for age, smoking, blood pressure, serum cholesterol, and body mass index. Based on the 16-year follow-up study of the Harvard alumni, Paffenbarger et al. (1990) have estimated that three to four hours of exercise per week added about 1.5 years to life. In the latter study, the effect was maximal around 35 years and became progressively smaller with aging. It is thought that an extension of 1.5 to 2 years of life expectancy represents a conservative estimate (Heyden, Schneider, & Schneider, 1991). With longer follow-up data, inclusions of all disease endpoints, and adjustment for other common risk factors, more reliable estimates of the average influence of habitual physical activity on lifespan will likely become available in the future.

THE TRADITIONAL VIEW OF EXERCISE AND FITNESS

For many years, most fitness specialists considered the concept of fitness in primarily cardiorespiratory terms. This belief was reflected in the 1978 American College of Sports Medicine position paper, "The Recommended Quantity and Quality of Exercise for Developing and Maintaining Fitness in Healthy Adults." The prevailing view then, and in the decades before, was that cardiorespiratory fitness was the single most important component of fitness and that other components were also positively influenced by an exercise program designed to cause training effects on the cardiorespiratory system. Maximal oxygen uptake was considered as the best overall indicator of fitness. The evidence in support of this view, although incomplete in some respects, was highly suggestive and, at times, quite persuasive (Shephard, 1969).

It was generally held that fitness benefits were obtained by engaging regularly in physical activities of fairly high intensity. This was perfectly logical, seeing as the expected outcome was a training effect on the performance of the heart and a corresponding increase in maximal aerobic power. Thus, after the early phases of adaptation to an exercise regimen, people of all ages and both sexes were typically advised to exercise three to five times a week, for at least 30 minutes, at an intensity approaching 70 to 80 percent of $\dot{V}O_2$max or maximal heart rate reserve. Although fitness specialists were also interested in weight control, muscular strength and endurance, and flexibility, these attributes did not receive the same attention as the cardiorespiratory component of fitness.

The logical extension of the preceding view of fitness was the development of the exercise prescription concept (American College of Sports Medicine, 1975). On the one hand, it was based on the most effective combination of mode, frequency, duration, and intensity of physical activity to induce training effects on the cardiorespiratory system. On the other hand, because of the intensity requirement of an exercise program designed to improve $\dot{V}O_2$max, the development of the exercise prescription concept was also motivated by the necessity to reduce the risks of exercising and to improve the safety of the participants. Today, exercise prescription remains an important tool for those involved in the fitness area, particularly when working with symptomatic persons, unfit asymptomatic individuals, or senior citizens who are setting new high-fitness goals for themselves (Bouchard & Landry, 1985).

GROWING RECOGNITION OF THE MULTIFACETED EFFECTS OF PHYSICAL ACTIVITY

The concept of fitness summarized in the preceding section has changed and is still evolving. One of the most important changes is the recognition that physical activity has pervasive influences on biological, behavioral, social, and other dimensions of a person. This is true in the acute phase of the response to a given activity episode, but particularly so in the adaptation to regular physical activity. The challenge of physical activity necessitates molecular, cellular, metabolic, physiological, and morphological responses depending upon its demands. It may also affect other behaviors, mental health, social adjustment, and so on.

When physical activity is evaluated in the context of the health-related fitness concept presented earlier in this chapter, it follows that physical activity must be seen in much broader circumstances than it was when cardiorespiratory fitness was the dominant goal. In other words, fitness and health benefits can be derived from participating in physical activities that do not meet the stringent frequency, duration, and intensity criteria of the exercise prescription designed to increase

$\dot{V}O_2$max. Important fitness benefits that have a predictable, favorable impact on a variety of health outcomes are prompted by all types of physical activity, including those with high and low metabolic demands. It is quite likely that fitness and health benefits associated with high-intensity and low-intensity activities are not the same. The greatest fitness and health benefits are probably obtained when a person includes both high- and low-intensity activities in his or her program of regular physical activity.

More research is needed on the dose-response relationship between the intensity or total volume of physical activity and fitness and health benefits. The total volume of activity results from the combination of frequency × duration × intensity of participation. Thus, many combinations will generate the same volume of physical activity. For some fitness and health outcomes, existing data suggest almost linear changes with the increase in the total volume of physical activity. This seems to be the case, for instance, for weight loss and weight control. In other cases, favorable effects are observed only when the exercise intensity is beyond a threshold. For example, an increment in cardiac output is not expected with regular physical activity at 30 percent of $\dot{V}O_2$max. Another illustration of the limited influence of some physical activity circumstances is provided by the response of bone tissue. While there may be positive influences on bone density of activities at various levels of intensities, maximum benefits are apparently achieved with weight-bearing activities and high-resistance exercise.

In some cases, the dose-response relationship is strikingly different. Thus, above a given level of total volume or intensity of exercise, there may be no further gains in fitness and health outcomes and, at times, misadaptation and negative consequences may occur. For instance, orthopedic problems become more frequent with high levels of intensity or high levels of participation. Coronary events may be precipitated by high-intensity exercise. High-intensity exercise may do more harm than good in hypertensive individuals. In brief, it is likely impossible to define a single set of circumstances that would have the potential of bringing about all the known fitness and health benefits of regular participation in physical activity.

The above view is gaining adherents, as illustrated by the recently published revision of the American College of Sports Medicine position paper (1990), even though the approach remains somewhat conservative on the issue of low-intensity physical activity. The concept that regular, low- to moderate-intensity physical activity can generate meaningful fitness and health benefits, with a minimum of risk to the participant and with good prospects for high adherence (Haskell, 1991), is becoming more accepted by the fitness community. This notion, combined with the increasingly accepted concept that the greatest fitness and health benefits occur when sedentary persons become moderately active or when unfit individuals become moderately fit (Blair et al., 1989; Haskell, 1991), sets the stage for regular physical activity to play a major role in health promotion efforts. Indeed, these new lines of evidence provide support for a broad definition of regular physical activity, one that encompasses physical activity over a wide range of energy costs and relative intensities.

LIMITATIONS OF THE PRECEDING GENERALIZATIONS

The preceding overview of the contributions of regular physical activity to fitness and health identified not only extensive positive influences, but also some potentially adverse consequences under specific activity volume and intensity conditions. It is fair to say that the bulk of the evidence suggests that physical activity programs with high volume at moderate intensity and high intensity with lower volume generally have favorable consequences on fitness and health. However, it should be emphasized that such a conclusion is based on the *average* effects observed in groups of boys and girls, men and women, or elderly subjects of both genders. The point is that these influences, documented at the level of the group, may not fully apply to each member of that group. Indeed, there are considerable individual differences in the response to regular physical activity, even when all members of the exercising group are exposed to the same volume of physical activity at the same relative intensity (Bouchard, 1983, 1986; Lortie et al., 1984).

Health is the culmination of many interacting factors, including genetic constitution. The genotype represents the characteristics of the individual at a given gene or set of genes. Needless to say, humans are genetically quite diverse. Current estimates are that each human being has about one variable DNA base for every 100 to 300 bases out of a total of about 3 billion base pairs. Variations in DNA sequence constitute the molecular basis of genetic individuality. Given genetic individuality, equality of health and physical and mental well-being, even under similar environmental and lifestyle conditions, is unlikely; some persons will thrive better than others and will remain free from disabilities for a longer period of time. Given such individuality, it should come as no surprise that a minority of adults remain relatively fit in spite of a sedentary lifestyle.

Genetic differences do not operate in a vacuum. They constantly interact with existing cellular and tissue conditions to provide a biological response commensurate with environmental demands. Genes are constantly interacting with everything in the physical environment (including the individual's lifestyle characteristics) that translates into signals capable of affecting the cells of the body. For instance, overfeeding, a high-fat diet, smoking, and regular endurance exercise are all powerful stimuli that may elicit strong biological responses. However, because of inherited differences at specific genes, the amplitude of adaptive responses varies from one individual to another. Inheritance is one of the important reasons why we are not equally prone to become diabetic or hypertensive or to die from a heart attack. It is also one major explanation for individual differences in the response to dietary intervention or regular physical activity.

Genetic individuality is important in the present context because of its impact on the physical activity, fitness, and health paradigm. There are inherited differences in the level of habitual physical activity (Pérusse, Tremblay, Leblanc, & Bouchard, 1989) and in most components of health-related fitness (Bouchard, 1986, 1990, 1991). Evidence also strongly suggests that genetic variation accounts for most of individual differences in the response to regular exercise of health-related fitness components and of various risk factors for cardiovascular disease and NIDDM (Bouchard, 1990). Not only is it important to recognize that there are individual differences in the response to regular physical activity, but research also indicates that there are nonresponders in the population. Typically, there is a three- to tenfold difference between low responders and high responders, depending upon the phenotype considered, as a result of exposure to the same standardized physical activity regimen for a period of 15 to 20 weeks (Bouchard, 1992; Bouchard, Dionne, Simoneau, & Boulay, 1992).

An appreciation of the critical role of DNA sequence variation in human responses to various challenges and environmental conditions has become essential to the study of the physical activity, fitness, and health paradigm. It augments our understanding of human individuality and makes us more cautious when defining the fitness and health benefits of a physically active lifestyle. Incorporating biological individuality into our thinking will increase the relevance of our observations to the true human situation.

IMPLICATIONS OF HOLISTIC APPROACHES FOR THE PROMOTION OF PHYSICAL ACTIVITY

The physical activity, fitness, and health model elaborated in this chapter is useful for understanding the biological implications of a broader approach to active living. It provides a highly flexible definition of physical activity while retaining all of the useful characteristics (intensity or energy cost, frequency, duration, and volume) for an appreciation of its morphological, physiological, and metabolic impact. The model broadens considerably the concept of physical fitness to include components that have emerged during the last decade and which may be of even greater significance for health in the broader sense than the traditional physical fitness factors. Finally, the model is anchored on a broadly defined health concept even though it acknowledges that the available evidence regarding the effects of variation in physical activity and fitness levels is generally limited to short-term, laboratory-controlled intervention studies and to mortality and morbidity data derived from a limited number of epidemiological studies.

Holistic visions of physical activity have been evident in a large segment of the physical activity sciences community for several decades. A review of several classic papers of the 1950s and 1960s quickly demonstrates that various manifestations of physical activity—not exercise programs and sports alone—were known to benefit active individuals (Larson, 1961, 1971; Johnson, 1960). It was already understood by the time of the 1966 International Conference on Physical Activity and Cardiovascular Health held in Toronto (Shephard, 1967), even though the program emphasized the cardiovascular outcomes.

The most striking illustration of a holistic view of physical activity, which has been with us for some decades, comes from the work of epidemiologists who probed the relationships between habitual physical activity and various health outcomes, starting with the paper by Morris et al. in 1953. These scientists did not focus exclusively on sports or exercise; indeed, they recognized early on that the level of habitual physical activity, including sport participation, other leisure activities, personal chores, and occupational work, was the most general and encompassing variable to consider. In a sense, habitual physical activity is the core concept behind notions such as active living. Even though the substance already existed about 40 years ago, it was not adequately incorporated into the theoretical models and praxis of most fitness leaders of the time.

All approaches to the study of physical activity—including the holistic—must recognize that physical activity cannot be studied in isolation; it is but one element of an individual's lifestyle. Nutritional habits, smoking, drinking, and other leisure activities deserve particular attention in this respect. Individual differences in level of habitual physical activity are superimposed on heterogeneity stemming from other lifestyle components and from the physical and social environments. Each of these factors varies from person to person because of biological individuality. It is important, therefore, that public pronouncements about the relative values and virtues of a physically active lifestyle are fully informed and show appropriate restraint. That is, promotional efforts must be solidly anchored in the most advanced knowledge available and undertaken in a context where safety and responsibility remain at the forefront of all initiatives.

A further word of caution: Terms like active living can be somewhat equivocal. For example, while some will clearly define active living as a physically active mode of life, others could perceive it as the ratio of hours awake to hours asleep, or as the amount or proportion of time allocated to intellectual or social pursuits unrelated to physical activity. Holistic concepts and approaches must be defined clearly and simply, so that these are immediately and readily recognized by all segments of the public to whom they are targeted.

In Canada, the promotion of active living has emphasized fun, pleasure, feelings, and experiences associated with a physically active lifestyle. At the same time, however, we must not neglect to emphasize frequency, intensity, or volume of activity requirements. The growing body of current knowledge on physical activity, health-related fitness, and health have identified two main requirements for positive physical health outcomes. On the one hand, *frequent* periods of activity (about four times a week or more), at *moderate intensity* (about 40 to 60 percent of maximum), for *30 to 60 minutes per session*, have been shown to generate an energy expenditure sufficient to affect energy balance and provide a healthy stimulus for various physiological systems and metabolic pathways. On the other hand, *occasional* periods of exercise at *higher intensities* seem to be particularly beneficial for heart health.

These findings must be taken into account in any holistic approaches to counseling or promoting physical activity in the general population—for example, "Active Living" in Canada and "Exercise Lite" in the United States. That is, promoting the positive outcomes of regular participation in physical activity must go hand in hand with promoting a physically active lifestyle *at sufficient levels* to influence both health-related fitness and physical health as well as mental health and emotional well-being.

Holistic approaches and concepts that have emerged from the activity, fitness, and health paradigm have significant implications for the professional preparation of fitness and health specialists, who work in a variety of settings. Such specialists should be comfortable with these concepts. They would benefit from a thorough understanding of the fitness and health implications of individual differences in the level of habitual physical activity. They also need to be knowledgeable about the determinants of the level of activity within and between populations, within and between genders, and in various circumstances.

IMPLICATIONS OF HOLISTIC APPROACHES FOR THEORY AND RESEARCH

All the issues discussed previously have implications for research. In the quest for knowledge about the role of physical activity and inactivity on our lives, we have no other valid choice but to rely on the scientific method. However, scientists must recognize that biological individuality constitutes an incredibly complex challenge, which many have failed to recognize thus far. It should not then come as a surprise to conclude that we are still quite ignorant about the details of the mechanisms by which physical activity affects the health of a given individual. Nonetheless, we must maintain a firm commitment to science as the only valid and acceptable path to achieving an understanding of the biological implications of active living. Attempts at shortcuts will lead to obscurantism, dogmatism, and, potentially, consumer fraud.

There appears to be a relationship between the dose of physical activity and the biological response in terms of improvement of fitness and health. The dose-response issue is quite complex and needs to be considered carefully in light of the diversity of fitness components and health objectives. The importance of age and gender in intensity and volume of regular physical activity should also be the focus of research.

Scientists interested by the biological aspects of active living must become familiar with the complexity of the fitness and health phenotypes if they want to make significant contributions. One example should suffice to illustrate this point. Research on the impact of regular physical activity or persistent inactivity on atherosclerosis will have little chance of making significant advances if it is not rooted in the most current understanding of the pathogenesis of atherosclerosis. Thus, the biology of the arterial wall, including the endothelium and the smooth muscle cells; the mechanisms leading to thrombosis; the role of several growth factors; monocytes, lymphocytes, and macrophages; and the biochemistry of lipoproteins, particularly the mechanisms by which the LDL are modified to become highly atherogenic, are some of the areas that need to be mastered by young scientists contemplating this field for a career.

CONCLUSIONS

Dr. Louis W. Sullivan, former Secretary of the U.S. Department of Health and Human Services, wrote recently that the typical family physician provides care for about 1,000 patients over a 10-year period. During that time, 25 will die from coronary heart disease, 20 from cancer, 6 from stroke, and 4 from injuries (Sullivan, 1990). He further estimated that about 29 of these 55 deaths will be premature, with 16 occurring before the age of 65. He speculated that at least 10 of these deaths could have been prevented. In the United States, the Healthy People 2000 initiative is the national framework to address these issues. Its main goal is to increase the span of healthy life. One of the cornerstones of the program is that much of the responsibility lies with the individual.

The Canadian "Active Living" initiative and other holistic approaches must be consistent with these views. They must also recognize the unique contribution to fitness and wellness of being physically active, while acknowledging that there are major gaps in our knowledge base about the influences of regular physical activity or sedentarism on fitness and health. Promoting regular physical activity and a physically active lifestyle in a context where fun, pleasure, and *joie de vivre* prevail should not be incompatible with reasonable recommendations concerning volume and intensity of participation.

While caution should moderate all new initiatives in the area, efforts to raise the level of habitual physical activity deserve strong support not only from fitness specialists but also from physicians, nutritionists, educators, and public health personnel. It would seem that the pioneers in the areas of epidemiology of physical activity, the health-oriented exercise physiologists, and the proponents of an active lifestyle as a part of an effective health promotion strategy were right: The level of habitual physical activity is important for health and well-being.

REFERENCES

Aloia, J.F. (1989). *Osteoporosis, a guide to prevention and treatment*. Champaign, IL: Leisure Press.

American College of Sports Medicine. (1975). *Guidelines for graded exercise testing and exercise prescription* (1st ed.). Philadelphia: Lea & Febiger.

American College of Sports Medicine. (1978). Position statement on the recommended quantity and quality of exercise for developing and maintaining fitness in healthy adults. *Medicine and Science in Sports, 10*, VII-X.

American College of Sports Medicine. (1990). The recommended quantity and quality of exercise for developing and maintaining cardiorespiratory and muscular fitness in healthy adults. *Medicine and Science in Sports and Exercise, 22*, 265-274.

Andres, R. 1985. Mortality and obesity: The rationale for age-specific height-weight tables. In R. Andres, E.L. Bierman, & W.R. Hazzard (Eds.), *Principles of geriatric medicine* (pp. 311-318). New York: McGraw-Hill.

Berlin, J.A., & Colditz, G.A. (1990). A meta-analysis of physical activity in the prevention of coronary heart disease. *American Journal of Epidemiology, 132,* 612-628.

Björntorp, P. (1990). Portal adipose tissue as a generator of risk factors for cardiovascular disease and diabetes. *Arteriosclerosis, 10,* 493-496.

Blair, S.N., Kohl, H.W., Paffenbarger, R.S., Jr., Clark, D.G., Cooper, K.H., & Gibbons, L.W. (1989). Physical fitness and all-cause mortality—A prospective study of healthy men and women. *Journal of the American Medical Association, 262*(Suppl. 17), 2395-2401.

Blanchet, M. (1990). Assessment of health status. In C. Bouchard, R.J. Shephard, T. Stephens, J.R. Sutton, & B.D. McPherson (Eds.), *Exercise, fitness, and health* (pp. 127-131). Champaign, IL: Human Kinetics.

Bø, K., Hagen, R.H., Bernt, K., Jørgensen, J., & Larsen, S. (1990). Pelvic floor muscle exercise for the treatment of female stress urinary incontinence: III. Effects of two different degrees of pelvic floor muscle exercises. *Neurourology and Urodynamics, 9,* 489-502.

Bouchard, C. (1983). Human adaptability may have a genetic basis. In F. Landry (Ed.), *Health risk estimation, risk reduction and health promotion. Proceedings of the 18th Annual Meeting of the Society of Prospective Medicine* (463-476). Ottawa: Canadian Public Health Association.

Bouchard, C., & Landry, F. (1985). La pratique des activités physiques. Dans J. Dufresne, F. Dumond, and Y. Martin (Eds.), *Traité d'anthropologie médicale* (pp. 861-904). Québec: Presses de l'Université du Québec, Institut québécois de recherche sur la culture et Presses Universitaires de Lyon.

Bouchard, C. (1986). Genetics of aerobic power and capacity. In R.M. Malina & C. Bouchard (Eds.), *Sport and human genetics* (pp. 59-89). Champaign, IL: Human Kinetics.

Bouchard, C. (1990). Discussion: heredity, fitness, and health. In C. Bouchard, R.J. Shephard, T. Stephens, J.R. Sutton, & B.D. McPherson (Eds.), *Exercise, fitness and health: a consensus of current knowledge* (pp. 147-153). Champaign, IL: Human Kinetics.

Bouchard, C., Bray, G.A., & Van Hubbard, V.S. (1990). Basic and clinical aspects of regional fat distribution. *American Journal of Clinical Nutrition, 52,* 946-950.

Bouchard, C., Shephard, R.J., Stephens, T., Sutton, J.R., & McPherson, B.D. (1990). *Exercise, fitness and health: a consensus of current knowledge.* Champaign, IL: Human Kinetics.

Bouchard, C., Shephard, R.J., Stephens, T., Sutton, J.R., & McPherson, B.D. (1990). Exercise, fitness and health: the consensus statement. In C. Bouchard, R.J. Shephard, T. Stephens, J.R. Sutton, & B.D. McPherson (Eds.), *Exercise, fitness and health: a consensus of current knowledge* (pp. 3-28). Champaign, IL: Human Kinetics.

Bouchard, C., Tremblay, A., Nadeau, A., Dussault, J., Després, J.P., Thériault, G., Lupien, P.J., Serresse, O., Boulay, M.R., & Fournier, G. (1990). Long-term exercise training with constant energy intake. 1: Effect on body composition and selected metabolic variables. *International Journal of Obesity, 14,* 57-73.

Bouchard, C. (1991). Heredity and the path to overweight and obesity. *Medicine and Science in Sports and Exercise, 23,* 285-291.

Bouchard, C., Tremblay, A., Després, J.P., Thériault, G., Nadeau, A., Lupien, P.J., & Moorjani, S. (1992). The response to exercise with constant energy intake in identical twins. *FASEB Journal*. (Abstract. Federation of American Societies for Experimental Biology, Anaheim, CA)

Bouchard, C. (1992). Genetic determinants of endurance performance. In P.O. Astrand & R.J. Shephard (Eds.), *The Olympic book of endurance in sports*. Oxford: Blackwell Scientific.

Bouchard, C., & Shephard, R.J. (1993). Physical activity, fitness and health: a model and key concepts. In C. Bouchard, R.J. Shephard, & T. Stephens (Eds.), *Proceedings of the International Consensus Symposium on Physical Activity, Fitness and Health*. Champaign, IL: Human Kinetics.

Bouchard, C., Després, J.P., & Tremblay, A. (1993). Exercise and obesity. *Obesity Research, 1*, 40-54.

Bouchard, C., Dionne, F.T., Simoneau, J.A., & Boulay, M.R. (1992). Genetics of aerobic and anaerobic performances. In J.O. Holloszy (Ed.), *Exercise and Sport Sciences Reviews, 20*, 27-58.

Bouchard, C. (1994). Active living from the biological sciences perspective: A word of caution. In A. Quinney, L. Gauvin, & A.E. Wall (Eds.), *Toward active living: Proceedings of the International Conference on Physical Activity, Fitness and Health* (pp. 277-279). Champaign, IL: Human Kinetics.

Bourey, R.E., & Santoro, S.A. (1988). Interactions of exercise, coagulation, platelets, and fibrinolysis—a brief review. *Medicine and Science in Sports and Exercise, 20*, 439-446.

Canada Fitness Survey. (1983a). *Canadian youth and physical activity*. Ottawa: Government of Canada Fitness and Amateur Sport.

Canada Fitness Survey. (1983b). *Fitness and lifestyle in Canada*. Ottawa: Directorate of fitness and amateur sport.

Cumming, D.C., Wheeler, G.D., & McColl, E.M. (1989). The effects of exercise on reproductive function in men. *Sports Medicine, 7*, 1-17.

Després, J.P., Bouchard, C., Savard, R., Tremblay, A., Marcotte M., & Thériault, G. (1984). The effect of a 20-week endurance training program on adipose tissue morphology and lipolysis in men and women. *Metabolism, 33*, 235-239.

Després, J.P., Moorjani, S., Tremblay, A., Poehlman, E.T., Lupien, P.J., Nadeau, A., & Bouchard, C. (1988). Heredity and changes in plasma lipids and lipoproteins after short-term exercise training in men. *Arteriosclerosis, 8*, 402-409.

Després, J.P., Tremblay, A., & Bouchard C. (1989). Sex differences in the regulation of body fat mass with exercise training. In P. Björntorp & S. Rossner (Eds.), *Obesity in Europe I* (pp. 297-304). London: Libbey.

Després, J.P., Bouchard, C., & Malina, R.M. (1990). Physical activity and coronary heart disease risk factors during childhood and adolescence. In K.B. Pandolf & J.O. Holloszy (Eds.), *Exercise and sport sciences reviews* (pp. 243-261). Baltimore: Williams & Wilkins.

Després, J.P., Moorjani, S., Lupien, P.J., Tremblay, A., Nadeau, A., & Bouchard, C. (1990). Regional distribution of body fat, plasma lipoproteins, and cardiovascular disease. *Arteriosclerosis, 10*, 497-511.

Després, J.P., Pouliot, M.C., Moorjani, S., Nadeau, A., Tremblay, A., Lupien, P.J., Thériault, G., & Bouchard, C. (1991). Loss of abdominal fat and metabolic response to exercise training in obese women. *American Journal of Physiology, 261,* E159-E167.

Dishman, R.K. (1990). Determinants of participation in physical activity. In C. Bouchard, R.J. Shephard, T. Stephens, J.R. Sutton, & B.D. McPherson (Eds.), *Exercise, fitness and health: a consensus of current knowledge* (pp. 75-101). Champaign, IL: Human Kinetics.

Ducimetière, P., & Richard, J.L. (1989). The relationship between subsets of anthropometric upper versus lower body measurements and coronary heart disease risk in middle-aged men. The Paris Prospective Study. *International Journal of Obesity, 13,* 111-112.

Ducimetière, P., Richard, J.L., & Cambien, F. (1986). The pattern of subcutaneous fat distribution in middle-aged men and the risk of coronary heart disease. The Paris Prospective Study. *International Journal of Obesity, 10,* 229-240.

Ernst, E. (1987). Physical exercise for peripheral vascular disease—a review. *Vasa, 16,* 227-231.

Evans, D.J., Hoffman, R.G., Kalkhoff, R.K., & Kissebah, A.H. (1984). Relationship of body fat topography to insulin sensitivity and metabolic profiles in premenopausal women. *Metabolism, 33,* 68-75.

Exercise and NIDDM. (1990). *Diabetes Care, 13,* 785-789.

Fitness Canada. (1991). Active living: A conceptual overview.Ottawa: Government of Canada.

Fujioka, S., Matsuzawa, Y., Tokunaga, K., & Tarui, S. (1987). Contribution of intra-abdominal fat accumulation to the impairment of glucose and lipid metabolism in human obesity. *Metabolism, 36,* 54-59.

Gledhill, N. (1990). Discussion: Assessment of fitness. In C. Bouchard, R.J. Shephard, T. Stephens, J.R. Sutton, & B.D. McPherson (Eds.), *Exercise, fitness and health: a consensus of current knowledge* (pp. 121-126). Champaign, IL: Human Kinetics.

Glueck, C.J., Taylor, H.L., Jacobs, D., Morrisson, J.A., Beaglehole, R., & Williams, O.D. (1980). Plasma high-density lipoprotein cholesterol: Association with measurements of body mass. The Lipid Research Clinics Prevalence Study. *Circulation, 62*(suppl. IV), 62-69.

Hagberg, J.M. (1989). Effect of exercise and training on older men and women with essential hypertension. In W.W. Spirduso & H.M. Eckert (Eds.), *Physical activity and aging* (pp. 186-193). Champaign, IL: Human Kinetics.

Hagberg, J.M. (1990). Exercise, fitness, and hypertension. In C. Bouchard, R.J. Shephard, T. Stephens, J.R. Sutton, & B.D. McPherson (Eds.), *Exercise, fitness and health: a consensus of current knowledge* (pp. 455-466). Champaign, IL: Human Kinetics.

Hanefeld, M. (1991). Exercise for patients with hyperlipo-proteinemia. In P. Oja & R. Telama (Eds.), *Sport for all* (pp. 271-279). Amsterdam: Elsevier.

Hardman, A.E., Hudson, A., Jones, P.R.M., & Norgan, N.G. (1989). Brisk walking and plasma high density lipoprotein cholesterol concentration in previously sedentary women. *British Medical Journal, 299,* 1204-1205.

Haskell, W.L. (1986). The influence of exercise training on plasma lipids and lipoproteins in health and disease. *Acta Medica Scandinavica* (Suppl. 711), 25-37.

Haskell, W.L. (1991). Dose-response relationship between physical activity and disease risk factors. In P. Oja & R. Telama (Eds.), *Sport for all* (pp. 125-133). Amsterdam: Elsevier.

Health and Welfare Canada. (1989). *Canadian guidelines for healthy weights*. Ottawa: Supplies and Services Canada.

Helmrich, S.P., Ragland, D.R., Leung, R.W., & Paffenbarger, R.S. (1991). Physical activity and reduced occurrence on non-insulin-dependent diabetes mellitus. *New England Journal of Medicine, 335*, 147-152.

Henley, K., & Vaitukaitis, J.L. (1988). Exercise-induced menstrual dysfunction. *Annual Review of Medicine, 39*, 443-451.

Heyden, S., Schneider, K.A., & Schneider, N. (1991). Physical fitness and longevity. In P. Oja & R. Telama (Eds.), *Sport for all* (pp. 333-342). Amsterdam: Elsevier.

Higgins, M., Kannel, W., Garrison, R., Pinsky, J., & Stokes, J. (1988). Hazards of obesity—The Framingham Experience. *Acta Medica Scandinavica* (Suppl. 723), 23-36.

Holmgren, A. (1967). Vasoregulatory asthenia. *Canadian Medical Association Journal, 96*, 904-905.

Johnson, W.R. (Ed.). (1960). *Science and medicine of exercise and sports*. New York: Harper & Brothers.

Kalkhoff, R.K., Hartz, A.H., Rupley, D., Kissebah, A.H., & Kelber, S. (1983). Relationship of body fat distribution to blood pressure, carbohydrate tolerance, and plasma lipids in healthy obese women. *Journal of Laboratory and Clinical Medicine, 102*, 621-627.

Kenyon, G.S. (1968). Six scales for assessing attitudes towards physical activity. *Research Quarterly, 39*, 566-574.

Kissebah, A.H., Vydelingum, N., Murray, R., Evans, D.V., Hartz, A.J., Kalkhoff, R.K., & Adams, P.W. (1982). Relation of body fat distribution to metabolic complications of obesity. *Journal of Clinical Endocrinology and Metabolism, 54*, 254-260.

Kissebah, A.H., & Peiris, A.N. (1989). Biology of regional body fat distribution: Relationship to non-insulin-dependent diabetes mellitus. *Diabetes and Metabolism Review, 5*, 83-109.

Kissebah, A.H., Freedman, D.S., & Peiris, A.N. (1989). Health risks of obesity. *Medicine Clinics of North America, 73*, 111-138.

Kohl, H.W., LaPorte, R.E., & Blair, S.N. (1988). Physical activity and cancer. An epidemiological perspective. *Sports Medicine, 6*, 222-237.

Krauss, H., & Raab, W. (1961). *Hypokinetic disease: Diseases produced by lack of exercise*. Springfield, IL: Charles C Thomas.

Krotkiewski, M. (1983). Physical training in the prophylaxis and treatment of obesity, hypertension and diabetes. *Scandinavian Journal of Rehabilitation Medicine* (Suppl. 9), 55-70.

Krotkiewski, M. (1985). Physical training in obesity with varying degree of glucose intolerance. *Journal of Obesity and Weight Regulation, 4*, 179-209.

Krotkiewski, M., Björntorp, P., Sjöström, L., & Smith, U. (1983). Impact of obesity on metabolism in men and women. Importance of regional adipose tissue distribution. *Journal of Clinical Investigation, 72*, 1150-1162.

Lampman, R.M., & Schteingart, D.E. (1991). Effects of exercise training on glucose control, lipid metabolism, and insulin sensitivity in hypertriglyceridemia and non-insulin dependent diabetes mellitus. *Medicine and Science in Sports and Exercise, 23*, 703-712.

Lapidus, L., Benftsson, C., Larsson, B., Pennert, K., Rybo, E., & Sjöström, L. (1984). Distribution of adipose tissue and risk of cardiovascular disease and death: A 12-year follow-up of participants in the population study of women in Gothenburg, Sweden. *British Medical Journal, 289*, 1261-1263.

Larson, L.A. (1961). *Health and fitness in the modern world.* Rome: The Athletic Institute in cooperation with the American College of Sports Medicine.

Larson, L.A. (Ed.). (1971). *Encyclopedia of sport sciences and medicine.* London: Collier-Macmillan and New York: Macmillan.

Larsson, B., Svardsudd K., Welin, L., Wilhelmsen, L., Björntorp, P., & Tibblin, G. (1984). Abdominal adipose tissue distribution, obesity and risk of cardiovascular disease and death 13 year follow-up of participants in the study of men born in 1913. *British Medical Journal, 288*, 1401-1404.

Leon, A.S. (1991). Physical activity and risk of ischemic heart disease—an update 1990. In P. Oja & R. Telama (Eds.), *Sport for all* (pp. 251-264). Amsterdam: Elsevier.

Leon, A.S., Conrad, J., Hunninghake, D.B., & Serfass, R. (1979). Effects of a vigorous walking program on body composition, carbohydrate and lipid metabolism of obese young men. *American Journal of Clinical Nutrition, 32*, 1776-1787.

Lortie, G., Simoneau, J.A., Hamel, P., Boulay, M.R., Landry, F., & Bouchard, C. (1984). Responses of maximal aerobic power and capacity to aerobic training. *International Journal of Sports Medicine, 5*, 232-236.

Malina, R.M. (1991). Darwinian fitness, physical fitness and physical activity. In C.G.N. Mascie-Taylor & G.W. Lasher (Eds.), *Applications of biological anthropology to human affairs* (pp. 143-184). Cambridge: Cambridge University Press.

Malina, R.M., & Bouchard, C. (1991). *Growth, maturation, and physical activity.* Champaign, IL: Human Kinetics.

Manson, J.E., Nathan, D.M., Krolewski, A.S., Stampfer, M.J., Willett, W.C., & Hennekens, C.H. (1992). A prospective study of exercise and incidence of diabetes among U.S. male physicians. *Journal of the American Medical Association, 268*, 63-67.

Manson, J.E., Rimm, E.B., Stampfer, M.J., Rosner, B., Hennekens, C.H., Speizer, F.E., Colditz, G.A., Willett, W.C., & Krolewski, A.S. (1991). Physical activity and incidence of non-insulin-dependent diabetes mellitus in women. *Lancet, 338*, 774-778.

Montoye, H.J. (1986). Physical activity, physical fitness, and heart disease risk factors in children. In G.A. Stull, & H.M. Eckert (Eds.), *Effects of physical activity on children. The Academy papers* (pp. 127-152). Champaign, IL: Human Kinetics.

Morris, C.K., & Froelicher, V.F. (1991). Cardiovascular benefits of physical activity. *Herz, 16*, 222-236.

Morris, J.N., Heady, J.A., Raffle, P.A.B., Roberts, C.G., & Parks, J.W. (1953). Coronary heart disease and physical activity of work. *Lancet, ii*, 1053-1057, 1111-1120.

National Heart, Lung, and Blood Institute Report of the Task Force on Research in Hypertension. U.S. Department of Health and Human Services, Public Health Service, National Institutes of Health, September 1991.

National Research Council. (1989). *Diet and health. Implications for reducing chronic disease risk* (pp. 563-592). Washington, DC: National Academy Press.

Oakes, B.W., & Parker, A.W. (1990). Discussion: bone and connective tissue adaptations to physical activity. In C. Bouchard, R.J. Shephard, T. Stephens, J.R. Sutton, & B.D. McPherson (Eds.), *Exercise, fitness and health: a consensus of current knowledge* (pp. 345-361). Champaign, IL: Human Kinetics.

O'Connor, G., Buring, J., Yusuf, S., Goldhaber, S., Olmstead, E., Paffenbarger, R., & Hennekens, C. (1989). An overview of randomized trials of rehabilitation with exercise after myocardial infarction. *Circulation, 80*, 234-244.

Oldridge, N., Guyatt, G., Fischer, M., & Rimm, A. (1988). Cardiac rehabilitation after myocardial infarction. *Journal of the American Medical Association, 260*, 945-950.

Oshida, Y., Yamanouchi, K., Hazamizu, S., & Sato, Y. (1989). Long-term mild jogging increases insulin action despite no influence on body mass index or $\dot{V}O_2max$. *Journal of Applied Physiology, 66*, 2206-2210.

Paffenbarger, R., Hyde, R.T., & Wing, A.L. (1990). Physical activity and physical fitness as determinants of health and longevity. In C. Bouchard, R.J. Shephard, T. Stephens, J.R. Sutton, & B.D. McPherson (Eds.), *Exercise, fitness and health: A consensus of current knowledge* (pp. 33-48). Champaign, IL: Human Kinetics.

Paffenbarger, R.S., Jung, D.L., Leung, R.W., & Hyde, R.T. (1991). Physical activity and hypertension: an epidemiological view. *Annals of Medicine, 23*, 319-327.

Pate, R.R., & Shephard, R.J. (1989). Characteristics of physical fitness in youth. In C.V. Gisolfi & D.R. Lamb (Eds.), *Perspectives in exercise science and sports: Vol. 2. Medicine, youth, exercise and sport* (pp. 1-45). Indianapolis: Benchmark Press.

Pekkanen, J., Nissinen, A., Marti, B., Tuomilehto, J., Punsar, S., & Karvonen, M.J. (1987). Reduction of premature mortality by high physical activity: a 20-year follow-up of middle-aged Finnish men. *Lancet, i*, 1473-1477.

Pérusse, L., Tremblay, A., Leblanc, C., & Bouchard, C. (1989). Genetic and familial environmental influences on level of habitual physical activity. *American Journal of Epidemiology, 129*, 1012-1022.

Pooling Project Research Group. (1978). Relationship of blood pressure, serum cholesterol, smoking habit, relative weight and ECG abnormalities to incidence of major coronary events: final report of the Pooling Project. *Journal of Chronic Disease, 31*, 202-306.

Powell, K.E., Thompson, P.D., Caspersen, C.J., & Kendrick, J.S. (1987). Physical activity and the incidence of coronary heart disease. *Annual Review Public Health, 8*, 253-287.

Rodnick, K.J., Haskell, W.L., Swislocki, A.L.M., Foley, J.E., & Reaven, G.M. (1987). Improved insulin action in muscle, liver, and adipose tissue in physically trained human subjects. *American Journal of Physiology, 253*, E489-E495.

Schoeller, D.A., Ravussin, E., Schutz, Y., Acheson, K.J., Baertschi, P., & Jéquier, E. (1986). Energy expenditure by doubly labeled water: validation in humans and proposed calculation. *American Journal of Physiology, 250*, R823-R830.

Seeman, E., & Allen, T. (1989). Risk factors for osteoporosis. *Australia and New Zealand Journal of Medicine, 19*, 69-75.

Shaper, A.G., & Wannamethee, G. (1991). Physical activity and ischaemic heart disease in middle-age British men. *British Heart Journal, 66*, 384-394.

Shephard, R.J. (Ed.). (1967). Proceedings of the International Symposium on Physical Activity and Cardiovascular Health. *Canadian Medical Association Journal, 96* No. 12.

Shephard, R.J. (1969). *Endurance fitness.* Toronto: University of Toronto Press.

Shephard, R.J. (1987). *Physical activity and aging* (2nd ed.). London: Croom Holm.

Shephard, R.J. (1990). Physical activity and cancer. *International Journal of Sports Medicine, 11,* 413-420.

Simons-Morton, B.G., Parcel, G.S., O'Hara, N.M., Blair, S.N., & Pate, R.R. (1988). Health-related physical fitness in childhood: status and recommendations. *Annual Review of Public Health, 9,* 403-425.

Skinner, J.S. (1981). *Body energy.* Mountain View, LA: Anderson World.

Smith, E.L., & Gilligan, C. (1989). Osteoporosis, bone mineral, and exercise. In W.W. Spirduso & H.M. Eckert (Eds.), *Physical activity and aging* (pp. 107-119). Champaign, IL: Human Kinetics.

Smith, E.L., Smith, K.A., & Gilligan, C. (1990). Exercise, fitness, osteoarthritis, and osteoporosis. In C. Bouchard, R.J. Shephard, T. Stephens, J.R. Sutton, & B.D. McPherson (Eds.), *Exercise, fitness and health: a consensus of current knowledge* (pp. 517-528). Champaign, IL: Human Kinetics.

Sopko, G., Jacobs, D.R., Jeffery, R., Mittelmark, M., Lenz, K., Hedding, E., Lipcjik, R., & Gerber, W. (1983). Effects on blood lipids and body weight in high risk men of a practical exercise program. *Atherosclerosis, 49,* 219-229.

Spirduso, W.W. (1989). Physical activity and aging: introduction. In W.W. Spirduso & H.M. Eckert (Eds.), *Physical activity and aging. The Academy papers* (pp. 1-5). Champaign, IL: Human Kinetics.

Stamler, J. (1979). Overweight, hypertension, hypercholesterolemia and coronary heart disease. In M. Mancini, B. Lewis, & F. Contaldo (Eds.), *Medical complications of obesity* (pp. 191-216). London: Academic Press.

Sullivan, L.W. (1990). Sounding Board—Healthy People 2000. *New England Journal of Medicine, 323* (Suppl. 15), 1065-1067.

Thompson, J.K., Jarvie, G.J., Lahey, B.B., & Cureton, K.J. (1982). Exercise and obesity: Etiology, physiology, and intervention. *Psychological Bulletin, 91,* 55-79.

Tipton, C.M., & Vailas, A.C. (1990). Bone and connective tissue adaptations to physical activity. In C. Bouchard, R.J. Shephard, T. Stephens, J.R. Sutton, & B.D. McPherson (Eds.), *Exercise, fitness and health: a consensus of current knowledge* (pp. 331-344). Champaign, IL: Human Kinetics.

Tremblay, A., & Bouchard, C. (1987). Assessment of energy expenditure and physical activity pattern in population studies. In F.E. Johnston (Ed.), *Nutritional anthropology* (pp. 101-116). New York: Alan R. Liss.

Tremblay, A., Després, J.P., & Bouchard, C. (1985). The effects of exercise training on energy balance and adipose tissue morphology and metabolism. *Sports Medicine, 2,* 223-233.

Tremblay, A., Després, J.P., & Bouchard, C. (1988). Alteration in body fat and fat distribution with exercise. In C. Bouchard & F.E. Johnston (Eds.), *Fat distribution during growth and later health outcomes* (pp. 297-312). New York: Alan R. Liss.

Tremblay, A., Després, J.P., Leblanc, C., & Bouchard, C. (1984). Sex dimorphism in fat loss in response to exercise training. *Journal of Obesity and Weight Regulation*, *3*, 193-203.

Tremblay, A., Nadeau, A., Després, J.P., St-Jean, L., Thériault, G., & Bouchard, C. (1990). Long-term exercise training with constant energy intake. 2: Effect on glucose metabolism and resting energy expenditure. *International Journal of Obesity*, *14*, 75-84.

Tucker, L.A., & Friedman, G.M. (1990). Walking and serum cholesterol in adults. *American Journal of Public Health*, *80*, 1111-1113.

U.S. Department of Health and Human Services. (1987). Protective effects of physical activity on coronary heart disease. *Morbidity and Mortality Weekly Report*, *36*, 426-430.

Van Itallie, T.B., & Abraham, S. (1985). Some hazards of obesity and its treatment. In J. Hirsch & T.B. Van Itallie (Eds.), *Recent advances in obesity research, IV* (pp. 1-19). London: John Libbey.

Vranic, M., & Wasserman, D. (1990). Exercise, fitness, and diabetes. In C. Bouchard, R.J. Shephard, T. Stephens, J.R. Sutton, & B.D. McPherson (Eds.), *Exercise, fitness, and health* (pp. 467-490). Champaign, IL: Human Kinetics.

Waaler, H. (1983). Height, weight and mortality. The Norwegian experience. *Acta Medica Scandinavica* (Suppl. 679).

Warren, M.P. (1991). Exercise in women. Effects on reproductive system and pregnancy. *Clinics in Sports Medicine*, *10*, 131-139.

Williams, P.T., Krauss, R.M., Wood, P.D., Lindgren, F.T., Giotas, C., & Vranizan, K.M. (1986). Lipoprotein subfractions of runners and sedentary men. *Metabolism*, *35*, 45-52.

Wood, P.D., & Stefanick, M.L. (1990). Exercise, fitness, and atherosclerosis. In C. Bouchard, R.J. Shephard, T. Stephens, J.R. Sutton, & B.D. McPherson (Eds.), *Exercise, fitness and health: a consensus of current knowledge* (pp. 409-423). Champaign, IL: Human Kinetics.

World Health Organization. (1968). Meeting of investigators on exercise tests in relation to cardiovascular function. *WHO Technical Report*, *388*.

Zurlo, F., Lilioja, S., Esposito-Del Puente, A., Nyomba, B., Raz, I., Saad, M., Swinburn, B., Knowler, W., Bogardus, C., & Ravussin, E. (1990). Low ratio of fat to carbohydrate oxidation as predictor of weight gain. *American Journal of Physiology*, *259*, E650-E657.

In Perspective

ACTIVITY, EXPERIENCE,
AND PERSONAL GROWTH

Mihaly Csikszentmihalyi

As a child in Europe during World War II, I was struck by an overwhelming sense of human stupidity. Even some of the nicest people acted cruelly, the smartest ones had no clue as to what was happening, the rich lost whatever they had, and the powerful were humiliated. I became a research psychologist in part to understand how such a potentially promising species as the human race could be so helpless.

I am not sure that I have made much progress in that direction since 1965, when I received my PhD from the University of Chicago: The roots of our misery are even deeper and more contorted than I had imagined. What I have learned, instead, are a few interesting facts about creativity and about optimal experiences—in other words, about what lies at the opposite extreme along the spectrum of behavior and phenomenology. It is from this perspective that I approach the study of human activity. By striving to understand what makes life meaningful and rewarding, I hope to complement the more obvious knowledge about what makes it painful.

Some of the more widely read accounts of my research have been reported in *Flow: The Psychology of Optimal Experience* (1990), which has been translated into ten languages, including Japanese and Chinese, and in *The Evolving Self* (1993), also written for a broad audience. Besides these publications, the findings on which my conclusions are based are reported in a large number of scholarly articles. The interested reader is referred to these for a more detailed discussion of research on flow, human activity, and experience.

Currently, as always, I am involved in several large-scale research projects, writing books and articles, and, whenever possible, hiking with my wife, friends, or family in the wilderness of the Rocky Mountains.

Chapter 2

ACTIVITY, EXPERIENCE, AND PERSONAL GROWTH

Mihaly Csikszentmihalyi

The topic I was invited to cover in my chapter for this volume has to do with the spiritual dimensions of physical activity. My approach is as follows. In the first place, I have assumed that activity, by definition, involves volition; in other words, we can choose to do or not to do an activity. I also assume that the activities one chooses will shape both the person who engages in them and his or her community. For example, it will make a difference whether I spend my free time hunting, playing slot machines, or volunteering in a hospital. Watching television in one's free time has a different impact on the ecology, on the community, and on the viewer's psychology than does reading poetry. However, there is not enough space in a single chapter to consider all the possible effects of every possible activity, so I will limit myself to a survey of the activities people in technologically advanced societies engage in most frequently, and consider briefly their impact on psychological processes of the sort we have traditionally thought of as being "spiritual."

We shall begin with a review of some of the present knowledge about the kind of activities people engage in and the psychological and social consequences they usually produce. The thesis of this review is that we are what we do, or become what we have done. The nature of the activities in which we invest psychic energy will determine the kind of individuals who will constitute our society. Before summarizing and interpreting the relevant empirical data, I shall briefly develop the theoretical position that informs my perspective, beginning with a definition of the first term in the title of this piece, that is, activity.

Activity, in this chapter, refers to any patterned, voluntary investments of attention. This may appear at first to be a strange definition, emphasizing the cognitive aspects of the phenomenon at the expense of its physical, emotional, and volitional aspects. But, as I hope to show, to "invest attention" involves an act of will as much as of knowledge, and it is a necessary step in order to have feelings and physical movements. Without attention we cannot be happy or sad, nor can we lift a tennis racquet or pedal a bike. Of course, like any definition, this one will exclude phenomena that others may wish to include in the concept. However, I hope that what the definition brings to light will compensate for what it excludes.

By *pattern* I mean that an activity should have a recognizable order, a set of rules, of interrelated goals and means. Most activities will be recursive, or habitual to a given individual. At the same time, it is useful to remember that even single instances of an activity may have an extraordinary impact. For example, a child might participate in a moving religious ceremony or an outstanding sport performance only once, but the experience could have permanent effects on that child's life.

The second condition specifies that an activity be *voluntary*. This restriction might be quite controversial, since many patterns of what otherwise we would think of as activities are not voluntary. For example, in the history of human evolution the development of bipedal locomotion could be seen as a fundamental change in activity patterns. In turn it resulted in the freeing of hands for carrying food, weapons, and offspring, and eventually in the ability to fashion tools of increasing complexity. According to some, walking also forced shorter gestation and longer periods of extra-uterine development, which in turn made it possible for learning to take precedence over instincts. The shift to walking is thus responsible not only for the development of culture, but for the peculiar organization of the human brain as well. Yet it would be frivolous to imagine that bipedal locomotion was the result of a voluntary choice. Presumably it evolved as a result of slow, random, and unconscious adaptations. Therefore an activity such as bipedal locomotion would not fall within the purview of the present definition.

If something as important as the development of walking is excluded, doesn't this mean that the definition is too restrictive? This could be true, but I shall argue that at the current stage of evolution, activities that are not voluntary in the sense of being the result of conscious choice would only confuse the issue and therefore are best excluded. Nowadays when a person decides to walk to work—instead of driving, taking a bus, or riding the subway—he or she makes a voluntary choice. In such a case, of course, walking would be an activity by our definition.

Finally, an activity involves investments of *attention*. Conceiving of activities in terms of behavior or motor patterns is too restrictive because it would leave out listening to music, thinking, chess, and similar processes where the overt behavioral component is trivial. Conversely, all true physical activities require investments of attention and thus are included. For example, it would be inconceivable to ski, swim, bowl, or fish without concentrating on the stimuli relevant to each activity.

Defining activities in terms of attention invested has important theoretical consequences. Attention is necessary to carry out all nonreflexive physical and mental activities. It is necessary for feeling, thinking, and doing. However, it is in limited supply: We can only pay attention to a few bits of information at the same time. This is what psychologists and neurophysiologists have to say about attention:

> The limit on attentional capacity appears to be a general limit on resources. . . . The completion of a mental activity requires two types of input . . . an information input specific to that [mental] structure, and a non-specific input which may be variously labeled "effort capacity" or "attention." To explain man's limited ability to carry out multiple activities at the same time, a capacity theory assumes that the total amount of attention which can be deployed at any time is limited. (Norman, 1976)

Others who share this approach include Kahneman (1973); Hasher and Zacks (1979); Hoffman, Nelson, and Houck (1983); and Simon (1969). Eysenck writes: "The original notion of attention has been replaced by a conceptualization in which attention is regarded as a limited power supply. The basic idea is that attention represents a general purpose limited capacity that can be flexibly allocated in many different ways in response to task demands" (Eysenck, 1982, p. 28). In fact, it makes sense to think of attention as *psychic energy*, because no complex mental or physical work can be accomplished without it.

This perspective on attention implies that the content and structure of a person's life depends in large part on the activities he or she focuses attention on (Csikszentmihalyi, 1978, 1990; Csikszentmihalyi & Csikszentmihalyi, 1988; Csikszentmihalyi & Massimini, 1985; James, 1890; Massimini & Inghilleri, 1986). The question is one of choice.

Consciously or not, voluntarily or reflexively, people select from among an enormous variety of possible activities the ones they will invest attention in. The sum of these choices describes a person's life.

The relevance of the definition should now be clearer. In studying activities this way, we should be able to understand better the pattern of choices that shapes the physical and mental lives of individuals. The activities people invest psychic energy in will determine not only the content of individual lives, but also some of the most important parameters of culture and social institutions. For example, few would disagree that when a large portion of the psychic energy of the leading citizens of Rome, Byzantium, or Ming China was channeled into the consumption of passive mass entertainment requiring low mental complexity, the viability of those civilizations became seriously compromised. What do people actually invest their attention in? For what reason? What are the consequences of different patterns of attention investment? It is difficult to think of any questions of comparable importance for the human sciences.

THE VARIETY OF HUMAN ACTIVITIES

The first question—What do people actually invest their psychic energy in?—seems relatively straightforward, but on closer examination it involves some rather complicated methodological and even epistemological issues. Let us take the example of a man sitting in his office, writing on a piece of paper. What is he doing? If we asked the man to describe his activity, he might give us several answers: "I was working," or "I was making a list," or "I was trying to solve a marketing problem," or (if he was paying attention to his internal states) he might say "I was thinking about when to have lunch," or "I was mad at my boss." It is not that one of these answers would be more correct than the others; all of them could legitimately represent the activity that the man was attending to. As Vallacher and Wegner (1987) have shown, different people construe their actions in terms of different principles: Some explain what they are doing in terms of momentary, concrete actions; others focus more on long-range goals or social contexts.

The problem in describing activities exactly is in some ways analogous to the uncertainty principle in quantum physics: Just as it is impossible to measure precisely both the position and the momentum of a subatomic particle at the same time, it is equally impossible to know where a person's attention will be at any given moment. And even if we were to ascertain that at time x all of a person's attention is invested in reading a book, the next moment he may get up to get a cup of coffee, make a phone call, or stare out of the window. Besides, the very act of finding out where a person's attention is focused will inevitably change that focus. If I asked, "What are you thinking about now?" you would stop thinking about whatever it was you were thinking of, because my question would have distracted you. Without trying to make too much of this issue, it should be pointed out that the analogy between the behavior of consciousness and subatomic particles is not that far-fetched. Many philosophers, including Spinoza, Whitehead, and Teilhard de Chardin, had anticipated it (Zohar, 1990); in the words of the physicist David Bohm, "The mental and the material are two sides of one overall process . . . separated in thought and not in actuality. . . . There is never any real division between mental and material sides at any stage of the overall process" (Bohm, 1986, p. 129).

There are two ways to circumvent the implications of this state of affairs. The first is to limit oneself to a single disciplinary perspective. For instance, the sociologist may decide not to worry about the details of a man's consciousness as he is sitting at his desk. The important thing is that he is in his office; therefore, the man is "working." The clinical psychologist may focus instead on the fact that the man is mad at his boss and might describe his activity as "experiencing hostility." The cognitive psychologist in turn ignores both of these dimensions and is interested only in the fact that the man is "problem solving." Although these are all very different descriptions of what the man does, each reflects part of the truth.

The second strategy for bringing some order to the indeterminacy of conscious processes is to adopt a statistical approach. This again is analogous to quantum mechanics, which allows one to predict accurately the position and velocity of particles on the average, even though it is not possible to make predictions about individual instances. Returning to our example, if we knew more about the man sitting at his desk, we might be able to predict that during his eight hours in the office he will be adding numbers half of the time, chatting with his co-workers 15 percent of the time, thinking about his boss 5 percent of the time, and so forth. The reason it is possible to make such predictions is that, while psychic energy can change direction in a fraction of a second without apparent cause, on the average it is invested in a finite number of tasks. These "attentional structures" define activities for which we are predisposed either genetically, culturally, or by our unique life experiences. By considering these recursive activities it is possible for the social scientist to begin to make some sense out of the bewildering variety of possibilities.

In my research I have used 150 to 200 codes to describe the elements of human activity. These basic codes can then be recombined into about a dozen major categories, which in turn can be collapsed into three very general classes: work, maintenance, and free time. To move from the basic codes to the general classes is like changing the magnification of a microscope: An entirely new picture emerges at each stage, even though one is looking at the same slice of reality. Which stage one wishes to stop at depends on one's objectives; neither is more "real" than the other. The finer resolution reveals more structural details, the coarser one shows contexts and relationships more clearly. Other investigators have found even more detailed descriptions of activities useful (e.g., Barker, 1968, 1978).

It might be useful at this point to describe briefly the research methodology I have been using for the past 15 years to study human activity. The findings reported in these pages are based on the Experience Sampling Method (ESM), which I developed with my students at the University of Chicago in the early 1970s. It involves the use of electronic pagers that respondents carry with them, usually for one week at a time. Whenever the pager signals, according to a random schedule set for between 8 a.m. and 11 p.m., the respondent writes down in a booklet provided for this purpose answers to a number of questions, some open-ended, some numerically scaled. There are usually eight signals each day, so that by the end of the week each respondent provides up to 56 "snapshots" of daily activity and experience.

Because the responses represent a random sampling of waking life, it is possible to extrapolate from them a reasonably accurate account of what people do, why they do what they do, and how they feel about it. This method revealed, for instance, that American teenagers spend on the average only one and a half minutes per day with their fathers, and that elderly Canadians enjoy the company of their friends more than that of their families—a finding replicated since with other samples of different ages and in different cultures (Larson, Mannell, & Zuzanek, 1986).

To date, the ESM has been used with many "normal" samples in the United States, Canada, Italy, Germany, and South Korea and with many special groups such as mountaineers on a Himalayan expedition, depressed adolescents, mothers of small children, and even chronic schizophrenics (e.g., Csikszentmihalyi, Larson, & Prescott, 1977; Csikszentmihalyi & Csikszentmihalyi, 1988; DeVries, 1992). The methodology itself and some of the psychometric characteristics of the ESM are discussed in Csikszentmihalyi and Larson (1987); Hormuth (1986); Larson and Delespaul (1992); Larson and Csikszentmihalyi (1983).

The ESM is simply one of many methods one can use to assess the frequency and psychological impact of activities. It has its advantages and its disadvantages; in some respects it provides a clearer picture than alternative methods; in some respects it is less comprehensive. For instance, the ESM alone cannot provide a good picture of an individual's long-term goals or life theme, yet such information provides a valuable context for the microanalysis of daily activities. For this reason, an in-depth interview is generally indicated as a complement to the ESM.

Since the 1920s, physicists have become reconciled to the idea that the only access to reality is through the particular lenses of the methods one uses to make one's observations. As the Nobel laureate chemist Ilya Prigogine wrote: "Whatever we call reality, it is revealed to us only through an active construction in which we participate" (Prigogine & Stengers, 1984, p. 293). Or in the words of the physicist John A. Wheeler: "Beyond particles, beyond fields of force, beyond geometry, beyond space and time themselves, is the ultimate constituent [of all there is], the still more ethereal act of observer-participancy" (Wheeler & Zurek, 1983, p. 199). Nevertheless, some social scientists still tend to cling strenuously to the belief that when they measure something, they gain a complete picture of reality as it actually is. Needless to say, this leads to much confusing reification, as when people take the IQ score to be synonymous with intelligence or conclude that a person who spends 40 hours in the office has been working for 40 hours.

The fact that research results are relative to the methods used to obtain them does not mean, of course, that all methods are equally good or that "everything is relative." If we want to ascertain the width of a window in order to hang a curtain, we want to use an accurate tape measure. And once we accept the conventions of the metric system, lengths and weights achieve an invariant value within that system.

Neither the ESM nor any other method used to measure the frequency and the psychological meaning of activities gives a direct picture of an absolute reality. However, within the parameters of its conventions it can give a useful and rather precise idea of what people do day in, day out, and how they feel about it.

THE MAJOR ACTIVITY CATEGORIES

At what level of magnification should we begin looking at people's typical daily activities? If we started with the 150 to 200 detailed codes, we would get a concrete, vivid picture, but one that does not generalize well to any particular group. At this level of analysis, patterns of activity would be quite idiosyncratic, differing by age, gender, occupation, and so forth. One would see many interesting trees, but no forest.

Moving to the level of a dozen or so major activity categories, however, the picture changes. The data reported in Table 2.1 refer to a cross-section of American workers, but the frequency and duration of the various activity categories are very similar to those obtained in other domestic samples as well as samples from around the world (Szalai, 1972; Robinson, 1977; Csikszentmihalyi & Graef, 1980). Here we begin to see a great deal of similarity and consistency in human activities. In practically all modernizing societies (including what are usually referred to as first- and second-world countries), the average adult invests comparable amounts of psychic energy into tasks that are structurally similar to each other. For example, the 40-hour work week is more or less standard across the board, and travel time to and from work is not that different whether one lives in the United States, Japan, or Mexico. More people drive their own cars to work in the United States than in Mexico, but otherwise the time and energy invested in commuting is likely to be of the same order.

Table 2.1 reveals that while the average American worker does indeed spend about 42 percent of his or her waking life on the job (corresponding to about 40 hours a week), only two thirds of this time is actually spent working; one third is spent socializing, daydreaming, snacking, or on other nonproductive activities.

Perhaps nothing shows as clearly how dependent our conclusions are on our methods of measurement as trying to answer the simple question, How much time do people watch TV?

According to the ESM, the answer is less than 7 percent of waking time, or about an hour each day on average. This is much less than the commonly accepted figure: Most studies report that people in our culture spend as much as half of their free time watching TV. The ESM estimate is only one fifth to one sixth of free time. The main reason for this discrepancy is that my low estimate is based on respondents recording that their *primary* activity was watching TV at the time of the signal. When TV provided a background for conversation, for studying, or for dinner, and the respondent recorded it as a secondary activity, I did not count it as watching TV. This is very different from defining TV viewing as every time a set is turned on. Which convention is more accurate? Clearly both are defensible.

The affective valence of the various activities clearly indicates that people report being happiest when they are involved with other people. For instance they report being the most cheerful, friendly, happy, and sociable when they make love, socialize, talk; and then when they eat, play sports, shop, cook, and pursue hobbies. People report being least happy when taking a nap during the day, watching TV, reading, working, and doing chores around the house (Kubey & Csikszentmihalyi, 1990, p. 83). The picture changes little when people report on how strong, active, and excited they feel participating in various

Table 2.1

Major Activity Categories in the Lives of Adult U.S. Workers (Based on 4,791 ESM Responses)

Location/activity	% of responses	
Work		
Working	27.5	
Talking, eating, daydreaming while at work	14.8	
		42.3
Home		
Watching television	6.6	
Cooking	2.4	
Cleaning	3.4	
Eating	2.3	
Drinking, smoking	0.9	
Reading	2.7	
Talking	2.2	
Grooming	3.1	
Hobbies, repairs, gardening	3.7	
Other chores	3.0	
Idling, resting	4.0	
Other, miscellaneous	5.8	
		40.1
Public, others' homes		
Leisure (sports, movies, restaurants)	8.8	
Shopping	3.1	
Transportation	5.7	
		17.6

Adapted, by permission, from K. Kubey and M. Csikszentmihalyi, 1990, *Television and the quality of life* (Champaign, IL: Human Kinetics), 70.

activities. The feeling of potency is highest when people make love, followed by sports, hobbies, driving, shopping, and socializing. The lowest sense of potency is reported when resting, watching TV, reading, and idling.

If we turn the resolution of our imaginary microscope even lower, only three main classes of activity remain visible: work (or productive activity), maintenance, and free time. The amount of psychic energy devoted to these broad classes seems to be very similar not only across most human groups, but also among nonhuman primates. They represent the main features of what it means to be alive.

Productive activities include all forms of energy transformation necessary for life, including, at the most general level, the provision of calories in food, of temperature control through building, clothing, and heating, and the creation and trade of surplus goods. Currently, of course, most productive activities involve secondary and tertiary transformations of energy, and the medium of exchange is currency rather than barter. If for young people we include time spent learning in this category, on the grounds that from childhood to young adulthood schools are supposed to prepare individuals for productive careers, then at any given time about 30 percent of the average person's waking life is spent in productive activities. If we assume that a person is awake 16 hours a day, for 112 hours a week, then approximately 37 hours each week are spent either studying or working. It is interesting to note that free-ranging baboons in Kenya also spend about the same proportion of their waking time foraging for food—the only productive activity in which they engage (Altmann, 1980).

What we call maintenance activities include all the time spent restoring the body's homeostatic balance (e.g., eating, resting), restoring the appearance of the body to the expected cultural standards (e.g., dressing, washing up), restoring one's living environment to expected standards (e.g., washing dishes, cleaning, mowing the lawn), and the preparations required to complete such tasks (e.g., travel, shopping, cooking). Maintenance activities, which take up approximately 40 percent of a teenager's or a working adult's life (and more if the person is a housewife), differ from productive activities in that the psychic energy invested in them does not produce goods that can be exchanged. Nevertheless, maintenance activities are felt to be necessary and sometimes compulsory, and thus they differ from free-time activities.

The average person has about 30 percent of his or her time free from productive or maintenance obligations. Some of this time is spent doing nothing—staring out the window with a vacant mind. A considerable amount is spent in informal social interaction, chatting with friends or family. A large part is spent in passive leisure: watching TV and movies; reading books or magazines. On the average, a very small proportion of free time is devoted to active leisure such as bowling, biking, golf, playing a musical instrument, or painting. However, as we shall see later, this small fraction of active leisure time has a disproportionate significance in terms of human growth potential.

Although this threefold division of activities may seem too broad to shed any light on the human condition, many basic philosophical questions are predicated on just such categories. For instance, Marx and his followers have claimed that the potentialities inherent in an individual are developed and expressed only through productive work (Marx, 1956). The "nature" of a person is not present at birth, nor does it unfold automatically with age, as it does for other animals. Instead, Marx argues, a person's nature is formed by attempts to survive in the natural and cultural environment—a woman who weaves for a living will turn out to be a different person from one whose subsistence is based on milking cows. Work not only transforms the environment, it transforms the worker as well.

Much of the classic Greek philosophical tradition implies the opposite: According to that line of thought, human potentialities can only be nurtured in leisure (Hemingway, 1988). Many contemporary thinkers, especially in the field of leisure and recreation, would agree that free time activities are the most conducive to experimenting with new skills and new experiences—and hence it is in leisure rather than in work that the greatest potential for personal growth is possible (Kleiber, 1985).

In my opinion, both of these arguments have merit but neither is entirely true. In fact, the whole issue needs to be recast in a new conceptual framework. The point is that "work" and "leisure" are not the appropriate categories for deciding what does and what does not contribute to personal growth. This is because work sometimes can be the most challenging, stimulating, and enjoyable part of life for one person—and the most routine, boring, and alienating part for another. Similarly, leisure can indeed promote growth for one person, while leading to a waste of time for another. There are many opportunities for development in both work and leisure, as long as the activity is *complex* and provides a *flow experience*.

PSYCHIC COMPLEXITY

It is the complexity of our psychic processes that distinguishes us from other animal species. Being able to remember, to abstract, to reason, and to control attention are some of the most important distinctions between people and their primate cousins. These functions made it possible for humankind to build the cultural systems—such as language, religion, science, and the various arts—that mark the evolutionary divide between humans and other species. Although each infant inherits the genetic potential for remembering, reasoning, and so forth, these abilities do not become effective unless developed through appropriate, socially constructed activities—that is, through patterned, voluntary investments of attention. Complex abilities require complex activities.

The complexity of any system is a function of two variables: differentiation and integration. *Differentiation* refers to the degree to which a system (i.e., an organ, such as the brain, or an individual, a family, a corporation, a culture, or humanity as a whole) is composed of parts that differ in structure or function from each other. *Integration* refers to the extent that the different parts communicate and enhance each other's goals. A system that is more differentiated and integrated than another is said to be more *complex*.

For example, a person is differentiated to the extent that he or she has many different interests, abilities, and goals, and is integrated in proportion to the harmony that exists between various goals and between thought, feelings, and action. A person who is only differentiated might be a genius, but is likely to suffer from inner conflicts. One who is only integrated might experience inner peace, but is not likely to contribute anything new. Similarly, in a differentiated family parents and children are allowed to express their distinct individuality; in an integrated family the members are connected by ties of care and mutual support. A family that is only differentiated will be chaotic, and one that is only integrated will be smothering. Complexity, at any level of analysis, involves the optimal development of both differentiation and integration.

Evolution is the history of the complexification of living matter. From protozoa swimming in a primeval soup there evolved, through time, organisms fit for all kinds of different niches equipped with all sorts of specialized skills: amphibians, reptiles, birds, and mammals. At least, this is our theory; it might be that the real story of evolution will turn out to be the survival of the cockroach—especially if we fail to develop integration between the human race and the rest of the planet at the same rate as we are differentiating. But given that we humans are living at the threshold of the third millennium AD, we cannot easily abdicate a certain preference for complexity.

The opposite of complexity at the level of psychological development is a form of *psychic entropy.* This concept describes a disorder within human consciousness that leads to impaired functioning. Psychic entropy manifests itself by an inability to use energy effectively either because of ignorance or conflicting emotions such as fear, rage, depression, or simply lack of motivation. Usually it takes encouragement, support, and teaching from others to reduce entropy and restore the order in consciousness necessary for complex functioning.

To maintain the gains of our ancestors and to keep increasing psychic complexity for the use of our descendants, it is necessary to take part in activities that are themselves differentiated and integrated. Education is the main institution charged with providing young people with complex experiences. From the earliest curricula, such as the Trivium (grammar, rhetoric, and logic) and the Quadrivium (arithmetic, geometry, astronomy, and music), to the bewildering variety of choices offered by modern universities, cultures have packaged what they deemed to be important knowledge for transmission to the following generation. However, formal schooling at its best tends to provide only complex *information*; it offers few experiences that help the growth of emotions, character, and sensitivity—and often does a poor job at integrating even the knowledge it does provide. Not so long ago, a chancellor of the California higher education system proudly announced that he was no longer presiding over a *uni*versity but a *multi*versity. Most people no longer even notice that the various data they absorb are not sensibly related to each other.

A community concerned about the survival of its skills and values must invest in more than schools if it wants to preserve, let alone advance, the complexity its former members have so painfully acquired. If families fail to both support and challenge their children, if the community fails to offer them diverse experiences, they are unlikely to grow into complex adults. Boring jobs, oppressive or excessively bland political arrangements, lack of trustworthy leadership, and leisure opportunities that cater to the least common denominator, all contribute to an environment that inhibits involvement in complex activities, with the result that psychic entropy in the population is bound to increase.

FLOW AND COMPLEXITY

At the level of phenomenological analysis—that is, when we consider how individuals perceive what is happening to them—complexity can be indexed by two basic variables. The first consists in the opportunities for action, or challenges, that a person perceives at any given moment of time. The second involves the capacity for action, or skills, that the person believes he or she has. Challenges are the stimulus for differentiation, and skills lead to integration. For instance, a tennis player confronting a more skilled opponent faces a challenge. The natural result of an increase in challenges is a certain amount of psychic entropy: Our player is getting worried whether he might lose the game.

One way to eliminate this worry is by trying to play better than the opponent; but this involves stretching abilities to a new level—that is, differentiation. Now let's suppose that our player actually learns to play so that he can defeat his more accomplished adversary. He has increased his skills; in other words, he has integrated new abilities into his repertoire of behaviors. The other way to eliminate the tension is to ignore or retreat from the challenge. The first solution increases complexity, the second does not.

Evolution proceeds when organisms develop new skills in response to opportunities for action. Adaptation to new niches and the acquisition of more efficient organs leads to increased complexity in a species. Of course, opposite trends also occur—organisms lose complexity when they learn to parasitize other life forms—but we shall ignore these trends because although they exist, they are not part of the story of evolution. Similarly, individuals grow in complexity by developing skills in response to challenges and learning to integrate different possibilities into their repertoire of action. Many of these growth processes are automated: Children learn spontaneously to use their hands to grasp, their legs to walk, and their tongues to speak. But a child will never learn a great deal of what adult humans can potentially do without investing attention in artificial patterns shaped by culture—habits, crafts, books, values—and this requires exposure to complex activities.

The astonishing thing about this state of affairs is that human beings seem to be predisposed to enjoy complexity. At least phenomenologically, people feel best when they use personal resources to confront a new opportunity. This is true in terms of one's entire lifetime: Our most memorable and cherished events are major obstacles overcome and unique opportunities seized. And it is true for the ordinary course of our lives as well: What makes each day meaningful are those occasions when we have done something well, when we have had an unusual experience, and when we have learned something new (Csikszentmihalyi, 1990; Myers, 1992).

It is as if our genetic program has been designed so that we enjoy complexity, which is necessary for growth and evolution, just as we are genetically programmed to find pleasure in food and sex, which are necessary for biological survival (Tiger, 1992). It is true that pleasure is more "natural" and therefore easier to enjoy than complexity. Most everyone enjoys sex; comparatively few enjoy writing sonnets. Yet it appears that when a few preconditions are present, confronting novel opportunities becomes as enjoyable as the rewards programmed in our genes.

When challenges are high and personal skills are used to the utmost, we experience a rare state of consciousness. The first symptom of this state is a narrowing of attention on a clearly defined goal. We feel involved, concentrated, absorbed. We know what must be done, and we get immediate feedback as to how well we are doing. The depth of concentration precludes worrying about temporarily irrelevant issues; we forget ourselves and become lost in the activity. We experience a sense of control over our actions, yet because we are too busy to think of ourselves, it does not matter whether we are in control or not, whether we are winning or losing. Often, we feel a sense of transcendence, as if the boundaries of the self have been expanded. Even the awareness of time disappears, and hours seem to pass by without us noticing. When these conditions are present we say that the person is in flow, because the experience resembles a smooth, almost automatic movement toward an inevitable outcome. Furthermore, flow is so enjoyable that a person will want to repeat whatever activity has produced it.

Some people experience flow when reading a good novel, others when playing the piano, praying, or playing chess. Some find it in their work, others in competitive sports. Navajo shepherds report flow when riding after their flocks in the desert, Japanese teenagers when they ride their motorcycles through the streets of Kyoto, farmers from the Italian Alps when they care for their orchards, and Koreans when they meditate on sacred texts. The activity can be wildly different, but when people are deeply involved meeting a manageable challenge, the state of mind they report is the same the world over (Sato, 1990; Han, 1988; Delle Fave & Massimini, 1988).

However, when a person has few skills, flow can be induced by activities of low complexity, such as burglarizing a home, shooting at an enemy, or playing games of chance (Csikszentmihalyi & Larson, 1978). The point is that flow motivates people to grow. It is a neutral form of energy that can be used for both positive and negative ends. It always leads to greater complexity, but when experienced by a person who is relatively undifferentiated and unintegrated it may produce conflict with the goals of a more complex community. For example, a young man without skills and who has learned no values may feel really alive only when he breaks into a car to steal its radio. This act may be the most complex he can accomplish, and fills him with exhilaration even though it increases entropy in the wider community.

The task of a sound education, Plato argued 25 centuries ago, is to teach young people to find pleasure in the right things. If children enjoyed math, they would learn math. If they enjoyed helping friends, they would grow into helpful adults. If they enjoyed Shakespeare, they would not be content watching most television programs. If they enjoyed life, they would take great pains to protect it. A complex community cannot survive unless it finds ways to provide flow in activities that present a diversity of meaningful opportunities for a variety of skills. Only then will people want to invest the psychic energy necessary to become more complex individuals.

FLOW IN THE ACTIVITIES OF EVERYDAY LIFE

In trying to ascertain which activities produce flow in people's lives, we encounter measurement problems similar to those mentioned earlier in this chapter. What standard should we use to decide whether a person is in flow or not? One defensible criterion is to define flow operationally as any ESM response in which a person reports facing challenges above the person's own average level of challenges, as well as using above-average skills (Massimini & Carli, 1988). This is an extremely liberal criterion, somewhat akin to using a very low level of magnification on the microscope, because one would expect on the average one fourth of all experiences to be flow by this definition (in actuality, the observed range varies from individuals with only 5 percent of the responses in flow to individuals with a high of 45 percent of the responses in flow by this definition). Of course, one could also stipulate that only the most intense experiences, occurring once in a thousand or once in a million times, should be considered flow; but to do so would miss the more modest events that make everyday life meaningful and enjoyable.

If we use above-average challenges/above-average skills as the mea-sure of flow, we find the surprising result that the typical working adult in the United States experiences flow on the job three times as often as in free time. In a representative sample of urban workers, above-average levels of both challenges and skills were reported 54 percent of the time when actually working, versus only 17 percent of the time in leisure (Csikszentmihalyi & LeFevre, 1989). Whenever they were in flow, whether at work or in leisure, these workers reported being very significantly more happy, strong, satisfied, creative, and concentrated than when not in flow. Analysis of variance showed conclusively that it was the presence of flow, rather than whether one was at work or at leisure, that determined the quality of experience. These results were essentially the same for managers and white- and blue-collar workers.

There was, however, one disturbing exception. Motivation was af-fected more by whether one worked or was at leisure than by the presence of flow. People in general preferred to be at leisure than to be working, regardless of whether they experienced flow or not. Thus, paradoxically, in current American culture the aversion to work is so ingrained that although it provides the bulk of the most complex and enjoyable experiences, people still prefer having more free time, even though a great deal of free time is relatively boring and depressing.

The activities that provide flow at work differ depending on the type of job. For managers, solving problems and writing reports tends to produce the most flow; for clerical workers it is typing and keypunching; for blue-collar workers it is fixing equipment and working with computers. The least flowlike work activities include paperwork for managers, filing for clerical, and assembly-line work for the blue-collar employees. The three occupational groups are more similar to each other in terms of what produces flow in free time. Surprisingly, across all occupations, driving a car is the most consistent source of flow experiences, followed by conversations with friends and family. The least flowlike activities in free time are watching TV and maintenance functions such as walking about or trying to sleep (Csikszentmihalyi & LeFevre, 1989). Reading for pleasure is generally a more positive experience than watching TV, but most of the time it falls short of providing a flow experience. On the rare occasions that people are involved in active leisure—such as singing, bowling, biking, or building a cabinet on the basement lathe—they report some of the highest levels of flow, but such activities occur so infrequently in the life of the average person that they leave hardly a trace.

One of the most intriguing mysteries these studies pose is why people spend so much time in passive leisure such as watching television—which is by far the most time-consuming leisure activity in the modern world—when they enjoy it so little. Watching television is universally reported as involving practically no challenges and requiring no skills (Kubey & Csikszentmihalyi, 1990). The fact that people prefer this low-complexity activity to others that provide greater potential for growth appears to contradict the assertion that flow is motivating. There are two ways of reconciling the facts with the theory. One is to recognize that when choosing where to invest attention in free time, people seek to balance the psychic energy they have to expend with the anticipated benefits. Television viewing provides little enjoyment, but it requires also very little effort. Playing the piano or taking a bike ride are much more enjoyable, but require greater expenditures of energy. There is some evidence that in part this is the reason why children end up watching television so much (Csikszentmihalyi & Larson, 1984).

The other explanation is that while children spontaneously enjoy flow, in most societies the mismatch between opportunities and abilities leads to a progressive atrophy of the desire for complexity. Having learned that boredom and worry are the norm in the family, in the school, and in the community at large, children lose their curiosity, their interest, and their desire to explore new possibilities and become used to passive entertainment. They no longer perceive the many opportunities for action around them; they no longer feel that they have skills they can use. Even though passive leisure provides no joy, they see it as the only way to spend free time that is within their means. There is also evidence that supports this explanation. For example, it seems that adults are bimodally distributed in terms of whether their motivation is highest in flow or in apathy—that is, when both challenges and skills are below average. Presumably those who are more motivated in apathy have already resigned themselves to choosing activities of low complexity when they have free time. In general, they are significantly less satisfied, happy, relaxed, and strong when working than people whose motivation is higher in flow (Csikszentmihalyi & LeFevre, 1989).

Our studies suggest that flow does not just improve the quality of experience momentarily, but it has also important long-term effects. For instance, Wells (1988) found that women who are often in flow have much higher self-esteem than women who experience flow rarely. Executives who spend more time in flow are less prone to stress-related illness (Csikszentmihalyi & Donner, 1992). Teenagers who report more flow tend to be happier (Csikszentmihalyi & Wong, 1991) and develop their academic talents further than teens who are in flow less often (Csikszentmihalyi, Rathunde, & Whalen, 1993).

Thus, when persons learn to enjoy complex activities that provide high challenges commensurate to their skills, they are likely to have a more positive sense of self, will enjoy work more, will develop further their innate abilities, and will be happier overall. The question, however, remains: How does a person begin to enjoy complexity?

Although there is no good evidence for answering this all-important question, we can venture some informed guesses. Borrowing the psychologist Brewster Smith's notion of benign spirals of development (Smith, 1969), it seems likely that the quality of response to complexity will have genetic and prenatal components. A baby who has a hard time coping with survival is less likely to search out new challenges; thus, there might be constitutional and temperamental differences beginning to show in the first months of life. After this point, parental treatment can either encourage or further dampen the infant's interest in exploring and playing with his or her environment.

After the first few months of life, our knowledge is on somewhat more solid ground. It seems that the parents of children who experience flow often do treat them differently from the way other parents treat their children. They are more supportive and at the same time more stimulating than parents usually are (Rathunde, 1989; Rathunde & Csikszentmihalyi, 1991; Csikszentmihalyi, Rathunde, & Whalen, 1993). In such a family environment children feel safe to invest attention in gradually more challenging opportunities. In other words, a complex family milieu is likely to produce children comfortable with complexity.

There is also evidence, however, for an opposite developmental path. It is possible for children who have been ignored and even abused by their parents to learn to invest their psychic energies in complex challenges as an escape from the painful family milieu. The early lives of a great many eminent men and women are punctuated by tragedies of various kinds, ranging from the death of parents to illness, alcoholism, and financial ruin (Goertzel & Goertzel, 1962). It is still an open question, however, whether the quality of the flow experience of individuals who escape into complexity is identical with that of those who have been nurtured into it. It is possible that the former may depend on flow more than the latter, and that therefore their optimal experiences are more likely to be surrounded by anxiety and depression.

Beyond parents and the family, every new social contact the child makes will affect whether the developmental spiral will move up towards complexity or down into entropy. The peer group, the special friends one makes, the quality of the schools, the teachers, and the opportunities presented by the neighborhood—each of these factors either reinforces or undermines the growing child's differentiation of individual potentialities and his or her integration into a network of social roles and cultural beliefs. Whether the spiral of development will be benign or not depends on the complexity of the activities the child learns to enjoy. If only mindless or violent opportunities of action are available in the environment, it is unlikely that the child will learn to recognize challenges of a more subtle nature and develop the appropriate skills.

THE DEVELOPMENT OF SPIRITUAL SKILLS

In most cultures, the skills held in highest esteem are those involved in the manipulation and control of mental processes of a certain kind, which for the lack of a better term might be called spiritual. Shamans, priests, philosophers, artists, and wise men and women of various kinds are respected and remembered, and even though they may not be awarded secular power and material benefits, their advice is sought out and their very existence is cherished by the community in which they live.

At first sight, it is difficult to understand the importance attached to such spiritual contributions. From an evolutionary viewpoint, it would seem that they have no practical survival value. The activity of soldiers, farmers, builders, traders, statesmen, scientists, and workers produces obvious benefits; what does spiritual activity accomplish?

The common denominator of spirituality is the attempt to reduce entropy in consciousness. Spiritual activity aims at producing harmony within conflicting desires, strives to find meaning among the chance events of life, and attempts to reconcile human goals with the natural forces that impinge upon it from the environment. It increases complexity by clarifying the components of individual experience—such as good and bad, love and hate, pleasure and pain—and it helps integrate these elements of consciousness with each other and with the external world.

These efforts to bring harmony to consciousness are often based on a belief in supernatural powers, but not always. Many Eastern "religions," and the Stoic philosophies of antiquity, attempted to develop a differentiated and integrated consciousness without recourse to a Supreme Being. Some spiritual traditions, such as Hindu yoga and Taoism, focus exclusively on achieving harmony and control of psychic processes without any interest in reducing social entropy; others, like the Confucian tradition, aim primarily at achieving social order. In any case, if the importance attached to such endeavors is any indication, the reduction of conflict and disorder through spiritual means appears to be very adaptive. Without them, it is likely that people would get discouraged and confused, and that the Hobbesian "war of all against all" would become an even more prominent feature of the social landscape than it already is.

Currently, however, spirituality is almost invisible in the more advanced technological societies. This is due in part to the fact that the cognitive belief systems that validate spiritual order tend to lose their validity with time and need to be reformulated in convincing ways again and again. At present we are living in an era when many of the basic tenets of Christianity, which has supported Western spiritual values for almost two thousand years, have come into conflict with the conclusions of science and philosophy. At the same time that religions have lost much of their credibility, science and technology have been unable to generate convincing value systems.

It seems clear that neither the liberal humanism of the West nor the historical materialism that has so spectacularly failed in eastern Europe and the former USSR have been able to provide sustenance for the spiritual needs of their respective societies (Massimini & Delle Fave, 1991). The United States, in the midst of unprecedented material affluence, is suffering from symptoms of increasing individual and societal entropy: rising rates of suicide, violent crime, sexually transmitted disease, and unwanted pregnancy—not to mention growing economic instability fueled by the irresponsibly selfish behavior of many politicians and businessmen. In the former Communist countries, a half century or more of a fanatical application of materialist ideology has left people confused, cynical, and thirsting for something credible to believe in, even to the point of embracing formerly discredited religious and nationalist ideas. A new synthesis on which to base a believable set of values, one that will unify the best wisdom of past religions with current knowledge, has not yet taken place (Csikszentmihalyi, 1991). In the meantime, however, we can learn about some of the factors that militate against the renewal of spirituality in our culture.

A basic precondition for the development of any kind of spirituality is the ability to tolerate, and even enjoy, solitude. Only in solitary calm can a person reflect on the contents of consciousness and learn to bring order to it. In addition, the development of any complex skill requires solitary practice; the forging of self-control required by every spiritual discipline demands that a person spend some time alone. One of the most consistent findings of ESM studies is that very few people, of any age or social class, can tolerate solitude. When they find themselves alone, most people become depressed and listless. Flow experiences are rare; the paramount state is apathy. Instead of reflecting and trying to control emotions, the typical reaction to solitude is to turn on the television set, grab the first available magazine, phone a friend, or do something useful around the house (Larson & Csikszentmihalyi, 1978; Csikszentmihalyi & Larson, 1984; Larson, Mannell, & Zuzanek, 1986). These strategies for coping with loneliness help to restore order in consciousness in the short run, but they prevent people from developing the inner strength necessary to cope with chaos autonomously.

Spiritual skills are not easy to cultivate; they require disciplined habits slowly acquired. The long apprenticeship of Zen monks, the painstaking exercises of the Yogi, and the ascetic practices of the Christian mystics are just some examples of the kind of training necessary to perfect the ability to bring order to consciousness. It is not enough to learn to be alone; one must also become involved in appropriate activities. Any activity that requires focusing attention inward, that involves learning to control ideas, feeling, and desires, helps to lay the groundwork for the growth of spiritual skills.

The majority of young people in our culture, and hence the majority of future adults, get very little exposure to activities of this kind. Most of the activities they choose in free time involve either unstructured leisure—such as informal conversation with peers, which is the single most frequent free-time occupation (40 percent) and usually reinforces conformity to peer norms and does little to promote individual thinking—or passive leisure, such as TV watching, which takes up 18 percent of free time and is typically very low on concentration and alertness. Yet young people do these things often and willingly. By contrast, thinking, which is the main activity of adolescents only 6 percent of the time, is also the one they enjoy the least; of the 16 main activities they do, adolescents report the lowest level of motivation when they think—just a shade lower than when they study (Csikszentmihalyi & Larson, 1984). A similar pattern is true of every ESM sample, including educated and successful adults. The reason for this seems to be that people say "thinking" is their primary activity only when they are confronted with a problem they cannot possibly avoid. And because they have few skills to cope with psychic entropy, thinking about problems tends to be frustrating and depressing.

The only other things teenagers do that might train them for future spiritual skills are art and hobbies, which occupy only about 3.8 percent of their free time, and reading, which takes up 8.8 percent. Unfortunately, most of the reading is not meant to encourage reflection, consisting mainly of newspapers, magazines, comics, and such. One might perhaps argue that sports and games (another 8.5 percent), inasmuch as they teach discipline and concentration, also contribute to laying down the foundations upon which some spiritual discipline could be built. So under the best of conditions we might assume that the average adolescent spends about 27 percent of his or her free time doing things conducive to spiritual development and 73 percent doing things that, if not actively inimical to learning how to impose order on inner processes, are at best neutral.

The time teenagers spend in school is left out of this reckoning. It would be comforting to believe that formal education, in addition to teaching rules, facts, and some deportment, also prepares young people to create harmony in their consciousness. While this probably happens occasionally (for instance, whenever an inspired teacher is able to surprise a student into reflection), it is not a frequent occurrence. The curricula of Western schools are not very big on providing skills that could lead to spiritual autonomy. In fact, psychic conformity and dependence are the more usual results of formal education.

All in all, the picture is very similar when one moves from adolescence to adulthood. An overwhelming majority of people's psychic energy is invested in mastering the external environment, even after all rational need for it has been exhausted; very little attention is left over to bring order into one's consciousness or into the human environment we share with others. In a recent study of thousands of burnout cases among lawyers and doctors, the reason most often mentioned was that "I never learned to set priorities in my life." We do not learn the skills needed to order experience. We have access to too few activities that make it possible for us to develop them. The opportunities that define our lifestyle risk leading us to spiritual poverty.

HOW RESEARCH CAN CONTRIBUTE
TO THE IMPROVEMENT OF LIFE

What can academic research do to improve this state of affairs? The outlook is not very promising when one considers that decades of research linking cigarette smoke to lung cancer, alcohol to accidents and violence, drug use to dependence, and the destruction of forests to the destruction of the atmosphere have hardly made a dent on societal behavior. Nevertheless, the task of scientists dedicated to improving the quality of life is to report the facts as precisely and clearly as possible, in the hope that eventually the weight of evidence will make a difference in the way people will choose to lead their lives.

Empirical research, however, is blind without sound theoretical foundations. It is essential that we come to agree on the important principles that should inform our investigations, the phenomena worth pursuing, and the measurements that will yield the most relevant information. Studies that don't take into account the entire context of human experience, focusing only on isolated aspects, are often useless. So are studies that fail to account for the long-range consequences of different activities and look only at what people do at the moment. The systems-theory–based approach sketched out in this chapter is one promising theoretical approach. It generates research questions such as the following: Do complex institutions provide complex activities? Do complex activities lead to complex psychological processes? Do complex psychological processes result in complex personalities? Of course, before such questions can be answered, it will be necessary to agree on measures of differentiation and integration applicable to a variety of systems ranging from the individual to the culture. This is by no means an easy task. Yet anything less would not be much worth doing.

Useful research must consider as many ramifications of behavior as possible. For example, in an ongoing study of sixth- to twelfth-grade students we are finding that the amount of time spent watching television has a very high inverse correlation—for boys—with the clarity of their future occupational choices and with the amount of information they have about the steps they will have to take in order to prepare themselves for a career (Bidwell, Csikszentmihalyi, Hedges, & Schneider, in press). The correlations for males are in the –.5 to –.7 range; for females they are around zero. What is the nature of this relationship? And why does it show only for males? Is watching too much TV a symptom of impaired social growth for boys, or is it a cause?

Perhaps no other issue that affects growth is as salient as understanding how people can learn to better use free time, and especially free time spent in solitude. Whatever we can discover about how early experience, parental interaction, education, and the media can help to make people autonomous and unafraid of solitude, able to control their attention, and willing to invest it in challenging opportunities, should be extremely important. At this point it seems that an enormous amount of potentialities for complex activity and experience is lost during unstructured free time, when people resort to passive entertainment to keep their consciousness in order. What difference would it make in the long run if a person reallocated 10 hours a week from low-complexity activities (e.g., hanging out in bars, watching TV, cruising in a car) to activities of higher complexity?

Research into the nature of the optimal flow experience is equally promising. While sports, art, and leisure activities in general are naturally enjoyable, it is in the general interest to find ways to transform everyday tasks, such as studying, work, family life, and community interaction into activities that are as rewarding as the best of games. Only when everyday life is enjoyable will people willingly give up drugs and scale down TV watching and other forms of passive or dangerous entertainment.

It is essential to learn more systematically how social interactions, communities, and institutions best serve the growth of spiritual skills. Because practically all activities are embedded in social structures, it is very difficult to change the nature of activities without first changing the social structure. For instance, most young people spend the major part of their life in schools. This is the context in which they are supposed to learn to control their attention and invest it in complex, symbolic patterns. Unfortunately, students in general find the way schools are structured alienating, resist identifying with educational goals, and can't wait to escape from the rigid blandness of the classroom in pursuit of more exciting experiences. A useful theory of human activity should be able to suggest better ways of organizing formal educational institutions.

Similarly, we must know more about how the culture helps or hinders the development of spiritual skills. The way values are defined and reinforced by the media affects how we experience different activities. Advertising and commercials try to indoctrinate the population in the completely baseless belief that drinking beer and playing volleyball on the beach are the most rewarding experiences to which human existence should aim. We know that although work provides more optimal flow experiences, both in absolute and in relative terms, than any other activity people usually engage in, most of us would still like to be working less—no doubt in part because we have been indoctrinated in the belief that free time, and not work, makes us happy.

Work—or any other activity, for that matter—is likely to be rewarding if one feels that one has chosen to do it; the very same activity will be resented as a burden if one feels obliged to do it. How much leeway is there in giving people an actual sense of choice over their jobs, their learning, their family responsibilities, their civic duties, and their free time? Can we train a majority to have a feeling of ownership for their life choices and therefore enjoy the process of becoming more complex individuals?

These considerations suggest that the kind of research needed is likely to be interdisciplinary and longitudinal. It will take patience, long-range commitment, and plenty of money. This last requirement seems especially forbidding given current fiscal conditions. Yet it seems to me that money is much less of a problem than it is usually made out to be. When one tackles important issues with good ideas and serious dedication—which involves bringing oneself up to state-of-the-art standards—funding is not so impossible to find. In the marketplace of ideas, too many dollars are still chasing too few good projects. But it is also true that over time trivial ideas can kill a promising endeavor. It is therefore imperative that those of us who are interested in understanding the consequences of human activity do not succumb to the temptations of mediocrity. Small dreams and cheap projects are not going to make enough of a difference to warrant continued interest in these topics.

REFERENCES

Altmann, J. (1980). *The ecology of motherhood and infancy in the Savannah baboon.* Cambridge, MA: Harvard University Press.

Barker, R.G. (1968). *Ecological psychology.* Stanford, CA: Stanford University Press.

Barker, R.G. (1978). *Habitats, environments, and human behavior.* San Francisco: Jossey-Bass.

Bidwell, C., Csikszentmihalyi, M., Hedges, L., & Schneider, B. (in press). *Images and experiences of work in American adolescents.* New York: Cambridge University Press.

Bohm, D. (1986). A new theory of the relationship of mind and matter. *The Journal of the American Society for Psychical Research*, 80, 2.

Csikszentmihalyi, M. (1978). Attention and the holistic approach to behavior. In K.S. Pope & J.L. Singer (Eds.), *The stream of consciousness* (pp. 335-358). New York: Plenum.

Csikszentmihalyi, M. (1990). *Flow: The psychology of optimal experience.* New York: Harper & Row.

Csikszentmihalyi, M. (1991). Consciousness in the twenty-first century. *Zygon, 26*, 7-25.

Csikszentmihalyi, M. & Csikszentmihalyi, I. (Eds.). (1988). *Optimal experience: Psychological studies of flow in consciousness*. New York: Cambridge University Press.

Csikszentmihalyi, M. & Donner, E. (1992). Transforming stress to flow. *Executive Excellence, 9,* 16-17.

Csikszentmihalyi, M. & Graef, R. (1980). The experience of freedom in everyday life. *American Journal of Community Psychology, 8,* 401-414.

Csikszentmihalyi, M. & Larson, R. (1978). Intrinsic rewards in school crime. *Crime and Delinquency, 24,* 322-335.

Csikszentmihalyi, M. & Larson, R. (1984). *Being adolescent*. New York: Basic Books.

Csikszentmihalyi, M. & Larson, R. (1987). Validity and reliability of the Experience Sampling Method. *Journal of Nervous and Mental Disease, 175,* 526-536.

Csikszentmihalyi, M., Larson, R., & Prescott, S. (1977). The ecology of adolescent activity and experience. *Journal of Youth and Adolescence, 6,* 281-294.

Csikszentmihalyi, M. & LeFevre, J. (1989). Optimal experience in work and leisure. *Journal of Personality and Social Psychology, 56,* 815-822.

Csikszentmihalyi, M. & Massimini, F. (1985). On the psychological selection of bio-cultural information. *New Ideas in Psychology, 3,* 115-138.

Csikszentmihalyi, M., Rathunde, K., & Whalen, S. (1993). *Talented teenagers: A longitudinal study of their development*. New York: Cambridge University Press.

Csikszentmihalyi, M. & Wong, M. (1991). The situational and personal correlates of happiness: A cross-cultural comparison. In F. Strack, M. Argyle, & N. Schwartz (Eds.), *The social psychology of subjective well-being*. London: Pergamon Press.

Delle Fave, A. & Massimini, F. (1988). Modernization and the changing contexts of flow in work and leisure. In M. Csikszentmihalyi & I. Csikszentmihalyi (Eds.), *Optimal experience: Psychological studies of flow in consciousness* (pp. 193-213). New York: Cambridge University Press.

DeVries, M. (Ed.). (1992). *The experience of psychopathology*. Cambridge: Cambridge University Press.

Eysenck, M.W. (1982). *Attention and arousal*. Bern: Springer Verlag.

Goertzel, V. & Goertzel, M.G. (1962). *Cradles of eminence*. Boston: Little, Brown.

Han, S. (1988). The relationship between life satisfaction and flow in elderly Korean immigrants. In M. Csikszentmihalyi & I. Csikszentmihalyi (Eds.), *Optimal experience: Psychological studies of flow in consciousness* (pp. 138-149). New York: Cambridge University Press.

Hasher, L. & Zacks, R.T. (1979). Automatic and effortful processes in memory. *Journal of Experimental Psychology, 108,* 356-388.

Hemingway, J. (1988). Leisure and civility: Reflections on a Greek ideal. *Leisure Sciences, 10,* 179-181.

Hoffman, J.E., Nelson, B., & Houck, M.R. (1983). The role of attentional resources in automatic detection. *Cognitive Psychology, 51,* 379-410.

Hormuth, S. (1986). The sampling of experiences in situ. *Journal of Personality, 54,* 262-293.

James, W. (1890). *The principles of psychology*. New York: Dover.

Kahneman, D. (1973). *Attention and effort*. Englewood Cliffs, NJ: Prentice Hall.

Kleiber, D. (1985). Motivational reorientation and the resource of leisure. In D. Kleiber & M. Maehr (Eds.), *Motivation and adulthood* (pp. 217-250). Greenwich, CT: JAI Press.

Kubey, R. & Csikszentmihalyi, M. (1990). *Television and the quality of life*. Hillsdale, NJ: Laurence Erlbaum.

Larson, R. & Csikszentmihalyi, M. (1978). Intrinsic rewards in school crime. *Crime and Delinquency, 24*, 322-335.

Larson, R. & Csikszentmihalyi, M. (1983). The experience sampling method. In H.T. Reis (Ed.), *Naturalistic approaches to studying social interaction*. San Francisco: Jossey-Bass.

Larson, R. & Delespaul, P.A.E.G. (1992). Analyzing experience sampling data: A guidebook for the perplexed. In M. DeVries (Ed.), *The experience of psychopathology* (pp. 58-78). Cambridge: Cambridge University Press.

Larson, R., Mannell, R., & Zuzanek, J. (1986). Daily well-being of older adults with family and friends. *Psychology and Aging, 1*, 176-186.

Marx, K. (1956). *Karl Marx: Selected writings in sociology and social philosophy*. (T.B. Bottomore & Maximilien Rubel, Eds.). London: Watts.

Massimini, F. & Carli, M. (1988). The systematic assessment of flow in daily experience. In Csikszentmihalyi, M. and Csikszentmihalyi, I. (Eds.), *Optimal experience: Psychological studies of flow in consciousness* (pp. 138-149, 266-287). New York: Cambridge University Press.

Massimini, F. & Delle Fave, A. (1991). Religion and cultural evolution. *Zygon, 26*, 27-48.

Massimini, F. & Inghilleri, P. (Eds.). (1986). *L'Esperienza quotidiana: Teoria e metodi d'analisi*. Milan: Angeli.

Myers, D.G. (1992). *The pursuit of happiness*. New York: William Morrow.

Norman, D.A. (1976). *Memory and attention*. New York: Wiley.

Prigogine, I. & Stengers, I. (1984). *Order out of chaos*. New York: Bantam.

Rathunde, K. (1989). The context of optimal experience: An exploratory model of the family. *New Ideas in Psychology, 7*, 91-97.

Rathunde, K. & Csikszentmihalyi, M. (1991). Adolescent happiness and family interaction. In K. Pillemer & K. McCartney (Eds.), *Parent-child relations throughout life* (pp. 143-162). Hillsdale, NJ: Erlbaum.

Robinson, J.P. (1977). *How Americans use aim: A social-psychological analysis of everyday behavior*. New York:

Sato, I. (1990). *The thundering tribe*. Chicago: University of Chicago Press.

Simon, H.A. (1969). *Sciences of the artificial*. Cambridge, MA: MIT Press.

Smith, M.B. (1969). *Social psychology and human values*. Chicago: Aldine.

Szalai, A. (Ed.). (1972). *The uses of time*. The Hague: Mouton.

Tiger, L. (1992). *The pursuit of pleasure*. Boston: Little, Brown.

Vallacher, R.R. & Wegner, D.M. (1987). *A theory of action identification*. Hillsdale, NJ: Erlbaum.

Wells, A. (1988). Self-esteem and optimal experience. In M. Csikszentmihalyi & I. Csikszentmihalyi (Eds.), *Optimal experience: Psychological studies of flow in consciousness* (pp. 342-363). New York: Cambridge University Press.

Wheeler, J.A. & Zurek, W.H. (Eds.). (1983). *Quantum theory and measurement.* Princeton, NJ: Princeton University Press.

Zohar, D. (1990). *The quantum self: Human nature and consciousness defined by the new physics.* New York: William Morrow & Co., Inc.

In Perspective

THE SOCIAL PSYCHOLOGY
OF PHYSICAL ACTIVITY

Leonard M. Wankel

My interest in motivation and factors influencing involvement in physical activity developed early in my career as a high school physical education teacher in the early 1960s. I was perplexed by the problem of how to make activity attractive to the poorly skilled, often overweight individuals who would use any excuse to avoid physical education class or school sports of any type. I observed that the most skilled, most fit individuals were the ones who were ready to use the gymnasia or playground facilities at every opportunity. I wondered then "how to turn the sedentary on to physical activity" so that they too could enjoy it and experience the health and fitness benefits. With these interests in mind, I set off to the University of Alberta to study in the emerging area of sport psychology. One year of master's study only served to whet my appetite for research, so at that time I decided to forego my high school teaching career and enroll in Alberta's newly established PhD program. Under the guidance of Dr. Rikk Alderman, I developed an appreciation for the research process and gained an entry into the fledgling world of sport psychology. From the passion and idealism of Professor Al Affleck I learned the importance of "asking big questions" and facing the challenge of making leisure and physical activity opportunities available to all. Looking back some 25 years later, it is humbling to realize that I am still pursuing some of the same basic research questions that I set out to investigate in my graduate program.

Even though it is easy to be pessimistic about the progress in sport and exercise psychology over the years, it is also important to realize that there has been considerable development. There are a number of well-established research organizations—some might argue too many—that hold annual conferences to present current research and publish highly credible journals. The quality and quantity of the research in the field has definitely improved. The original, narrow emphasis on controlled experimental social psychology research, with relatively little attention given to actual sport and exercise contexts, has given way to a more balanced approach using varied methodologies to investigate applied and theoretical issues. Distinct trends or themes are evident in the evolution of the field. The powerful influence of the "Illinois approach to sport psychology," as reflected in the work of Rainer Martens, Dan Landers, Glyn Roberts, their students, and, in turn, their students' students, has contributed greatly to the development of systematic, high-quality, theory-guided research. The rapid development of the field of sport and exercise psychology through the 1970s and 1980s is in large part due to this productive group of scholars. On the negative side, the dominant influence of this group over the major organizations and research journals in the field has tended to stifle alternate approaches. "Hot" topics tended to dominate the conferences and journals of the day. Emphasis on a positivistic, theory-driven approach tended to discourage the basic descriptive research essential to the establishment of any new field of inquiry. The emphasis on quantitative research tended to narrow the focus of sport and exercise research to that of behavior, particularly performance, without paying attention to the broader experiential aspects of the overall phenomenon.

It was left to other areas, particularly leisure studies and, more generally, human development studies, to emphasize the study of the meaning of different experiences, including physical activity involvement. Mihaly Csikszentmihalyi, who is represented in this volume, contributed a number of landmark volumes to this line of research. His original book on the flow experience, *Beyond Boredom and Anxiety*, by providing a systematic method for examining the quality of diverse leisure experiences, has had a major impact upon the direction of leisure and recreation research. Subsequent research on the flow model and its demonstrated applicability to optimal human functioning in diverse applied contexts, both work- and non-work-related, indicated the model to be one of the most fruitful ways of viewing human motivation and development (see also *Flow: The Psychology of Optimal*

Experience, The Evolving Self, and *Optimal Experience: Studies of Flow in Consciousness*).

Another line of research complementing the mainstream focus of sport and exercise psychology has been that within behavioral medicine and public health. The work of individuals such as Jim Sallis, Rod Dishman, Bess Marcus, Gaston Godin, John Martin, Neville Owen, Abby King, and Neil Oldridge has contributed greatly to understanding the determinants of, and factors facilitating, physical activity for health benefits. Progress has been made in delineating different stages of activity involvement (Prochaska & Marcus, 1994) and how different situational and educational interventions might facilitate involvement (Dishman, 1988; Dishman & Sallis, 1994).

A major challenge for the future is to bring these different orientations together in a more integrated, holistic study of the process of becoming and remaining involved in regular physical activity. Although physical activity or exercise is a health-related behavior, and the behavioral medicine research is useful in understanding it as such, it is also important to recognize that physical activity is also a leisure activity and in this regard has a whole additional set of meanings and motivations. Such general social cognitive theories as self-efficacy theory and the theory of planned behavior can help to understand physical activity, or any other intentional behavior. However, consideration must be given also to the uniqueness of the activity context and the particular meaning to the individual. In this regard, basic descriptive research on activity contexts and in-depth, qualitative research on the personal meanings of activity must complement the mainlines of research currently evident. We must be open to all sources of knowledge and different ways of knowing. And always we must keep going back to, talking to, and watching those grade nine students and those "average" adults to check the validity of our models and explanations. Only then will we be sure that we are making progress in answering the big questions.

Chapter 3

THE SOCIAL PSYCHOLOGY OF PHYSICAL ACTIVITY

Leonard M. Wankel

Active living is defined as "a way of life in which physical activity experiences are valued and integrated into daily living" (Fitness Canada, 1988). From this perspective, physical activity is front and center, and active living is considered multifaceted behavior.

1. It involves a behavioral component—engaging regularly in physical activity. The particular type, intensity, duration, and context of the activity however may vary markedly from individual to individual and within the same individual over time.

2. It involves a cognitive component—the knowledge of how to be active and make activity an integral component of one's life.

3. It involves an affective component—the positive valuing of activity and the positive feelings associated with being active.

Active living connotes that to be oneself, to be fully living, one must be active and reap all of the associated physical, psychological, social, and spiritual benefits. This does not imply a hassled, compulsive view that one *should* be active. It does not mean frantically trying to squeeze an obligatory trip to the health spa into an already overcrowded day. Rather, it is a holistic perspective; one *wants t*o be active, and activity is a natural, rewarding, and indeed essential element of everyday life. This perspective of personal autonomy, whether one consciously chooses certain activities or whether they are routinely practiced as an automatic, enjoyable aspect of one's daily routine, is an important feature.

Beyond the individual level, active living involves a societal or cultural dimension—the collective valuing or establishing a norm of being active. While choice and autonomy are key features for individual well-being, individual decisions are always made within a social context (Health and Welfare Canada, 1986). Society models and reinforces certain types of behaviors and values and directly influences the type of opportunities that are available. The importance of this normative influence on individual lifestyles was formally recognized in the vision statement adopted at the 1986 Canadian Fitness Summit, which referred to making regular physical activity a generally accepted "Canadian cultural trademark" (Fitness Canada, 1986). It was recognized that active living is not only desirable from an individual perspective but that it contributes to community well-being and harmony with the physical environment.

While the concept of active living is new, there are definite parallels with other concepts. Revised perspectives of both health and leisure, which have gained broad acceptance in contemporary usage, share many features with active living.

Traditionally, health has been viewed narrowly as the absence of illness or disease. More recently, there has been a move away from this narrow focus to a more positive view of health. Health is viewed more holistically as a state characterized by mental and emotional, as well as physical, well-being (Health and Welfare Canada, 1989-1990). In adopting this broader perspective of health, government initiatives to enhance health have become much more diverse. The focus has shifted from a narrow emphasis on remedial health care (a curative model) to a broader focus on health enhancement (a health promotion model). In embracing such a perspective, Health and Welfare Canada, in its landmark document *A Framework for Health Promotion* (1986), emphasizes the major importance of individual lifestyle choices and environmental factors to population health. While recognizing the importance of personal responsibility for lifestyle choices, the framework emphasizes that these choices are made within a particular physical, social, and cultural milieu. To facilitate more equitable opportunities for healthy lifestyles and health outcomes, the framework suggests, "from a strategic point of view, more public involvement is needed in health issues, as well as improved supports and services at the community level, and a set of public policies that are internally consistent and coordinated in their approach to health issues" (Health and Welfare Canada, 1989-1990).

Active living can be seen to be an important facet of an overall healthy lifestyle. The emphasis upon personal responsibility and individual flexibility, the inclusive orientation (applies to all regardless of personal circumstances or resources), the social interdependence, and the importance of the environment (physical, social, and economic) are all common to both active living and healthy living. The main difference lies in the scope of the concepts. *Active* living refers to the facet of healthy living that emphasizes the relationships to physical activity. Overall *healthy* living, and a broader focus on a healthy lifestyle, would also encompass such other dimensions as nutrition, stress management, interpersonal relationships, and safety. While these aspects may have interrelations with active living (for example, to get the most enjoyment and satisfaction out of a physical activity an individual would have to practice reasonable nutritional and safety practices), these are not directly encompassed by the concept.

Another parallel may be seen in the contemporary view of leisure. Whereas some authors view leisure as discretionary time or activities, passive or active, which are engaged in during discretionary time, many contemporary writers view leisure in terms of experience (Iso-Ahola, 1980; Neulinger, 1984; Shaw, 1984). Less emphasis is placed on the particular activity itself than on what it means or does to the individual. The quality of the leisure experience is viewed in terms of the benefits to the participant, which may be of a physical, psychological, social, spiritual, or economic nature (Driver, Brown, & Peterson, 1991). Such a benefits emphasis necessarily draws attention to the dynamic nature of the relationship between the individual, the experience, the activity, and the context. In other words, such a perspective and the active living perspective share similar characteristics: holistic, personal or individualistic, contextually based (social and physical environment), and dialectical (the individual influences and is influenced by the immediate event).

The purpose of this chapter is to examine the relevance of the concept of active living to research in the social psychology of sport and physical activity. In pursuing this end, two general objectives will be emphasized. First, existing research in the social psychology of physical activity will be reviewed with a view to identifying themes pertinent to clarifying the meaning and relevance of the concept of active living. Second, the implications and the potential advantages and disadvantages of adopting an active living perspective for research in the social psychology of physical activity will be considered.

PSYCHOLOGICAL RESEARCH ON PHYSICAL ACTIVITY

Much of the psychological research on sport and physical activity has been performance oriented. Emphasis has been placed upon studying factors which influence the learning and performance of physical skills. Only relatively recently has significant attention been addressed to broader issues, such as the nature of the experience and the health outcomes of physical activity. The broader scope of interest within sport psychology research was reflected in the changing of the title of the major research journal in the field in 1988 from the *Journal of Sport Psychology* to the *Journal of Sport and Exercise Psychology*. The formation of the Association for the Advancement of Applied Sport Psychology and its subsequent publication of the *Journal of Applied Sport Psychology* has also helped to foster broader study of sport and physical activity from a psychological perspective.

   Psychological research relevant to a broader, more holistic approach may be categorized into two major groupings: (1) psychological perspectives of physical activity involvement and exercise adherence and (2) psychological benefits of physical activity. Within each area, major theories and trends will be identified. No attempt will be made to exhaustively review research in the field. Rather, reference will be made to existing reviews while highlighting aspects most pertinent to holistic studies of physical activity.

PSYCHOLOGICAL CONSIDERATIONS FOR UNDERSTANDING PHYSICAL ACTIVITY INVOLVEMENT AND EXERCISE ADHERENCE

A number of reviews have been written of the research pertaining to exercise adherence and/or motivation for involvement in physical activity (Dishman, 1988, 1990, 1991; Dishman, Sallis, & Orenstein, 1985; Godin & Shephard, 1990; Martin & Dubbert, 1982, 1985; Sallis & Hovell,

1990; Wankel, 1984, 1987, 1988). While each provides a somewhat different emphasis and varying interpretations, the major trends and approaches described are similar. A number of common themes are addressed.

Definitions

One common theme is the high level of confusion caused in the literature by the failure of authors to agree on a common definition of key terms in the field. What is meant by physical activity involvement? What does exercise adherence mean? There has been a general failure to agree on common terminology. Further, many researchers have not specified their terms precisely enough to enable meaningful comparisons between studies nor replicated their studies to establish reliable findings. A useful beginning in establishing some consistent definitions has been made by Caspersen, Powell, and Christenson (1985). They define physical activity as "any bodily movement produced by skeletal muscles that results in energy expenditure. The amount of energy required to accomplish an activity can be measured in kilojoules (kJ) or kilocalories (kcal); 4.184 kJ is essentially equivalent to 1 kcal" (p. 126). Overall physical activity may be segmented in different ways representing different life components (e.g., sleep, work, leisure; light, moderate, heavy; voluntary, compulsory; weekday, weekend). Caspersen et al. state with respect to these various means of categorizing physical activity that "all of these are acceptable ways of subdividing physical activity. The only requirements are that the subdivisions be mutually exclusive and that they sum to the total caloric expenditure due to physical activity" (p. 127). The authors make a clear distinction between exercise and physical activity. They state:

> Exercise, however, is not synonymous with physical activity: it is a subcategory of physical activity. Exercise is physical activity that is planned, structured, repetitive, and purposive in the sense that improvement or maintenance of one or more components of physical fitness is an objective. (1985: p. 128)

Measurement Issues

Closely tied to the problem of arriving at definitions is the problem of how to adequately operationalize the concepts of physical activity and exercise involvement. Patterns of activity have been almost exclusively established through self-report measures, many of which have questionable reliability and validity.[1] While the weaknesses of these measures has been clearly identified, no new, more advanced measure has gained widespread acceptance. Sallis and Hovell observe:

> Over 30 different methods for assessing physical activity have been reported, including self-report, direct observation, and mechanical and electronic monitoring, and new measures are proposed with regularity. Few of these measures combine affordability, practicality of use, and high validity, so physical activity is usually measured with considerable error. (1990: p. 309)

In the more delimited field of exercise adherence within a specified program context, more objective class attendance records are available. Hence it has been possible to more accurately assess the effects of various program interventions on adherence to exercise within delimited program contexts (Martin & Dubbert, 1982, 1984; Wankel, 1984, 1987). It is commonly noted, however, that program attendance itself may not be an adequate measure if interest is in increasing the level of activity involvement adequate for health benefits. Most scheduled class programs do not meet frequently enough for a sufficient time span to have significant health benefits unless supplemented by additional activity. Hence, program leaders recommend that participants also increase their participation in "nonclass" activity.

This measurement issue will become even more problematic with the broadened lifestyle perspective implied by holistic concepts such as active living. Self-reports are most accurate for specific, clearly identifiable, significant events. When the subject of inquiry is the total activity that an individual participates in throughout his/her diffuse daily activities, it is extremely difficult to obtain acceptable behavioral measures using self-report techniques (Baranowski, 1988). Even more difficult will be the assessment of the affective and cognitive aspects of active living. Here, the absence of agreed-upon objective indicators against which to validate self-report measures presents a major obstacle. Only recently has much attention been turned to the assessment of activity-related affect and cognition (see Hobson & Rejeski, 1993; Kendzierski & DeCarlo, 1991; McAuley, 1991).

Factors Affecting Physical Activity Involvement

Descriptive research has identified a number of personal and situational/environmental factors associated with different levels of activity involvement (Dishman, 1990; Wankel, 1988). In general, it has been noted that physical activity involvement is positively associated with income level, educational level, and occupational level and negatively associated with age. Although the percentages of males and females who are involved in leisure-time physical activity is not markedly different, males tend to participate at a higher intensity level (Stephens & Craig, 1990). A greater percentage of unmarried than married individuals participate. Table 3.1 from Dishman, Sallis, and Orenstein (1985) summarizes the evidence concerning variables that may affect physical activity involvement.[2] It is important to note that many of these factors are interrelated. It might be that two factors, age and educational level, account for most of the differences.

No integrated model of physical activity involvement has been developed to specifically incorporate these factors. However, they may be included to varying degrees in general models of behavior. A number of these will be discussed in the following section.

PSYCHOLOGICAL MODELS

A number of psychological models have been used to explain physical activity involvement (Godin, 1994; Godin & Shephard, 1990; Sonstroem, 1988). These models will be briefly examined with particular attention to their relevance for research on active living. Emphasis will be placed on those models that encompass cognitive and affective as well as behavioral components.

Health Belief Model

The Health Belief Model (HBM)(Becker, 1974; Rosenstock, 1974) was developed to explain individual decision making and subsequent health-related action. The overall model is outlined in Figure 3.1. The model posits that the likelihood of taking a given recommended health-related action (e.g., obtaining a chest x-ray or an inoculation) is the joint product of the perceived threat of the relevant disease/illness times the difference of the perceived benefits of the preventive action minus the perceived barriers to the preventive action.

Other variables influence the likelihood of taking action through their effects on these more direct influences. For example, perceived threat of the disease is jointly determined by the product of the perceived susceptibility to the disease times the perceived seriousness of the disease and cues to action (e.g., media, physician, modeling influences). Demographic variables (e.g., age, gender, ethnicity) and socio-psychological variables (e.g., personality, attitudes) are viewed as modifying factors, which may affect the taking of preventive action through their influence on the other predictors.

Table 3.1

Summary of Variables That May Determine the Probability of Exercise

	Changes in probability	
	Supervised program	*Spontaneous program*
Personal characteristics		
Past program participation	++	
Past extra-program activity	+	
School athletics, 1 sport	+	0
School athletics, > 1 sport		+
Blue-collar occupation	– –	–
Smoking	– –	
Overweight	– –	
High risk for coronary heart disease	++	
Type A behavior	–	
Health, exercise knowledge	–	0
Attitudes	0	+
Enjoyment of activity	+	
Perceived health	++	
Mood disturbance	– –	– –
Education	+	++
Age	00	–
Expect personal health benefit	+	
Self-efficacy for exercise		+
Intention to adhere	0	0
Perceived physical competence	00	
Self-motivation	++	0
Evaluating costs and benefits	+	
Behavioral skills	++	
Environmental characteristics		
Spouse support	++	+
Perceived available time	++	+
Access to facilities	++	0
Disruptions in routine	– –	
Social reinforcement (staff, exercise partner)	+	
Family influences		++
Peer influences		++

	Changes in probability	
	Supervised program	*Spontaneous program*
Environmental characteristics (cont.)		
Physical influences		+
Cost		0
Medical screening	–	
Climate	–	
Incentives	+	
Activity characteristics		
Activity intensity	00	–
Perceived discomfort	– –	–

++ = repeatedly documented *increased* probability; + = weak or mixed documentation of *increased* probability; 00 = repeatedly documented that there is *no change* in probability; 0 = weak or mixed documentation of *no change* in probability; – = weak or mixed documentation of *decreased* probability; – – = repeatedly documented *decreased* probability. Blank spaces indicate no data.

Reprinted, by permission, from R.K. Dishman, J.F. Sallis, and D.R. Orenstein, "The determinants of physical activity and exercise," *Public Health Reports* 100:158-171.

Although the model has received considerable support in some areas of preventive health (Health and Welfare Canada, 1989-1990), especially those involving single behavioral acts (e.g., receiving an inoculation or diagnostic x-rays), it has not gained much support in predicting more complex, ongoing exercise behavior. Beyond behavioral complexity, exercise may differ from these other health behaviors in important, underlying, motivational factors. In this regard, after reviewing the literature in the field, Godin and Shephard (1990) concluded:

> Existing data thus provide no clear indication that the HBM is appropriate for the study of exercise behavior. The likely explanation lies in the diversity of motives for exercising.

If the area of interest shifts from relatively delimited exercise behavior to a more diverse and holistic study of physical activity, the HBM will have further limitations. For example, research and promotional strategies associated with notions such as active living are not restricted to preventing specific health problems. Similarly, from a holistic perspective, only a small portion of the overall cognitions and feelings associated with physical activity pertain to avoiding health problems. Hence,

Individual perceptions	Modifying factors	Likelihood of action

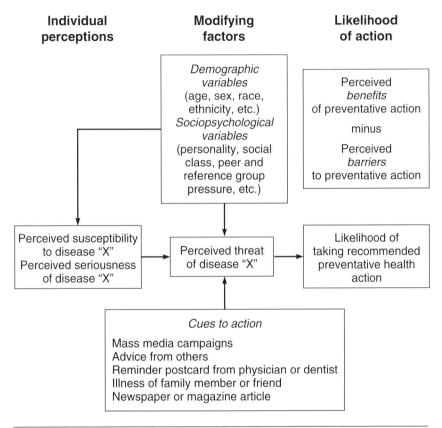

Figure 3.1 The Health Belief Model.
Reprinted, by permission, from M.H. Becker and L.A. Maiman, "Sociobehavioral determinants of compliance with health and medical care recommendations," *Medical Care* 13: 12.

the model would appear to be too restricted for research which takes a holistic approach to the study of physical activity.

Psychological Model for Physical Activity Participation

Sonstroem (1978, 1988; Sonstroem & Morgan, 1989) has developed a model to specify how psychological factors affect physical activity involvement, and in turn how physical activity involvement influences psychological adjustment. As depicted in Figure 3.2, the model posits that global self-esteem is affected by estimates of one's physical ability, which is shaped by one's experiences in physical activity. At the same time, it is hypothesized that estimation influences attraction to physical

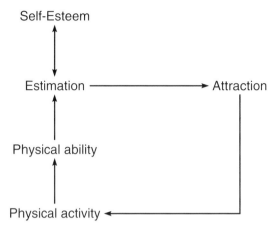

Figure 3.2 The psychological model for physical activity participation.

Reprinted, by permission, from R.F. Sonstroem, 1978, "Physical estimation and attraction scales: Rationale and research," *Medicine and Science in Sports* 10: 101.

activity (an attitude factor), which is a direct predictor of activity involvement.

Although the aspect of the model that deals with the psychological effects of physical activity has gained considerable support, the prediction of physical activity involvement, the aspect of greatest importance to the current discussion, has not (Sonstroem, 1988). It is not clear whether this failure is due to inadequacies of the model itself or to weaknesses in the Physical Estimation and Attraction Scale (PEAS) instruments used to operationalize the two key variables, estimation and attraction. It would appear that there may be limitations in both areas (Sonstroem, 1988).

A particular strength of the Sonstroem model, from a holistic perspective, is that it does attempt to integrate cognition, affect, and behavior. Although the operationalization of the concepts to date has been problematic, there is a potential for operationalizing the model in a broader, more holistic manner. A key consideration in any such operationalization, however, is that the measures of all variables must be at a similar level of specificity (Ajzen & Fishbein, 1980). The two variables in Sonstroem's model which are presented as predictors of physical activity involvement—estimation and attraction—can be viewed as parallel concepts to efficacy expectancies and outcome expectancies in Bandura's (1986) more general social cognitive theory of behavior. The increasing popularity of this theory with exercise researchers (McAuley, 1992) has tended to shift attention away from the more specific model of attraction to physical activity.

Bandura's Social Cognitive Theory

Building upon his earlier social learning theory (Bandura, 1977; Bandura & Walters, 1963), Bandura (1986) developed a social cognitive theory for explaining diverse behaviors. A basic tenet of this theory is that behavior, personal factors (e.g., cognition and affect), and environmental influences are all interactively related in a system of reciprocal determinism. That is, all three have an impact upon and are in turn affected by the others. This argues for a very dynamic, fluid perspective to understanding behavior. In other words, a basic assumption of social cognitive theory is a need to adopt a process view to understand ongoing behavior. Despite this general caveat, the most extensive application of the theory has been to make delimited, time-bound predictions. This type of operationalization within a physical activity context places emphasis on the importance of cognition.

Bandura (1986) has emphasized the importance of two types of expectancies, efficacy expectations and outcome expectancies. These are delineated as follows. "Perceived self-efficacy is defined as people's judgments of their capability to organize and execute courses of action required to attain designated types of performances. It is concerned not with the skills one has but with the judgments of what one can do with whatever skills one possesses" (p. 391). An outcome expectation is "a judgment of the likely consequences [such] behavior will produce" (p. 391). These two factors are felt to be of considerable importance to an individual's behavior beyond actual environmental influences and personal capabilities. As outcome is often influenced significantly by perception of efficacy, Bandura views efficacy as a more central determinant of behavior than outcome expectancy. Consistent with this view, research pertaining to exercise involvement has shown efficacy to be a better predictor than outcome expectancy of subsequent exercise behavior (Desharnais et al., 1986; Dzewaltowski, 1989; Dzewaltowski, Noble, & Shaw, 1990). Other research within a rehabilitative exercise program context (Ewart, Stewart, Gillilan, & Keleman, 1986; Ewart, Taylor, Reese, & DeBusk, 1983; Kaplan, Atkins, & Reinsch, 1984) with selected populations (McAuley & Jacobson, 1991), and in community participation studies (Sallis et al., 1986, 1989) has reported self-efficacy to be an important variable for understanding activity involvement.

The basic orientation of social cognitive theory may be applied in a generalist approach to the study of physical activity. However, much of the research based on the theory has adopted a much more delimited, focused emphasis than that implied by a broad, holistic perspective. Emphasis has been placed upon relatively specific tasks. Self-efficacy, the major referent, is a specific concept in contrast to more general conceptions of self (e.g., self-concept). In addition, this specific time and event focus seems somewhat inconsistent with a very general, more holistic construct, such as active living. It might be pertinent, however, to how active living is manifested in a large number of specific ways. According to social cognitive theory, the manifestations of specific behaviors would be expected to reflect the individual's expectancies concerning self-efficacy and outcomes related to the specific behaviors. Also, affect can have an impact on both cognition and behavior. Recent research by McAuley and associates (McAuley, 1991, 1992; McAuley & Courneya, 1992) has provided some support for social cognitive theory's predictions of how self-efficacy, affect, and behavior would interrelate in a physical activity context.

The Theory of Reasoned Action and the Theory of Planned Behavior

Fishbein (1973, 1980; Fishbein & Ajzen, 1975) formulated a theory of reasoned action (TRA) to predict and explain voluntary behavior. Figure 3.3 illustrates the posited structural relationship of different variables to behavior. According to this theory, the most immediate determinant of an individual's behavior is his/her specific behavioral intention—the intention to perform a specific act in the given situation. Intention, in turn, is determined by two factors: the individual's attitude toward the act and the individual's subjective norm. Attitudes are defined as the individual's affective reactions to the specific behavioral act. They are based upon the individual's salient behavioral beliefs concerning the likelihood of certain outcomes arising as a result of the intended behavior weighted by (i.e., multiplied by) the individual's evaluation of those outcomes. Subjective norm is the perceived social pressure to engage in the act; it is a combination of the individual's beliefs concerning salient reference groups' views about his/her engaging in the act and his/her motivation to comply with those referent groups' wishes. Other variables, such as personality factors, previous experiences, age, gender, and so on, are treated as external variables whose effects upon behavior are mediated through the individual's beliefs.

The theory has enjoyed great popularity in social psychology. The simplicity of the model, its straightforward operationalization, and its general applicability has led to widespread application (Ajzen & Fishbein, 1980). The theory has been shown to predict voluntary behavior with considerable accuracy across a wide variety of contexts (Ajzen & Fishbein, 1980; Davidson & Jaccard, 1975; Norman, 1989). Despite this general support, a number of researchers have questioned the completeness of

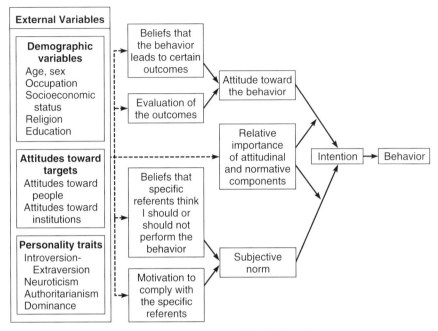

----→ Possible explanations for observed relations between external
       variables and behavior
——→ Stable theoretical relations linking beliefs to behavior

Figure 3.3 The theory of reasoned action: indirect effects of external variables on
behavior.
Icek Ajzen/Martin Fishbein, *Understanding attitudes and predicting social behavior,* © 1980, p. 84.
Reprinted by permission of Prentice-Hall, Englewood Cliffs, New Jersey.

the model and the accuracy of some of its tenets. Attitudes have been
reported to have direct as well as indirect (mediated through behavioral
intention) effects on behavior, and previous behavior has been found to
have a direct influence on behavior intentions and on behavior (Godin
& Shephard, 1990).

Research applying TRA to physical activity and exercise contexts has
yielded results generally consistent with those in other areas. Behavior
intention has generally been found to be a reasonably effective predictor
of behavior (Bentler & Speckart, 1979, 1981; Godin, Valois, Shephard, &
Desharnais, 1987; Riddle, 1980; Valois, Desharnais, & Godin, 1988).
Wurtele and Maddux (1987) and Dzewaltowski (1989), however, reported behavior intention to account for less than 10 percent of the
variance in exercise behavior. Although the attitudinal and subjective
norm components have been found useful for predicting behavior

intention (Godin, Cox, & Shephard, 1983; Riddle, 1980; Wankel & Beatty, 1975), as in other areas, and contrary to the theory, other factors (especially prior exercise behavior) have been found to affect behavior intentions directly (Godin, Cox, & Shephard, 1983; Godin & Shephard, 1986; Godin et al., 1987).

Ajzen (1985, 1987) has proposed an extension to the theory of reasoned action to overcome some of the noted limitations. Specifically, the original theory is restricted to behavior that is completely under volitional control. This is a major limitation when it is recognized that much behavior, including much physical activity behavior, is subject to external factors that limit the availability of opportunities. To account for this, in the theory of planned behavior (TPB), Ajzen adds a perceived behavioral control component to the original attitude and social norm predictors of the theory of reasoned action (see Figure 3.4). Behavioral control in this context is very similar to the perception of self-efficacy in Bandura's social cognitive theory.

Research on a variety of topics is generally supportive of the major tenets of TPB (Ajzen, 1991). Also, the theory has received some support in the physical activity domain. Dzewaltowski (1989) found self-efficacy to significantly add to behavior intention's ability to predict exercise behavior. Although Dzewaltowski interpreted his results as indicating the superiority of social cognitive theory over TRA, the results might also be interpreted as being consistent with TPB if the self-efficacy

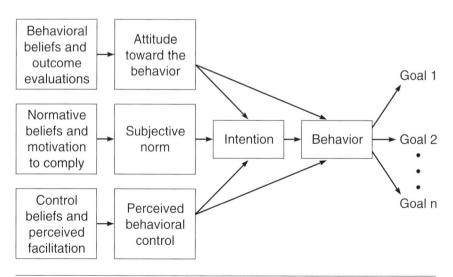

Figure 3.4 The theory of planned behavior.

Driver, B.L., Brown, P.J., & Peterson, G.L. (Eds.). (1991). *Benefits of leisure.* (p. 414). State College, PA: Venture Publishing, Inc.

measure is considered to be a measure of perceived behavioral control. In a subsequent study, Dzewaltowski, Noble, and Shaw (1990) obtained results consistent with TPB. Intention predicted physical activity participation, and attitude and perceived behavioral control predicted intentions. Subjective norms did not significantly contribute to the prediction of intention. It should be noted that consistent with the earlier Dzewaltowski (1989) study, self-efficacy was the best single predictor of behavior, thus supporting Bandura's social cognitive theory.[3] Further research should investigate whether this result simply reflects a measurement issue, as conceptually perceived behavioral control and self-efficacy seem very similar. Two recent research projects pertaining to regular physical activity involvement (Wankel, Sefton, & Mummery, 1991) and leisure choices (Ajzen & Driver, 1992) have supported the predictive utility of TPB.

Like social cognitive theory, both TRA and TPB have largely focused on the explanation and prediction of relatively specific behaviors. Ajzen and Fishbein (1977) have emphasized that, for social psychological variables such as intentions, attitudes, and perceived social norms to predict behaviors, all variables must be operationalized at the same level of specificity. In order to predict specific behaviors (e.g., engaging in a particular activity program), all variables must use the same specific referent (e.g., attitude toward the act of engaging in the specific activity) rather than more general measures (e.g., attitude toward physical activity). This caveat could be followed while conducting research on active lifestyles across a full continuum of topics. At a general level, research might focus on the general idea of maintaining an active lifestyle, with all measures operationalized at this general level. Or, the research could extend throughout the whole continuum, focusing on different dimensions of active living (e.g., leisure-time physical activity, activity during routine tasks of daily living, physical activity at work—right down to engaging in specific types of activity within specified contexts in a defined time frame).

The theory of reasoned action and the theory of planned behavior are consistent with the orientation of active living in that they do encompass cognitive, affective, and behavioral components. Furthermore, there is provision for environmental, personal, and situational influences through the effects of "external variables" mediated through the more direct social psychological predictor variables. Although to date most research attention has been devoted to testing the relative efficacy of the direct predictors (e.g., attitude, subjective norms, perceived behavioral control) for predicting different behaviors, the theory could be used as well to investigate the cognitive and affective aspects of active living. The model is quite flexible and can be applied to very specific or very general behavioral areas. Given its comprehensiveness, adaptability, and ease of operationalization, the theory of planned behavior would appear to be a useful model for investigating active living.

INTERVENTIONS FOR FACILITATING ACTIVITY INVOLVEMENT

A number of researchers have addressed behavior change rather than general predictions of physical activity involvement. Their focus has been on delimited samples, that is, on individuals who join particular activity programs rather than the general population. Although a variety of intervention strategies have been investigated for facilitating program attendance, they essentially fall into two categories: behaviorist techniques (Lees & Dygdon, 1988; Martin & Dubbert 1982, 1984), and cognitive, decision making–based strategies (Kendzierski & Lamastro, 1988; Wankel, 1984, 1987, 1988). Behavioral techniques that have been investigated include material and token reinforcement, social reinforcement, cueing, chaining, and behavioral contracting. Cognitive interventions have included goal setting, decision making (decision-balance sheet), attitude change through belief messages, and attribution training for relapse prevention. In general, the results of this research indicate that a variety of different interventions may facilitate regular activity involvement, at least in formal exercise programs. The long-term effectiveness of these techniques and the relative superiority of any given technique over another, however, has not yet been demonstrated (Dishman, 1991; Wankel, 1987).

Although the interventions used to modify exercise program attendance are general techniques, which have been utilized in other areas of behavior change (e.g., smoking cessation, diet), their utility for more general lifestyle changes (e.g., active living) is not known. For such diffuse behaviors there is likely a broad variety of personal and environmental factors that have led to and reinforce the current lifestyle; therefore, it will be more difficult to successfully apply the behavior change techniques than in relatively circumscribed, specific behavior contexts. It is possible, however, that lifestyle changes are mutually reinforcing—change in one area augments changes in others. Recent research (Ornish et al., 1990) suggests that a comprehensive lifestyle change program could bring about significant reduction in coronary heart disease over a one-year period. Further research, however, is required to determine the relative contributions of the various components (e.g., diet, smoking cessation, stress management, exercise) and factors related to adherence to the prescribed lifestyle changes. Beyond the behavior changes themselves, additional emphasis must be placed upon thoughts and feelings, which are important aspects of lifestyle changes (Wankel & Sefton, 1994).

RESEARCH ON YOUTH SPORT INVOLVEMENT

Although statistics generally indicate that the youngest age groups within a population are the most active and that there is a successive decline across successive age categories (Stephens & Craig, 1990), there is increasing evidence to indicate that large numbers of children lead relatively sedentary lives (Sallis & McKenzie, 1991). This has produced concern that many children may be deprived of the potential enjoyment of active living and also may suffer greater incidence of health conditions related to underactivity, such as increased obesity, serum cholesterol, and blood pressure. Further, there is concern that activity patterns established in the early years may carry over into adulthood.

The majority of the extant literature on physical activity in youth has been within a sport context. Much of this research has been of a descriptive nature, describing factors related to sport involvement and lack of involvement. The most commonly reported reasons or motives reported for engaging in sport are to improve skills, to have fun, to be with friends and to make friends, to succeed or to achieve some goal, and to get exercise (Gould & Horn, 1984). Frequently reported reasons for withdrawing from sport participation include desire to participate in other activities, lack of playing time, lack of success, lack of fun, boredom, and injury (Gould, 1987). Although the major factor, desire to do another activity, is not a negative result from an active living perspective (because the individual remains active), some of the other factors are troubling. Dissatisfaction with the quality of the experience raises concern, especially if this is not for a specific activity but is generalized to all activities. Such dissatisfaction might "rob" young people of the opportunity to participate in healthy physical activity and to engage in positive social interaction with peers. Further, such experiences may have long-term implications for later activity involvement. Thus, the quality of the youth sport or physical activity experience is of considerable importance.

Some progress has been made in identifying those factors that lead to a positive, enjoyable experience and conversely those that do not. Personal competence (e.g., a perception that one has played well), challenge, excitement, and skill development have been shown to be major contributors to fun, with such social factors as being part of a team and being with friends being of secondary importance (Wankel & Kreisel, 1985; Wankel & Sefton, 1989). Excessive emphasis on winning and criticism has been associated with high anxiety and lack of enjoyment (Scanlan & Lewthwaite, 1986; Scanlan & Passer, 1978, 1979).

No comprehensive theory of motivation has been utilized to guide the youth sport research. Csikszentmihalyi's flow model and Deci's cognitive evaluation theory perspective of intrinsic motivation have guided the research on enjoyment conducted by Wankel and associates (Wankel & Kreisel, 1985; Wankel & Sefton, 1989a, 1989b). Harter's Competence Theory and Nicholls' developmental model of achievement motivation have also received support (Weiss, Bredemeier, & Shewchuk, 1986; Duda, 1987). Gould and Petlichkoff (1988) have combined elements of these different theories, as well as other concepts, into a multicomponent model of youth sport motivation. To date, however, no research has tested the viability of the model.

Even though a beginning has been made in identifying the factors that influence enjoyment of organized youth sport, major questions are unanswered as to its importance for long-term activity involvement. Furthermore, it is unknown whether these factors are equally important in less structured activity settings. Further, do these results generalize across youth populations or are they restricted to those who chose to participate in organized youth sport programs? Cross-sectional research indicates that there is considerable change in activity involvement across age groups (Yoesting & Burkhead, 1973). Longitudinal research is necessary to investigate changes in activity involvement over time and to identify the significant factors affecting it.

Although theory development pertaining to youth sport involvement, like that with respect to adult physical activity involvement, has been essentially restricted to borrowing theories from general social psychology, youth sport research has broadened the scope of the research by going beyond the simple act of involvement to examine the quality of the experience. The research on fun and anxiety is compatible with approaches advocating that physical activity should be studied holistically. The experience and meaning of the activity—and not just the simple behavioristic act of being active—are significant in their own right. The longitudinal approach adopted in the Wankel and Sefton (1989) research, and the qualitative in-depth approach of Scanlan, Stein, and Ravizza (1989), are methodologies which would contribute to a holistic approach to the study of physical activity. Recent research by Bocksnick (1991) into the physical activity experiences of older females also has demonstrated the value of supplementing quantitative methods with qualitative approaches in order to gain greater insights into individual lifestyles.

PSYCHOLOGICAL OUTCOMES OF PHYSICAL ACTIVITY INVOLVEMENT

Involvement in regular physical activity has been associated with a number of desirable psychological outcomes (Brown, 1990; Morgan & Goldston, 1987; Wankel & Berger, 1990). These outcomes include such health-related aspects as generally feeling better, reduced anxiety, reduced depression, and enhanced self-esteem, as well as such enhanced attitudinal states as enjoyment and satisfaction. While these psychological benefits of activity are generally accepted both by participants and medical professionals, there is a lack of evidence to indicate how physical activity mediates these outcomes (Morgan & Goldston, 1987). A number of alternate hypotheses have been proposed to account for these effects (Brown, 1990; Morgan & O'Connor, 1988; Petruzzello, Landers, Hatfield, Kubitz, & Salazar, 1991). In general, these alternate models may be grouped into physiological models (e.g., beta-endorphins, norepinepherine, increased body temperature, physical fitness–enhanced stress resiliency) and psychological models (e.g., distraction or time-out, achievement-competence, enjoyment-positive affect) (Wankel & Berger, 1990). No definitive research has been conducted to conclusively support any of the proposed models. Further, none of the models has been clearly eliminated, although both Dishman (1990b) and Petruzzello et al. (1991) argue that physiological research discounts the viability of the beta-endorphin explanation for post-exercise mood changes.

FUTURE RESEARCH DIRECTIONS

A more holistic approach to the study of physical activity may encompass both physiological and psychological models relating physical activity to psychological outcomes. The broad concept of an active, healthy lifestyle has important implications for such psychological maladies as anxiety and depression. A key antecedent of both nonpathological anxiety and depression is a general sense of lack of involvement or control. Holistic, lifestyle-oriented approaches to viewing physical activity, on the other hand, tend to emphasize personal control, as well as physical, psychological, and emotional involvement and well-being. The individual chooses to engage in activities which are personally meaningful.

It is important that research address neurophysiological explanations for positive physical activity influences on psychological well-being.

This kind of research is essential to establish any unique advantage for physical activity over other modes of involvement or interventions. Such an approach calls for collaborative research of psychologists and physiologists/neurologists. In his critical evaluation of the current status of sport psychology, Dishman (1990) presents a strong case for collaborative research between psychologists and other exercise scientists.

> The role of autonomic, neuroendocrine, and limbic systems in regulating mental health responses to exercise must be studied by exercise psychologists employing physiological and pharmacological methods or teaming with physiologists and pharmacologists. Psychological responses to exercise cannot be interpreted by social, behavioral, or cognitive methods alone. The physiological and pharmacological responses to the exercise stimulus must be controlled and quantified.

More specific research questions must be addressed. Rather than posing such general questions as "Does involvement in regular aerobic activity affect anxiety levels?" attention should focus on delineating the delimiting conditions (e.g., specific activity dose) for specific effects for specific target groups. Some results are available concerning the effectiveness of different levels of activity (e.g., type, duration, intensity, frequency) for different groups (e.g., age, gender, health status) (Petruzzello et al., 1991; Landers & Petruzzello, 1994). Further research of this type is needed. Beyond such delimited controlled research, exploratory community studies employing more qualitative approaches are also important. Are particular individual characteristics or different lifestyles prevalent in different communities systematically related to different psychological health characteristics? Longitudinal studies of the psychological health implications of changing lifestyles within individual communities would be of particular value. Such studies might be patterned after previous heart health studies in selected communities (e.g., Shea & Basch, 1990a, 1990b; Farquhar et al., 1989; Farquhar et al., 1990).

There are a number of additional problems and gaps in the research literature pertaining to the psychology of physical activity. For example, there continues to be a problem with the definition and measurement of key concepts pertaining to active living and physical activity involvement. Although it would be desirable to have some generally accepted definitions and standard operational measures for key terms, these are not likely to be available for some time. The relatively slow progress in coming to any generally accepted definitions of such long-standing terms as exercise and physical activity should temper any optimism about any rapid closure on diffuse, holistic concepts such as active living. In the absence of widely accepted conceptual and operational definitions, however, it is critical that each author clearly define key terms and describe in adequate detail how the terms are operationalized so that the study might be replicated. This would enable a meaningful interpretation of the results from different studies.

An additional problem in this field is a lack of coordination or meaningful information exchange between different research areas studying physical activity involvement (e.g., epidemiology, public health, physical education, recreation and leisure studies, youth sport). There is a tendency toward tunnel vision in conducting research: Researchers within each area tend to cite the same research studies and utilize similar research approaches without crossing over into other areas and exploring their relevant research. An example of this provincial orientation is the utilization of Csikszentmihalyi's flow model, which was published in book form in 1975 and has been part of the recreation and leisure studies area since that time, but only recently has received central attention in sport psychology (*Journal of Applied Sport Psychology*, 1992, *4*, 2).

A specific, coherent theory of physical activity involvement is also lacking. Although each discipline (e.g., psychology, sociology, physiology) has its own theories and has applied them to physical activity involvement, no general, multidisciplinary theory of physical activity involvement has been developed. As stated earlier, Dishman (1990b) has argued strongly for including physiological variables when conducting psychological studies of involvement. Similar arguments can be made for including pertinent sociological and anthropological variables. It should be noted that the theory of planned behavior does attempt to include these other variables. It posits that such factors as ethnicity, race, age, physique, and so on would only influence behavior indirectly through their influences on attitudes, social norms, and perceived behavioral control. Current theoretical attempts to explain physical activity involvement fall short in that they are static models, whereas physical activity is dynamic and changing. Although a number of authors have called for more dynamic process models to explain activity involvement, to date no satisfactory model has been developed. Bandura's social cognitive theory adopts a process-oriented, dynamic orientation, but the research generated by the theory has been of a very delimited, static nature. One of the most promising process models is the trans-theoretical model of behavior change of Prochaska and associates (Prochaska & DiClemente, 1984; Prochaska, Nordcross, & DiClemente, 1994). This model has been successfully applied to physical activity

(Prochaska & Marcus, 1994) and has been found to provide a useful framework for investigating the behavioral and experiential processes individuals utilize in progressing through five common stages for making a health-related behavior change:

1. *Precontemplation*: not intending to change in the foreseeable future (e.g., next six months).
2. *Contemplation*: seriously thinking about changing within the next six months.
3. *Preparation*: seriously intending to take action and have made some action plans to do so and may have implemented some changes but not at the criterion level.
4. *Action*: have implemented the desired behavior change within the past six months.
5. *Maintenance*: have maintained the desired behavior change for six months or more.

Another consideration in the psychology of physical activity is the relative lack of systematic programmatic research. Research in the field has been characterized by isolated, one-shot studies. More systematic programmatic research, wherein the results of one study set the problem for the next, is needed.

Similarly, there is a need for more social change or action research. If it is accepted that physical activity involvement does produce benefits (at least under specified conditions), action research within the field situation is required to investigate how these benefits might be brought about. How can positive change be effectively implemented in the field of practice, for example? Such research might effectively combine the commitment and zeal of the programmer with the systematic objectivity of the researcher. Examples of such change-oriented or policy-oriented research are the attempts to initiate change in youth sport programs (McPherson, 1986) and implement policy changes in recreation programs to enhance benefits (Driver, 1989).

Greater sophistication in conceptualizing research problems is also indicated. Too much attention has been addressed to simplistic approaches—for instance, "What effect does X have on Y?" Greater value would accrue from asking such questions as "What are the delimiting conditions for certain effects?" and "What is the dose-response for specified populations given certain conditions?" This recommendation applies equally to research pertaining to how various factors affect the physical activity involvement (cognitive, behavioral, and affective engagement) as well as how different types and levels of activity involvement affect different psychological outcomes (e.g., depression, anxiety, self-esteem, enjoyment).

In short, there remain a number of pressing research questions requiring investigation, which are particularly pertinent to this discussion. These are summarized below.

1. How can holistic concepts such as active living be conceptually and operationally defined? What are the antecedents and consequences of active living? Do these vary across the affective, cognitive, and behavioral domains of active living?

2. What is the dose-response relationship of different types of activity to various psychological outcomes? Is this relationship stable or is it influenced by various personal, situational, and sociocultural factors?

3. What is the relationship of active living to other lifestyle behaviors? Is this consistent across different population subgroups?

4. From a longitudinal perspective, what are the implications of youth activity involvement for involvement at later life stages and for health in later life? Are there significant early life experiences that have lasting health implications throughout life? What is the relationship of participation in various organized activity programs (e.g., youth sports, physical education, fitness classes) to maintaining an ongoing active lifestyle?

5. What are the key factors underlying enjoyment of physical activity for different populations, and how might these be utilized to enhance commitment to active living?

6. What types of intervention and promotion strategies are most effective for promoting and sustaining activity involvement for specific populations (e.g., age, gender, culture, socioeconomic status)?

IMPLICATIONS OF A HOLISTIC APPROACH FOR THEORY AND RESEARCH ON PHYSICAL ACTIVITY

An emphasis on a holistic approach would provide a philosophical or theoretical backdrop against which research on physical activity might be framed. It would provide a gestalt which might assist in integrating or linking many discrete, delimited research studies. It would not necessarily dictate that current lines of inquiry would no longer be pursued, but rather that they would be placed more effectively in context. Such individual studies would be viewed as addressing one small part of the overall, complex puzzle, not pursued as isolated ends in themselves.

There is no one theoretical model that would appear most compatible with the holistic approach embodied by concepts such as active living. Rather, as pointed out in the previous discussion, a number of existing theories, such as Ajzen's theory of planned behavior and Bandura's social cognitive theory, might be adapted to embrace this kind of approach. Perhaps the one psychological theory which has best bridged the scientific and naturalistic paradigms is the flow model of Csikszentmihalyi (1975, 1990; Csikszentmihalyi & Csikszentmihalyi, 1988). Chapter 2 presents this perspective and discusses its relevance to active living and human activity more generally.

In addition, a holistic active living orientation would draw attention to the need for addressing aspects of the physical activity experience which have been to a large extent ignored in current theory and research. More emphasis must be placed upon the broader experiences of the individual (physical, psychological, emotional, social, and spiritual), not just the fact of having engaged or not engaged in physical activity. Research within the psychology of leisure area (e.g., Iso-Ahola, 1980; Shaw, 1984) has indicated that involvement in any activity can have totally different meanings to different individuals. The psychological meaning of an activity to an individual, and the level of satisfaction it provides, depend more on such subjective factors as perceived freedom and competence, rather than objective activity factors (Shaw, 1984). Further, research has indicated that level of enjoyment or satisfaction from sport is more dependent upon subjective factors (e.g., how well one perceived that he/she played) rather than objective game outcome factors (Spink & Roberts, 1980; Wankel & Sefton, 1989).

To accommodate the broadened scope implied by a holistic orientation, new methods of research must be embraced. Greater emphasis should be placed upon naturalistic research (see Guba & Lincoln, 1983), which would be more compatible with the holistic, dynamic active living philosophy. This is not an "either-or" situation, however. It is not a matter of replacing scientific methods, controlled research, and conventional survey studies, but rather supplementing these to a greater extent than has been done to date with various qualitative, naturalistic techniques (e.g., participant observation, in-depth interviews). These latter approaches are particularly appropriate for studying lifestyle and broad community influences. At the same time, scientific methods can be effectively used to systematically investigate hypotheses concerning the relationship of specified variables (e.g., the dose-response effects of exercise). McGrath (1964) proposed a model (shown in Figure 3.5) to illustrate how different methods of research might fit into a systematic program of research.

This model should be interpreted loosely. That is, although the different types of research might be most valuable or most prevalent at different stages of a research program, it is quite possible that they might be utilized productively at all stages. An open stance should be taken toward methodology: The strengths and advantages of a particular methodology for investigating a given question, within the constraints of the particular situation, should dictate the selection of method. A good researcher will not be method-bound but rather will have the flexibility to select, or adapt, appropriate methods to the task at hand.

Part of this adaptable approach to research (tailoring the method to the problem at hand) would be a greater emphasis upon interdisciplinary and multidisciplinary research. Such an approach requires the active collaboration of researchers from all different disciplines.

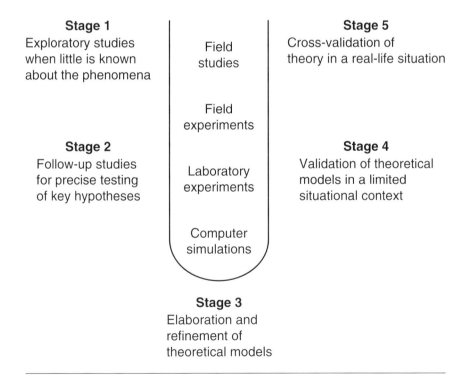

Figure 3.5   Diagram of a five-stage logical path for programmatic research.

Reprinted, by permission, from J.E. McGrath, 1964, Toward a "theory of method" for research on organizations. In *New perspectives in organizational research*, edited by W.W. Cooper (New York: John Wiley and Sons).

STRENGTHS AND WEAKNESSES OF HOLISTIC APPROACHES FOR THEORY AND RESEARCH

The major advantage of adopting a holistic perspective for studying physical activity is that it provides an inclusive and integrative orientation. It encourages observing the way the total being acts and reacts in an ongoing, dynamic way with the environment; one's work, leisure, and home life are all viewed as part of an integrated whole. This overcomes the problem of earlier, fragmented research, which tended to examine involvement in organized exercise programs in isolation from other, ongoing daily activity. A holistic, active living perspective also broadens the focus from a simple appraisal of the behavior of being active to a consideration of the entire experience. What are the antecedents, correlates, and outcomes, broadly viewed, of the total experience? In a dynamic, ongoing process, how does one experience lead into and shape subsequent experiences and mold one's overall lifestyle and quality of life?

The strength of this perspective, however, may also be its greatest weakness. By becoming too broad, such an approach may lose focus. The problem of lack of control and precision of measurement may become more pronounced, which would detract from the reliability and validity of a scientific approach. In scientific terms, such an approach may emphasize external validity but be deficient in demonstrated internal validity. Broad, holistic concepts have ecological validity in that they are tied to everyday life; their weakness is the lack of precision in definition and generally accepted methods for operationalizing the concepts.

Essentially, the issue here is the relative advantage of the scientific versus the naturalistic paradigms for studying human behavior (see Guba & Lincoln, 1983). The bulk of the extant research in sport psychology has been framed within the scientific paradigm. This may have seemed appropriate when the emphasis was on the need for control and replication to understand exercise within a delimited context; however, if a shift is to be made to a more holistic, active living orientation, the relative strengths of the naturalistic paradigm become more salient. This will simply be a matter of degree, however, as no single approach will ever suffice. Each approach has its own inherent limitations which means that complementary approaches must be employed to compensate for those limitations.

Notes

[1]Lamb and Brodie (1990) provide a valuable review of the measurement qualities of many of the most popular questionnaire measures of leisure-time physical activity.

[2]For reviews of research published since this summary table, see Dishman, 1990; Dishman and Sallis, 1994; and Sallis and Hovell, 1990.

[3]Godin (1994) has noted that the self-efficacy and intention measures in the Dzewaltowski, Noble, and Shaw (1990) study were highly correlated and hence may in fact represent two measures of the same variable.

REFERENCES

Ajzen, I. (1985). From intentions to actions: A theory of planned behavior. In J. Kuhl & J. Beckman (Eds.), *Action-control: From cognition to behavior* (pp. 11-39). Heidelberg: Springer.

Ajzen, I. (1987). Attitudes, traits and actions: Dispositional predictions of behavior in personality and social psychology. In L. Berkowitz (Ed.), *Advances in experimental social psychology* (Vol. 20, pp. 1-63). New York: Academic Press.

Ajzen, I. (1991). The theory of planned behavior. *Organizational Behavior and Human Decision Processes, 50*, 179-211.

Ajzen, I. & Driver, B. (1992). Application of the theory of planned behavior to leisure choice. *Journal of Leisure Research, 24*, 207-224.

Ajzen, I. & Fishbein, M. (1977). Attitude-behavior relations: A theoretical analysis and review of empirical research. *Psychological Bulletin, 84*, 888-918.

Ajzen, I. & Fishbein, M. (1980). *Understanding attitudes and predicting social behavior.* Englewood Cliffs, NJ: Prentice Hall.

Ajzen, I. & Madden, T.J. (1986). Prediction of goal-directed behavior: Attitudes, intentions, and perceived behavioral control. *Journal of Experimental Social Psychology, 22*, 453-474.

Bandura, A. (1977). Self-efficacy: Toward a unifying theory of behavioral change. *Psychological Review, 84*(2), 191-215.

Bandura, A. (1982). Self-efficacy mechanisms in human agency. *American Psychologist, 37*(2), 122-147.

Bandura, A. (1986). *Social foundations of thought and action: A social cognitive theory.* Englewood Cliffs, NJ: Prentice Hall.

Bandura, A. & Walters, R.H. (1963). *Social learning and personality development.* New York: Holt, Rinehart & Winston.

Baranowski, T. (1988). Validity and reliability of self report measures of physical activity: An information-processing perspective. *Research Quarterly for Exercise and Sport, 59*, 314-327.

Becker, M.H. (1974). The health belief model and personal health behavior [Monographs]. *Health Education, 2*, 1-326.

Becker, M.H. & Maiman, L.A. (1975). Sociobehavioral determinants of compliance with health and medical care recommendations. *Medical Care, 13*, 12.

Bentler, P.M. & Speckart, G. (1979). Models of attitude behavior relations. *Psychological Review, 86*, 452-464.

Bentler, P.M. & Speckart, G. (1981). Attitudes "cause" behavior: A structural equation analysis. *Journal of Personality and Social Psychology, 40*, 226-238.

Bocksnick, J. (1991). *Effectiveness of a physical activity adherence counselling program with older females*. Unpublished doctoral dissertation, University of Alberta, Edmonton.

Brown, D.R. (1990). Exercise, fitness and mental health. In C. Bouchard, R. Shephard, T. Stephens, J. Sutton, & B. McPherson (Eds.), *Exercise, fitness and health: A consensus of current knowledge*. Champaign, IL: Human Kinetics.

Caspersen, C.J., Powell, K.E., & Christenson, G.M. (1985). Physical activity, exercise, and physical fitness: Definitions and distinctions for health related research. *Public Health Reports, 100*, 126-130.

Csikszentmihalyi, M. (1975). *Beyond boredom and anxiety*. San Francisco: Jossey-Bass.

Csikszentmihalyi, M. (1990). *Flow: The psychology of optimal experience*. New York: Harper & Row.

Csikszentmihalyi, M. (1994). *The evolving self: A psychology for the third millennium*. New York: Harper Collins.

Csikszentmihalyi, M. & Csikszentmihalyi, I. (Eds.). (1988). *Optimal experience: Psychological studies of flow in consciousness*. New York: Cambridge University Press.

Davidson, A.R. & Jaccard, J.J. (1975). Population psychology: a new look at an old problem. *Journal of Personality and Social Psychology, 31*, 1073-1082.

Desharnais, R., Bouillon, J., & Godin, G. (1986). Self-efficacy and outcome expectations as determinants of exercise adherence. *Psychological Reports, 59*, 1155-1159.

Dishman, R. (Ed.). (1988). *Exercise adherence: Its impact on public health*. Champaign, IL: Human Kinetics.

Dishman, R. (1990a). Determinants of participation in physical activity. In C. Bouchard, R. Shephard, T. Stephens, J. Sutton, & B. McPherson (Eds.). *Exercise, fitness and health: A consensus of current knowledge* (pp. 75-101). Champaign, IL: Human Kinetics.

Dishman, R. (1990b). The failure of sport psychology in the exercise and sport sciences. *New possibilities, new paradigms*? (American Academy of Physical Education papers, No. 24, pp. 39-47). Champaign, IL: Human Kinetics.

Dishman, R. (1991). Increasing and maintaining exercise and physical activity. *Behavior Therapy, 22*, 345-378.

Dishman, R. & Dunn, A.L. (1988). Exercise adherence in children and youth: Implications for adulthood. In R.K. Dishman (Ed.), *Exercise adherence: Its impact on public health* (pp. 155-200). Champaign, IL: Human Kinetics.

Dishman, R.K. & Sallis, J.F. (1994). Determinants and interventions for physical activity and exercise. In C. Bouchard, R. Shephard, & T. Stephens (Eds.), *Physical activity, fitness and health: International proceedings and consensus statement* (pp. 214-238). Champaign, IL: Human Kinetics.

Dishman, R.K., Sallis, J.F., & Orenstein, D.R. (1985). The determinants of physical activity and exercise. *Public Health Reports, 100*, 158-171.

Driver, B.L. (1989). Applied leisure research: Benefits to scientists and practitioners and their respective roles. In E.L. Jackson & T.L. Burton (Eds.), *Understanding leisure and recreation: Mapping the past, charting the future* (pp. 597-609). State College, PA: Venture.

Driver, B., Brown, P., & Peterson, G. (1991). *Benefits of leisure.* State College, PA: Venture.

Duda, J.L. (1987). Toward a developmental theory of children's motivation in sport. *Journal of Sport Psychology, 9,* 130-145.

Dzewaltowski, D. (1989). Toward a model of exercise behavior. *Journal of Sport and Exercise Psychology, 11,* 251-269.

Dzewaltowski, D., Noble, J.M., & Shaw, J. (1990). Physical activity participation: Social cognitive theory versus the theories of reasoned action and planned behavior. *Journal of Sport and Exercise Psychology, 12*(4), 388-405.

Ewart, C.G., Stewart, K.J., Gillilan, R.E., & Keleman, M.H. (1986). Self-efficacy mediates strength gains during circuit weight training in men with coronary artery disease. *Medicine and Science in Sports and Exercise, 18,* 531-544.

Ewart, C.K., Taylor, C.B., Reese, L.B., & DeBusk, R.F. (1983). Effects of early postmyocardial infarction exercise testing on self-perception and subsequent physical activity. *American Journal of Cardiology, 51,* 1076-1080.

Farquhar, J.W., Fortmann, S.P., Flora, J.A., Taylor, C.B., Haskell, W.L., Williams, P.T., Macoby, N., & Wood, P.D. (1989). Lifestyle research: An overview. In D.G. Russell & D.H. Buisson (Eds.), (pp. 16-38). Dunedin, NZ: Human Performance Associates.

Farquhar, J.W., Fortmann, S.P., Flora, J.A., Taylor, C.B., Haskell, W.L., Williams, P.T., Macoby, N., & Wood, P.D. (1990). Effects of community-wide education on cardiovascular disease risk factors: The Stanford five-city project. *Journal of the American Medical Association, 264,* 359-365.

Fishbein, M. (1973). The prediction of behavior from attitudinal variables. In C.D. Mortenson & K.K. Sereno (Eds.), *Advances in communication research* (pp. 3-31). New York: Harper & Row.

Fishbein, M. (1980). A theory of reasoned action: Some applications and implications. In M.M. Page (Ed.), *Nebraska symposium on motivation* (pp. 65-116). Lincoln, NB: University of Nebraska Press.

Fishbein, M. & Ajzen, I. (1975). *Belief, attitude, intention and behavior: An introduction to theory and research.* Reading, MA: Addison-Wesley.

Fitness Canada. (1986). *Fitness . . . the future. Canadian Summit on Fitness.* Ottawa: Government of Canada.

Fitness Canada. (1988). *Active living.* Unpublished materials. Ottawa: Fitness Canada.

Godin, G. (1994). Social-cognitive models. In R.K. Dishman (Ed.), *Advances in exercise adherence* (pp. 113-136). Champaign, IL: Human Kinetics.

Godin, G., Cox, M., & Shephard, R.J. (1983). The impact of physical fitness evaluation on behavioral intentions towards regular exercise. *Canadian Journal of Applied Sport Sciences, 8,* 240-245.

Godin, G. & Shephard, R.J. (1986). Psychosocial factors influencing intentions to exercise of young students from grades 7 to 9. *Research Quarterly for Exercise and Sport, 57,* 41-52.

Godin, G. & Shephard, R.J. (1990). Use of attitude—behavior models in exercise promotion. *Sports Medicine, 10*(2), 103-121.

Godin, G., Valois, P., Shephard, R.J., & Desharnais, R. (1987). Prediction of leisure time exercise behavior: A path analysis (LISREL V) model. *Journal of Behavioral Medicine*, *10*(2), 145-158.

Gould, D. (1987). Understanding attrition in children's sport and physical activity. In D. Gould & M.R. Weiss (Eds.), *Advances in pediatric sport sciences* (Vol. 2). Champaign, IL: Human Kinetics.

Gould, D. & Horn, T. (1984). Participation motivation in young athletes. In J.M. Silva & R.S. Weinberg (Eds.), *Psychological foundations of sport* (pp. 359-370). Champaign, IL: Human Kinetics.

Gould, D. & Petlichkoff, L. (1988). Participation motivation and attrition in young athletes. In F.L. Smoll, R.A. Magill, & M.J. Ash (Eds.), *Children in sport* (pp. 161-178). Champaign, IL: Human Kinetics.

Gould, D. & Weiss, M. (Eds.). (1987). *Advances in pediatric sport sciences* (Vol. 2). Champaign, IL: Human Kinetics.

Guba, E.G. & Lincoln, Y.S. (1983). *Effective evaluation: Improving the usefulness of evaluation research through responsive and naturalistic approaches*. San Francisco: Jossey-Bass.

Health and Welfare Canada. (1986). *Achieving health for all: A framework for health promotion*. Ottawa: Minister of Supply and Services.

Health and Welfare Canada. (1989-1990). Developing knowledge for health promotion in Canada. *Health Promotion*, *3*, 1-14.

Hobson, M. & Rejeski, W.J. (1993). Does the dose of acute exercise mediate psychophysiological responses to mental stress. *Journal of Sport and Exercise Psychology*, *15*, 77-87.

Iso-Ahola, S. (1980). *The social psychology of leisure and recreation*. Dubuque, IA: Brown.

Kaplan, R.M., Atkins, C.J., & Reinsch, S. (1984). Specific efficacy expectations mediate exercise compliance in patients with COPD. *Health Psychology*, *3*, 223-242.

Kendzierski, D. & DeCarlo, K.J. (1991). Physical activity enjoyment scale: Two validation studies. *Journal of Sport and Exercise Psychology, 13*, 50-64.

Kendzierski, D. & Lamastro, D. (1988). Reconsidering the role of attitudes in exercise behavior: A decision theoretical approach. *Journal of Applied Social Psychology*, *18*, 737-759.

Lamb, K.L. & Brodie, D.A. (1990). The assessment of physical activity by leisure-time physical activity questionnaires. *Sports Medicine*, *10*, 159-180.

Landers, D.M. & Petruzzello, S. (1994). Physical activity, fitness and anxiety. In C. Bouchard, R. Shephard, & T. Stephens (Eds.), *Physical activity, fitness and health: International proceedings and consensus statement* (pp. 868-915). Champaign, IL: Human Kinetics.

Lees, L.A. & Dygdon, J.A. (1988). The initiation and maintenance of exercise behavior: A learning theory conceptualization. *Clinical Psychology Review*, *8*, 345-353.

Martin, J. & Dubbert, P. (1982). Exercise applications and promotion in behavioral medicine: Current status and future directions. *Journal of Consulting and Clinical Psychology*, *50*, 1004-1017.

Martin, J. & Dubbert, P. (1984). Adherence management strategies for improving health and fitness. *Journal of Cardiac Rehabilitation, 4*(5), 200-208.

Martin, J. & Dubbert, P. (1985). Adherence to exercise. In R.L. Terjung (Ed.), *Exercise and sport sciences reviews* (pp. 137-167). Syracuse, NY: Macmillan.

McAuley, E. (1991). Efficacy, attributional, and affective responses to exercise participation. *Journal of Sport and Exercise Psychology, 13*, 382-393.

McAuley, E. (1992). Understanding exercise behavior: A self-efficacy perspective. In G.C. Roberts (Ed.), *Motivation in sport and exercise* (pp. 107-127). Champaign, IL: Human Kinetics.

McAuley, E. & Courneya, K.L.S. (1992). Self-efficacy relationships with affective and exertion responses to exercise. *Journal of Applied Social Psychology, 22*, 312-326.

McAuley, E. & Jacobson, L.B. (1991). Self-efficacy and exercise participation in sedentary adult female exercise patterns. *American Journal of Health Promotion, 5*, 185-191.

McGrath, J.E. (1964). Toward a "theory of method" for research on organizations. In W.W. Cooper et al. (Eds.), *New perspectives in organizational research* (pp. 533-556). New York: Wiley.

McPherson, B.D. (1986). Policy-oriented research in youth sport: An analysis of the process and product. In C.R. Rees & A.W. Miracle (Eds.), *Sport and social theory* (pp. 255-287). Champaign, IL: Human Kinetics.

Morgan, W.P. & Goldston, S.E. (Eds.). (1987). *Exercise and mental health.* Washington, DC: Hemisphere.

Morgan, W.P. & O'Connor, P.J. (1988). Exercise and mental health. In R. Dishman (Ed.), *Exercise adherence: Its impact on public health* (pp. 91-123). Champaign, IL: Human Kinetics.

Neulinger, J. (1984). Key issues evoked by a state of mind conceptualization of leisure. *Society and Leisure, 71*, 25-36.

Norman, R. (1989). The nature and correlates of health behavior. *Health Promotion* (Series. No. 2, p. 163). Ottawa: Health and Welfare Canada.

Ornish, D., Brown, S.E., Scherwitz, L.W., Billings, J.H., Armstrong, W.T., Ports, T.A., McLanahan, S.M., Kirkeeide, R.L., Brand, R.J., & Gould, K.L. (1990). *Lancet, 336*, 129-133.

Petruzzello, S.J., Landers, D.M., Hatfield, D.B., Kubitz, K.A., & Salazar, W. (1991). A meta-analysis on the anxiety-reducing effects of acute and chronic exercise. *Sports Medicine, 11*, 143-182.

Prochaska, J.O. & DiClemente, C.C. (1984). *The transtheoretical approach: Crossing traditional boundaries of therapy.* Pacific Grove, CA: Brooks/Cole.

Prochaska, J.O., Nordcross, J.C., & DiClemente, C.C. (1994). *Changing for good.* New York: Morrow.

Prochaska, J.O. & Marcus, B.H. (1994). The transtheoretical model: Applications to exercise. In R. Dishman (Ed.), *Advances in exercise adherence* (pp. 161-180). Champaign, IL: Human Kinetics.

Riddle, P.K. (1980). Attitudes, beliefs, behavioral intentions, and behaviors of women and men toward regular jogging. *Research Quarterly for Exercise and Sport, 51*(4), 663-674.

Rosenstock, I.M. (1974). Historical origins of the health belief model. *Health Education Monographs*, *2*, 328-335.

Sallis, J.F., Haskell, W.L., Fortmann, S.P., Vranizan, K.M., Taylor, C.B., & Solomon, D.S. (1986). Predictors of adoption and maintenance of physical activity in a community setting. *Preventive Medicine*, *15*, 331-341.

Sallis, J.F. & Hovell, M.F. (1990). Determinants of exercise behavior. In K.B. Pandolf & J.O. Holloszy (Eds.), *Exercise and sport sciences reviews* (Vol. 18, pp. 307-330). Baltimore: Williams & Wilkins.

Sallis, J.F., Hovell, M.F., Hofstetter, C.R., Faucher, P., Elder, J.P., Blanchard, J., Caspersen, C.J., Powell, K.E., & Christenson, G.M. (1989). A multivariate study of exercise determinants in a community sample. *Preventive Medicine*, *18*, 20-34.

Sallis, J.F. & McKenzie, T.L. (1991). Physical education's role in public health. *Research Quarterly for Exercise and Sport*, *62*, 124-137.

Scanlan, T. & Lewthwaite, R. (1986). Social psychological aspects of competition for male youth sports participants: IV. Predictors of enjoyment. *Journal of Sport Psychology*, *8*, 25-35.

Scanlan, T. & Passer, M. (1978). Factors related to competitive stress among male youth sport participants. *Medicine and Science in Sports*, *10*, 103-108.

Scanlan, T. & Passer, M. (1979). Sources of competitive stress in young female athletes. *Journal of Sport Psychology*, *1*, 151-159.

Scanlan, T.K., Stein, G.L., & Ravizza, K. (1989). An in-depth study of former elite figure skaters: II. Sources of enjoyment. *Journal of Sport and Exercise Psychology*, *11*, 65-83.

Schifter, D.B. & Ajzen, I. (1985). Intention, perceived control, and weight loss: An application of the theory of planned behavior. *Journal of Personality and Social Psychology*, *49*, 843-851.

Shaw, S.M. (1984). The measurement of leisure: A quality of life issue. *Society and Leisure*, *71*, 91-106.

Shea, S. & Basch, C.E. (1990a). A review of five major community-based cardiovascular disease prevention programs: Part I. Rationale, design, and theoretical framework. *American Journal of Health Promotion*, *4*, 203-213.

Shea, S. & Basch, C.E. (1990b). A review of five major community-based cardiovascular disease prevention programs: Part II. Intervention strategies, evaluation methods, and results. *American Journal of Health Promotion*, *4*, 279-287.

Sonstroem, R. (1978). Physical estimation and attraction scales: Rationale and research. *Medicine and Science in Sports*, *10*, 97-102.

Sonstroem, R. (1988). Psychological models. In R. Dishman (Ed.), *Exercise adherence: Its impact on public health* (pp. 125-153). Champaign, IL: Human Kinetics.

Sonstroem, R. & Morgan, W.P. (1989). Exercise and self-esteem: Rationale and model. *Medicine and Science in Sports and Exercise*, *21*(3), 329-337.

Spink, K.S. & Roberts, G. (1980). Ambiguity of outcome and causal attributions. *Journal of Sport Psychology*, *2*, 237-244.

Stephens, T. & Craig, C. (1990). *The well-being of Canadians: Highlights of the 1988 Campbell's survey*. Ottawa: Canadian Fitness and Lifestyle Research Institute.

Valois, P., Desharnais, R., & Godin, G. (1988). A comparison of the Fishbein and Ajzen and Triadis attitudinal models for the prediction of exercise intention and behavior. *Journal of Behavioral Medicine, 11*, 459-472.

Wankel, L.M. (1984). Decision-making and social support strategies for increasing exercise adherence. *Journal of Cardiac Rehabilitation, 4*, 124-135.

Wankel, L.M. (1987). Enhancing motivation for involvement in voluntary exercise programs. In M. Maehr & D. Kleiber (Eds.), *Advances in motivation and achievement: Enhancing motivation* (pp. 239-286). Greenwich, CT: JAI Press.

Wankel, L.M. (1988). Exercise adherence and leisure activity: Patterns of involvement and interventions to facilitate regular activity. In R. Dishman (Ed.), *Exercise adherence: Its impact on public health* (pp. 369-396). Champaign, IL: Human Kinetics.

Wankel, L.M. & Beatty, B.D. (1975). Behavior intentions and attendance of an exercise program: A field test of Fishbein's model. *Movement actes du le Symposium Canadien en Apprentissage Psycho Moteur et Psychologie du Sport* (pp. 381-386).

Wankel, L.M. & Berger, B. (1990). The psychological and social benefits of sport and physical activity. *Journal of Leisure Research, 22*, 167-182.

Wankel, L.M. & Kreisel, P.S. (1985). Factors underlying enjoyment of youth sports: Sport and age group comparisons. *Journal of Sport Psychology, 7*, 51-64.

Wankel, L.M. & Sefton, J.M. (1989a). A season-long investigation of fun in youth sports. *Journal of Sport and Exercise Psychology, 11*(4), 355-366.

Wankel, L.M. & Sefton, J.M. (1989b). Factors distinguishing high—and low—fun experiences in ice hockey. *World Leisure of Recreation, 31*(3), 29-31.

Wankel, L.M. & Sefton, J.M. (1994). Physical activity and other lifestyle behaviors. In C. Bouchard, R. Shephard, & T. Stephens (Eds.), *Physical activity, fitness and health: International proceedings and consensus statement* (pp. 530-550). Champaign, IL: Human Kinetics.

Wankel, L.M., Sefton, J.M., & Mummery, W.K. (1991). *Testing the theory of planned behavior and developing physical activity promotion strategies for specific target groups with data from the Campbell Survey of Well-Being (CSWB).* Ottawa: Canadian Fitness and Lifestyle Research Institute. (Final report of research project #0095-760-3046).

Weiss, M.R., Bredemeier, B.J., & Shewchuk, R.M. (1986). The dynamics of perceived competence, perceived control, and motivational orientation in youth sports. In M.R. Weiss & D. Gould (Eds.), *Sport for children and youth* (pp. 89-101). Champaign, IL: Human Kinetics.

Weiss, M.R. & Gould, D. (Eds.). (1986). *Sport for children and youth.* Champaign, IL: Human Kinetics.

Wurtele, S.K. & Maddux, J.E. (1987). Relative contributions of protection motivation theory components in predicting exercise intentions and behavior. *Health Psychology, 6*, 453-466.

Yoesting, D.R. & Burkhead, D.L. (1973). Significance of childhood recreation experience on adult leisure behavior: An exploratory analysis. *Journal of Leisure Research, 5*, 25-36.

In Perspective

SOCIOLOGICAL PERSPECTIVES ON PHYSICAL ACTIVITY

Nancy Theberge

My work on physical activity grew out of my work in the sociology of sport, which I began while completing a master's degree in sociology at Boston College. A course in race relations inspired me to write a paper on black athletes. I remember my instructor's response to my choice of topics: It was an interesting issue, but he didn't know how much literature I would find. This was in 1971, and as I looked for research, I found that literature on both black athletes and the field of sport sociology were rapidly expanding. Having grown up in a home where sport was a passion, which I adopted at a young age, that there was such a field as the sociology of sport seemed to me too good to be true.

In 1973, I returned to the University of Massachusetts, where I had completed my undergraduate degree in sociology in 1970, for a PhD in sociology with a specialization in the sociology of sport. These doctoral studies were rather far removed from a concern with active living as we now know the term. For me and many others at the time, interest in the sociology of sport for the most part meant a concern with *organized* sport, heavily focused on professional and amateur sport at the elite level, such as at the Olympics. My choice of dissertation topic reflected the times' elite focus: It was a study of the careers and work of women on the Ladies Professional Golf Association Tour.

The major career move that steered me in the direction of studying physical activity was accepting a position with the Kinesiology Department at the University of Waterloo in 1976. This move was significant in two respects. Working in the Kinesiology Department, I came to recognize the breadth of interest and disciplinary approaches to studying human movement, including the variety of activities that are today captured under the term active living. The second important aspect of coming to Waterloo was my relocation to Canada. In short order, I came to appreciate some of the significant political and social differences between Canada and the United States and their implications for sport and physical activity. I also learned of the significant influence of political economy on Canadian sociology. The role of the state in the organization and support of amateur sport and in health promotion and fitness became major interests, which I incorporated into my teaching and research.

In 1985, I spent a six-month sabbatical in Norway and traveled extensively throughout Europe. During visits to a number of universities and institutes, I heard much about the study of "body culture" and began to read systematically in the rapidly growing field of the sociology of the body. These interests now imbue my work; while I still teach the sociology of sport, I also teach one course in the sociology of physical activity (which deals with the variety of forms of physical activity within kinesiology) and another, in the Sociology Department, in the sociology of the body.

A continuing interest from the earliest stages of my career is a concern with social inequality. Schooled first in the civil rights movement of the 1960s, which focused on race relations, I, along with many other women, discovered and embraced feminism and feminist analysis in the 1970s. My decision to write a dissertation on women in sport was a first indication of the influence of that period on my own thinking. Since completing my dissertation, I have done a good deal of research on gender issues. In recent years, I have turned particularly to questions of ideology and the cultural construction of gender. This work is informed by the critical approach taken in the interdisciplinary field of "cultural studies."

My contribution to this volume discusses the influences on the study of active living that have come from political economy, cultural studies, and feminism as well as from the sociology of the body. As this chapter indicates, my own work has been significantly affected by each of these traditions. That work has been enormously interesting and rewarding, and I look forward to continued involvement in the field.

Chapter 4

SOCIOLOGICAL PERSPECTIVES ON PHYSICAL ACTIVITY

Nancy Theberge

In the 1960s, physical activity, physical education, sport, health, and fitness gained recognition as subjects appropriate for, and in need of, scholarly, critical analysis. Of course, these subjects had long been concerns of university programs in physical and health education, public health, and the like, but throughout the first half of this century an applied focus, often infused with a missionary-like zeal to "spread the word" on the beneficial effects of physical activity and active living. As part of a general effort to improve the quality and prestige of North American universities, the study of physically active lifestyles underwent an extensive overhaul, its applied and missionary character replaced by a more scientific and scholarly approach.

The model of scientific scholarship adopted to study physical activity had significant consequences for the development of the field and its professional practice. Greatly influenced by medicinal studies that emphasized systems, production, and technical intervention, the conception of active living that evolved emphasized the biophysical aspects of physical activity, with a focus on issues of human performance (Demers, 1988). This approach was evident not only in the study of the physiology and biomechanics of activity, but also in research on the behavioral and social dimensions.

The sociology of physical activity and sport, in the formative years of its institutionalization, also was dominated by mechanistic approaches to conceptualizing and understanding its subject matter and a quest to establish the scientific legitimacy of the field. Science then was understood to be objective and value-free, and quantitative methodologies were favored over interpretive and historical approaches, which were thought to be less rigorous and hence less scientific.

The early period of work in sport sociology, from the mid-1960s to the mid-1970s, produced a wealth of descriptive material about the characteristics of participants in sport and physical activity and the correlates of this activity. Among correlational studies, concern with socialization predominated, and numerous studies attempted to identify factors associated with socialization into physical activity and the socialization effects or outcomes of participation. Work in this decade extensively documented the importance of sport in society through its connection to other major institutions—political, economic, and educational.

Although sport sociologists in this period established the legitimacy of the sociology of sport and physical activity as an area of study and compiled and disseminated extensive information about participants and the institutional structure of sport and physical activity, there were some serious limitations. In large measure, the work reflected a mechanistic model of science: Physical activity was conceptualized either as the product of "inputs" (gender, class, and age) or the determinant of certain "outputs" (attitudes, orientations, educational, and occupational attainment).

Another feature of early sociological thinking about active living was its conformance to the functionalist tradition in sociology, which conceives of societies as relatively stable systems of interrelated parts, characterized by some degree of shared beliefs and values (Hagedorn, 1990, p. 13). Following this tradition, there was little concern in analyses of active living with the dynamic processes of social life or with power and ideology, "the values and beliefs that help to maintain the position of more powerful groups" (Giddens, 1991, p. 865).

Finally, in the tradition of most of western social science, the study of physical activity embraced a Cartesian dualism, separating mind from body and culture from nature and elevating the first elements of these dyads to positions of prominence (Turner, 1984). In a curious irony, the study of physical activity took little account of the bodily aspects of these processes.

RECENT THEORETICAL DEVELOPMENTS IN THE SOCIOLOGY OF SPORT

Important challenges to assumptions about physical activity emerged in the mid-1970s as work in sport sociology and physical activity gained theoretical maturity and researchers began to adopt a consciously critical perspective. The most significant feature of this work was an increasing concern for and sophistication in dealing with issues of inequality, power, and ideology. Writers from different theoretical perspectives moved the sociology of sport and physical activity away from mechanistic models and the implicit functionalism of such approaches. This work brought us a much better understanding and appreciation of the conflicts inherent in active living, differences in experiences and access, and the power of dominant groups (gender, class, and racial) in defining and setting limits on the experience of active living. Among the most important influences on thinking about physical activity was the research informed by political economy, cultural studies, and feminism. Analyses from these perspectives highlighted different concerns and interpretations.

Work Informed by Political Economy

Political economy stressed the role of the state and capital in structuring the development and organization of sport and physical activity. Research examined the growth and development of sport and physical culture under industrial capitalism and the implications of government policies and state intervention in health and welfare for quality of life and equality of condition. Among works in this area, a volume edited by Cantelon and Gruneau (1982) is notable for the scope of the analyses of sport and the state in both capitalist and state socialist societies. Another important contribution is the research by Jean Harvey (1983, 1988) on the involvement of the Quebec and Canadian governments in the promotion and professionalization of physical activity. Developments in the political economy of sport have yielded greater insight into some of the historical agents and conditions that shape the experience of active living.

Work Informed by Cultural Studies

A fundamental assumption of the cultural studies perspective is that cultural practices, including sport, are an arena of contest (Donnelly,

1988). What form an activity takes often involves struggle, such as the emphasis on some activities over others, and the values, meanings, and ideologies associated with these activities. These struggles occur between groups with different interests and resources, both economic (i.e., income to pay for equipment and memberships) and cultural (i.e., information and skills). Groups differ in their capacities for mobilizing these resources. For example, in Britain and North America, middle- and upper-class males historically have utilized their power and influence in sport organizations and schools to fashion a particular definition of sporting practice (Mangan, 1981; Kidd, 1988) favoring the values of achievement and competition: This definition was an important element of masculine socialization. An indication of the power of these groups to implement a dominant definition of physical activity is that other forms of activity, including noncompetitive games and other recreational physical activity, still are viewed as alternatives.

A contemporary example of the utilization of resources can be seen in certain practices by the media. The media, particularly television, exert a powerful influence on ideas about physical activity and active living. The concentration is on men's professional sport. Studies show that, with occasional exceptions, media coverage consists mainly of men's sport. For example, a recent analysis of television sports news in the United States showed that 94 percent of air time was devoted to men's sport, 5 percent to women's sport, and 1 percent to gender-neutral topics (Amateur Athletic Foundation, 1994). Another U.S. study of the coverage of women's sport in four daily newspapers showed that 81 percent of stories were about men only and only 3.5 percent were about women only (Amateur Athletic Foundation, 1991). Analyses of newspaper coverage in Canada show similar patterns (CAAWS, 1989, 1994). This selective emphasis shapes ideas about who athletes are and what is legitimate or "real" sport.

The dominance of cultural practices is never total or fixed but is continually challenged by alternative forms. In the contemporary period, the "Sport for All" movement, which attempts to broaden the conception of active living, is an effort to counter the elitist emphasis on skill and performance. Advocates of "Sport for All" particularly are concerned with extending the experience to groups that were formerly excluded, important examples being the disabled and the elderly.

Cultural studies provide a needed corrective to mechanistic conceptions of social life, including the notion that sporting practice is somehow "determined" by dominant groups or institutions, such as the economy or polity. Research attempts to identify the means by which groups exercise power and influence and the struggles that occur in this process. An exemplar of this work is John Hargreaves' *Sport, Power and*

Culture (1986), which examines the development of popular sporting forms in Britain in the context of class relations and the emergence of mass culture. Other recent contributions include a 1992 issue of the *Sociology of Sport Journal* devoted to "British Cultural Studies and Sport," another discussion of the linkage of British cultural studies and sport by Andrews and Loy (1993), and an edited collection by Ingham and Loy (1993). A particular strength of the Ingham and Loy volume is the cross-disciplinary and cross-cultural range of the contributions, which include pieces from historical, sociological, and political economic perspectives examining sport in North America, Latin America, Britain, and the ancient world. The emphasis in cultural studies on the process of cultural production, material and historical analysis, and the struggle between dominant and subordinate groups have been significant contributions from this perspective to the analysis of active living.

Work Informed by Feminism

Feminism presented a third important challenge to assumptions about active living. The first stage in the feminist challenge was identification of gender inequality and exclusionary practices, including bias in the study of sport and physical activity (Birrell, 1984) as well as exclusionary practices in sport and physical activity (Theberge, 1985). Unequal access to active living continues and is most evident at the highest levels of organized sport; professional sport is still nearly exclusively male, and men predominate at the highest levels of organized amateur sport. In the 1992 Barcelona Olympics, for example, men competed in 159 official medal events, women competed in 86 medal events, and there were 12 "mixed" events in which both competed (*Olympian*, 1990, p. 58).

Although organized competitive sport is still largely a male domain, the differences between men's and women's participation in other forms of physical activity and active living are becoming less pronounced. In Canada, national survey data show that when considering the amount of time spent in physical activity, there are few differences in the proportion of men and women who are active. That is, in 1988, 82 percent of males and 79 percent of females reported engaging in some form of activity at least three hours a week for more than nine months of the preceding year. This measure, however, takes no account of intensity of activity, and several of the measures included in the survey item that measured involvement, like walking and gardening, involve relatively low levels of energy expenditure (Stephens & Craig, 1990, p. 53).

In the same study, greater gender differences are evident in another measure of activity that considers energy expenditure or intensity of activity. This analysis shows that in every age category, males are more active than females. Additional analysis shows that gender differences in intensity of activity are partly due to men's greater participation in vigorous physical activity (Stephens & Craig, 1990, p. 52). Men also are more likely to engage in competitive activities (Stephens & Craig, 1990, p. 58).

Joining Feminism and Cultural Studies

The analysis of patterns of involvement has been complemented in recent years by work that explores how images and ideals of gender and gender differences are constructed and realized in physical activity and sport. In this respect, the recent joining of feminism with work informed by a cultural studies approach has been an important development in the study of active living (Theberge & Birrell, 1994a). In "Women's Athletics and the Myth of Female Frailty," Theberge (1989) shows how women's sport has historically been a setting for a struggle over both the institutions that controlled their participation and the meanings of their activity. The struggle is a legacy of the Victorian ideal of womanhood, which held that women were morally and spiritually strong but physically and intellectually weak.

This ideal was seriously challenged by women's increasing involvement in sport and physical activity in the early 20th century. A debate that ensued among physicians and physical educators over the wisdom and propriety of this activity was ultimately "resolved" by the adoption of a "modified" model of sport and physical activity, wherein girls and women participated in adapted versions of men's activities that were less strenuous and competitive and thus deemed more suitable for women. Among the best known examples of the modified model are restrictions on the length of women's races in sports such as track and swimming. (For example, the women's marathon was only added to the Olympics in 1984, after an enormous lobbying effort, to be followed by the addition of the 10,000-meter race in 1988.) An additional outcome was emphasis on women's involvement in activities deemed appropriately feminine, such as figure skating and gymnastics (Theberge, 1989).

Recent decades have witnessed tremendous changes in women's participation in physical activity. In an era in which women are boxing, playing sports like rugby and ice hockey in expanding numbers, and engaging in other types of active living at rates comparable to men's, the "myth of female frailty" would seem finally to be laid to rest. While the fact of women's physical activity is now evident, the meaning and implications of this activity are still very much a matter of cultural struggle. One element of this struggle involves a renewed emphasis on the feminization of fitness and physical activity; well-known instances of this include feminized versions of fitness and exercise activities, such as jazzercise and aerobics classes, which are targeted to women and emphasize appearance and weight control. An insightful analysis of the feminization of fitness activities is MacNeill's analysis of the popular television show, "Twenty-Minute Workout." MacNeill shows how a variety of audio and visual practices involving camera angle, lighting and contrast, commentary, and background music "create sexual images rather than images of physical activity" (1988, p. 199).

Evidence of the association between exercise and body image among adolescent women is found in research by Susan Shaw (1991). A survey of 563 female and 513 male Nova Scotia high school students found that 53.8 percent of the females and 34.3 percent of males were dissatisfied with their weight. Among males who were dissatisfied, the majority wished to gain weight. Among females, most of those who were dissatisfied wished to lose weight, although less than 10 percent of them were overweight, based on standards indicated in *Canadian Guidelines for Healthy Weights* (1988). Moreover, among males and females there was no relationship between desired body weight and overall participation in sport and physical activity, or participation in specific activities, with one notable exception—females who wished to lose weight were more likely to participate in aerobics. Shaw (1991, p. 363) notes that her cross-sectional data do not allow for establishing the causal direction of this relationship but expresses concern that "the fitness subculture, as maintained by organizers and leaders as well as by participants, may be encouraging an obsession with body weight and body fat, either explicitly or implicitly. The fitness clothing industry and the ways in which fitness activities are advertised and promoted may also be reinforcing the anti-fat ideology" (see Shaw & Kemany, 1989).

The sexualization of women's fitness is also evident in the print media. When it began publication in 1974, the American magazine *WomenSports* was devoted to increasing women's and girls' involvement in physical activity and sport and promoting this activity as a means of enjoyment and empowerment. Over the years, the magazine, now known as *Women's Sports and Fitness* has moved away from this focus and now promotes physical activity and fitness primarily in terms of physical attractiveness. The conscious activism of the magazine's early years has been muted by a more conventional emphasis on appearance and desirability (Endel, 1991; Birrell & Theberge, 1994).

A second element in the struggle to legitimize women's physical activity concerns the construction and reconstruction of gender difference. In the past, when girls' and women's physical activity was discouraged or restricted to alternative practices that were clearly distinguished from "real" male sport, sport and physical activity served as a clear and powerful marker of gender and gender differences. In this "simpler" time, sport and strenuous physical activity were for boys and men; women who violated this canon did so at considerable cost to their standing as "true" women.

As contemporary women increasingly engage in activities formerly reserved for men and claim other activities, such as aerobics, for themselves, the meanings of active living for the construction of gender is being challenged and renegotiated. An ideology of natural difference, which asserts that although women may take part in physical activity, essential differences between the sexes guarantee men's superiority and justify their favored status in the world of sport and physical activity, complicates this process.

This point has been developed by several authors. In his essay on "Women in Sport and Ideology," Paul Willis (1982) discusses the particular power of sport to contribute to an ideology of natural difference. Central to this is the "indisputable" claim of the biological basis of physical performance. Willis argues that:

> Ideology can claim biological discrepancy fully for its own: to present cultural legitimations as biological factors. The fact that no one can deny female difference becomes the fact of female inferiority, becomes the fact that females are innately different from men, becomes the fact that women who stray across the defining boundary are in a parlous state. An ideological view comes to be deposited in our culture as a common sense assumption—of course women are different and inferior. (p. 130)

Willis' piece was presented as an "essay in ideas" (Willis, 1982, p.117). Subsequent work has provided evidence of the ways in which sport and other forms of active living are ideologically constructed so as to support the view of natural and essential differences between men and women. Much of this work has focused on media constructions. Michael Messner (1988) suggests that the undeniable advances in women athletes' achievement prompted a change in media strategies of portraying female athletes. The media have abandoned their former practices of sexualizing and trivializing women's sport in favor of a strategy that Messner (1988, p. 206), paraphrasing the media, describes as "[women athletes] want to be treated the same as men? Well, let's see what they can do." As Messner indicates, however, given the history of advantage that men have enjoyed and the current organization of sport around definitions that favor men (i.e., faster, higher, stronger), this strategy is again a prescription for defining masculine superiority.

Margaret Carlisle Duncan (1990) has provided additional insight into media constructions of gender differences. Duncan examined photographs that accompanied sport stories concerning the 1984 and 1988 Olympic Games in five American and one Canadian magazines. From a sample of nearly 1,400 pictures, she identified 186 that suggested sexual difference. Her analysis considered both the content of photographs, including camera angle and subjects' appearances, poses, body positions, expressions and emotional displays, and the context, including visual space, caption, accompanying text, and substance of the article.

The results indicate how the media continue to gender athletic performance and sexualize female athletes. A picture of the 1984 gold medalist Romanian gymnastics team stooping to shake hands with members of an opposing team captures this effectively. The shot is taken from the rear, and the result is a picture of six female bottoms, with the accompanying caption: "First but hindmost, the conquering Romanians stoop to congratulate the third place Chinese team." The sexualization of women's athletics is also accomplished through the emphasis on glamorous women champions like sprinter Florence Griffith Joyner and figure skater Katarina Witt. For example, the Canadian magazine *Maclean's* published five photographs of Witt, including two of her in skin-tight jeans, in comparison to one of Canadian medalist Elizabeth Manley (Duncan, 1990).

Constructions of gender differences in the sports photographs occur in a variety of ways. In addition to being sexualized, women athletes are presented as emotional and prone to crying. Neither of these features is evident in the photographs of men. Furthermore, camera angles depict women athletes below eye level and men above, suggesting positions of inferiority and superiority, respectively. Hierarchical relations are also indicated in a number of photos that feature a man in the foreground surrounded by a number of women; the effect is that the male appears to tower over the smaller females (Duncan, 1990).

Duncan's (1990) analysis indicates the persistence of subtle yet powerful efforts to legitimate assumptions about gender difference.[1] The influx of strong, powerful women like Florence Griffith Joyner has provided an assault on the formerly masculine stronghold of sport. Duncan suggests that the threat posed by the possibility of female equality in sport has prompted a renewed effort to reassert masculine superiority. Photographs of women athletes suggest that women are not like men and imply that they can never be like men. In this construction, the challenge to the myth of female frailty posed by modern sportswomen has been subverted and the ideology of natural difference once again reasserted.

The recent joining of cultural studies and feminist analysis has been an important advancement in our understanding of physical activity and active living. Going beyond descriptive accounts of patterns of participation, this work indicates the significance of active living for an ideology of gender and for gender relations. Cultural studies and feminism share a common concern to explore the processes that structure and constrain the experience of active living and a common emphasis on the realities and implications of power and ideology. The contributions of these approaches, as well as those from political economy, have led the study of physical activity and active living to a stage of theoretical and conceptual maturity.

Sociology of the Body

Another recent development in thinking about physical activity is the rapidly expanding literature on the sociology of the body. In his influential book, *The Body and Society* (1984), Bryan Turner discussed the absence of the body from social theory: "Contemporary sociology," he wrote, "has little to say about the most obvious fact of human existence, namely that human beings have, and to some extent are, bodies." Turner traced this phenomenon to the "epistemological foundations" of sociology and its rejection of the 19th-century belief that human behavior could be explained by biology. This, of course, is different from the adoption of biological *metaphors*, such as structural functionalism and systems analysis, which have exerted a tremendous influence in sociological theory and, as noted earlier, in sociological interpretations of active living.

In response to this "analytical gap," Turner proposed a return of the body to social theory (1984). This issue, and its relevance to active living, will now be considered.

ACTIVE LIVING AND THE BODY: CONTEMPORARY THEMES AND ISSUES

Since the publication of Turner's book, interest in the body has expanded greatly, a development leading one observer to write that "bodies are 'in,' in academia and in popular culture" (Frank, 1990, p. 131). The literature includes work in several substantive areas of particular relevance to a consideration of physical activity. The following discussion considers several issues that are key to an understanding of active living.

An analysis of commodification and consumerism, the role of the state and the media in the definition and organization of physical activity, and the rationalization of bodily practices all offer insights into the limits and possibilities of a holistic practice of active living that is concerned with quality of life. Although the themes are considered separately, the discussion will show that they are dynamically related.

Commodification and Consumerism

One of the most far-reaching influences on active living has been its incorporation into consumer culture, "the way of life in the modern era which is organized around the consumption of goods and services for the mass market" (Hargreaves, 1987, p. 140). The most obvious aspect of this process is a fitness industry that embraces an ever expanding set of products and services. These include equipment, clothing (including varieties of athletic shoes), foods and dietary aids, memberships in clubs, and services by varieties of fitness and body specialists. An important aspect of this process is the marketing of fitness imagery based on physical attractiveness. "Fundamental to the linking of the cultural concept of attractiveness to the concept of health, through exercise, is the assumption that 'healthy' is something that can be 'looked'" (Allard, 1987, p. 3).

The penetration of consumer culture into active living involves an effective integration of cultural, political, and social conditions. At the cultural level, body practices provide a particularly fertile field for the expansion of consumer culture. John Hargreaves (1987, p. 150) notes that this culture, above all, "valorizes self-expression through the meticulous attention that is paid to aspects of their lives that are deeply personal to people." Through their focus on appearance, feelings, and other aspects of individual needs and desires, body practices fuel the expansion of consumer culture.

Consumer culture, Hargreaves (1987, p. 150) argues, is a "specifically modern version of the good life." The historical conditions that have enabled the incorporation of the body into consumer culture and the valorization of appearance and form have been elaborated by others. Bryan Turner (1984, p. 113) has suggested that in late capitalism there is a "representational crisis of self-management." Mass consumerism, including mass leisure and entertainment, have masked traditional indicators of social status. Social success nonetheless continues to depend on the management of successful images, particularly body image, accomplished by rigorous training and discipline:

The new ethic of managerial athleticism is thus the contemporary version of the Protestant ethic, but, fanned by the winds of consumerism, this ethic has become widespread throughout the class system as a lifestyle to be emulated. The commodified body has become the focus of a keep-fit industry, backed up by fibre diets, leisure centers, slimming manuals and outdoor sports. (Turner, 1984, p. 112)

The incorporation of body practices into consumer culture, then, is in part a cultural manifestation of changes in the conditions for status representation and affirmation. In the contemporary period, these concerns are tied more closely to body presentation and image management. Practices have been highly commodified and the pursuit of a "healthy look" often is accompanied by a sense of duty and commitment that is strikingly similar to the asceticism of the Protestant ethic.

The Fitness Boom and Consumer Culture

The notion that "healthy can be looked" (Allard, 1987, p. 3) drives a lucrative fitness industry. This industry is central to the phenomenon known as the "fitness boom," the impressive rise in consciousness about exercise and physical activity that has occurred in the last decade or so. The growth of this industry has been aided greatly by state-sponsored public relations campaigns, such as the ParticipAction program launched by the Canadian government in the early 1970s, the "Life—Be In It" campaign in Australia, and the "Exercise Lite" campaign recently launched in the United States.

The fitness boom and the supporting lifestyle ideology need to be considered critically. One problematic feature is the shift in responsibility from the collective to the individual. The fitness boom as a contemporary manifestation of the incorporation of the body into consumer culture is a highly personalized approach to well-being. Within this personalized conception, the emphasis on appearance and image management is at odds with a holistic view of physical activity that integrates "mental, emotional, social and spiritual dimensions" (e.g., active living) (Fitness Canada, 1991, p. 4).

Second, the fitness boom and its incorporation into consumer culture serve to reproduce social divisions and maintain the position of dominant groups (Hargreaves, 1987). This process occurs at connected material and ideological levels. Materially, the commodification of physical activity favors the access and involvement of the economically advantaged. Ideologically, class differences in access and types of participation, as well as in leisure lifestyles (i.e., club memberships versus use of public facilities; designer clothing; high-tech equipment) publicly confirm and reproduce class relations. The commodification of fitness and expansion of the fitness industry is at odds with a vision of mass participation such as that embodied by the "Sport for All" movement in Europe or "Active Living" in Canada.

The divisions engendered by the fitness boom encompass much more than class relations. The fitness boom is grounded in the glorification of images of young, white, heterosexual, attractive, and able-bodied persons (Theberge & Birrell, 1994b). This bias is muted to some extent in noncommercial sectors; for example, in Canada, the public sector promotional campaign ParticipAction. Nonetheless, the strength of the commercial fitness industry and of media representations ensure the dominance of a restrictive and oppressive interpretation of active living. This further contradicts a vision of mass involvement.

Organized Sport, Commercialization, and the Glorification of the Individual

The extensive literature on the commercialization of sport tends to focus on the sometimes astounding incomes of professional athletes, the costs of facility construction, and the values of broadcast contracts and professional sport franchises. However, the impact of the commodification of sport goes well beyond the costs and rewards of professional sport. Less well recognized is the manner in which this process has contributed to perceptions and definitions of sporting practices.

Any account of the commodification of sport must consider the central place of the media. Television broadcast contracts enable the huge prize moneys and contracts awarded to athletes and organizations like the International Olympic Committee. One result of this situation is that media interests influence the content of broadcasts, often in ways that are not readily recognized. In addition to focusing on certain sports (primarily male team sports, in addition to selected Olympic events) and thereby contributing to the definition of who athletes are, the media present a definition of what constitutes good sporting practice. In this definition, good sport is highly specialized and oriented to spectacular individual performances and economic reward.

This point is evident in Gruneau's (1989) analysis of television coverage of a men's World Cup downhill ski race in British Columbia. By emphasizing particular aspects of the competition (for example, a racer's place in the overall season's rankings), and through the use of commentary, camera work, and technical devices like graphics display, television constructs a selective account of an event. In this account "specialization is the modern definition of excellence . . . enjoyment is tied to skill acquisition and . . . economic reward is an integral and necessary component of sporting entertainment" (Gruneau, 1989, p. 152).

The State, Consumer Culture, and Active Living

The incorporation of the body into consumer culture has also been fostered by a marriage between commercial and state interests. Several aspects of state activity and interests are of concern here. One of these is the ways in which state policies affect the nature and distribution of leisure opportunities. There is considerable literature on the role of national and federal governments in sport; a recent collection of articles on "Sport and the State" in capitalist and socialist countries is contained in Landry, Landry, and Yerles (1991).

The connections between state intervention at all levels and other forms of recreational physical activity are too little recognized. In fact, state policies and programs exert a wide-ranging impact on these concerns. Whitson (1987) identified five types of state involvement that have particular implications for sport and physical recreation and, more broadly, for active living. These include:

1. Direct provision and grant support. This ranges from municipal support or operation of facilities and programs to the variety of services and support offered by governments at different levels.

2. Regulation and taxation of popular enjoyments. Taxation policies on sport and recreation have an obvious impact on access and participation. In general, the reach of regulatory controls has declined over the last century. For example, 19th-century restrictions on recreation on Sunday, the Christian Sabbath, would now be seen to constitute an unreasonable state intrusion into private life and leisure time. State interest in regulating physical recreation persists, however, in a variety of areas where the public interest is judged to be at risk. Debate arising from calls to ban the sport of boxing (Kidd, Corner, & Stewart, 1983), or at least to increase safety and control, is an instance of state intervention through regulation.

3. Subsidies and incentives to leisure industries. This includes grants and assistance to local business ventures in the areas of sport and fitness as well as large-scale projects, such as stadium construction. A discussion of the contributions of federal and local governments in the financing and construction of facilities for large-scale events, such as the Olympics and Commonwealth Games, is contained in Whitson and Macintosh (1993).

4. Business environment. Whitson (1987, p. 230) identifies three aspects of the business environment that are relevant to forms of active living. The first is the enforcement of regulations affecting health and safety (for example, the regulation of fitness clubs). The second is land use regulation affecting parks and wilderness areas. The third is government policies concerning privatization of services or the ownership of facilities (for example, the management of park facilities).

5. Professionalization of recreation and leisure. State interest in all the preceding concerns has been marked by increasing rationalization and professionalization. The implications of this for a consideration of active living are discussed later in this section.

In the first four forms of state interest in physical recreation, the selective allocation or application of the policy or program in question is perhaps the most critical feature. State involvement or intervention may be in the interest of supporting business and commercial interests or participants and consumers; it may have the effect of increasing access or imposing barriers, as in the case of taxation policies or subsidization. An example of selective allocation of support occurred in the Canadian province of Ontario in the early 1980s. At the same time that the Ontario government spearheaded the formation of a consortium of businesses to support the financing of the Toronto Skydome, and governments at all levels contributed $85 million in public funds for the project (Kidd, 1990), a group of women in the city of London, Ontario, who were attempting to establish a women's fitness center, were unsuccessful in their efforts to gain sufficient support from various levels of government.

As Whitson and others (Harvey, 1988; Ingham, 1985) have noted, over the course of the last century the state has come to play an increasingly important role in the provision of welfare and social services, including those concerned with sport and physical recreation. In the period of economic growth following World War II, state expenditures on health, welfare, and social services increased greatly. Part of the expansion of state activity in many countries was attributable to increased government expenditures and bureaucracies in sport and fitness. The growth of the welfare state was radically challenged by the economic downturn of the 1980s, which simultaneously resulted in dwindling state resources and expanding claims on these resources in the form of expectations for services and entitlements. In response, neoconservative governments (including those in Canada, the United States, and Great Britain) stressed the limits of reliance on the state and the virtues of private enterprise and self-reliance. One outcome of this emphasis was an effort to restrict public expenditures and to shift the burden for the provision of many services to individuals and the private sector. In Canada, this is evident in efforts to increase corporate sector involvement in fitness and health issues (for example, the 1981 Canada Fitness Survey became the 1988 Campbell's Survey on the Well-Being of Canadians) and the sponsorship of activities (e.g., road races) and programs (e.g., a learn-to-swim program sponsored during the 1980s by Esso Canada).

A second major aspect of state involvement in physical activity and active living is its movement directly into the "discourse of the body"; that is, public discussion and debate about physical activity. Alan Ingham (1985) argues that the current preoccupation with bodies and lifestyles has arisen as a response to the fiscal crisis of the welfare state. Conservatives' emphasis on the limits of reliance on government and the virtues of private enterprise and self-reliance led to the identification of the "lifestyle solution" to the problems of the welfare state. This involves a shift in the definition of responsibility for health and wellness from the state to the individual. In Canada, a major turning point in this regard was the release in 1974 of the federal government policy statement, "A New Perspective on Health for Canadians." The Lalonde Report, as it is commonly known, identified lifestyle and behavioral change as keys to managing health care in the future.

The lifestyle solution is in some measure an ideological response to the structural problems of late capitalism. In this formulation, each of us is responsible for his or her health and can act on this responsibility by, for example, exercise, weight control and dietary management, avoidance of risk behaviors like smoking and alcohol consumption, and reducing our stress levels. Structural problems of unemployment, inequitable distribution of resources and opportunities, and community responsibility to maintain healthy environments, including work environments, are not addressed (Labonte, 1982).

Rationalization, the Body, and Active Living

This section considers the transformation of physical activity and other elements of body culture into appropriate subjects for management and control. The discussion develops several themes. First is a review of the manner in which the rationalization of bodily practices has become central to conceptions of active living. Second, the role of the "kinesiological and health professions" (Ingham, 1985) in this process is examined. Finally, an account is offered of the rationalization of bodily practices as an instance of a Foucauldian concern with the domination and subjugation of bodies. A theme that runs throughout the discussion and extends the analysis of the previous section is the connections between the process of rationalization and the interests of the state and capital.

The rationalization of bodily practices contends that, in place of activity pursued for joy, pleasure, and self-expression, we exercise for fitness, the enhancement of appearance, stress management, or some other achievement or purpose. As Turner (1984, p. 112) puts it, "we jog, slim and sleep not for intrinsic enjoyment, but to preserve our chances at sex, work and longevity." Often, these associations take on a moral connotation, and working at fitness becomes an obligation.[2]

A study by Crawford (1984) provides an interesting account of the rationalization of bodily practices. Crawford interviewed 60 adults in the Chicago area about the meaning of health and their explanations for their state of health. The interviews suggested two seemingly contradictory interpretations of health. On the one hand, respondents viewed health as a goal to be achieved through discipline, denial, and will power. This view was often accompanied by moral attributions that associated health with self-control, as in the comments that "You have to be man enough, woman enough, you have to be adult enough to control your own life" and "People bring it on themselves" (Crawford, 1984, p. 70).

The second theme was a view of health as the satisfaction (rather than suppression) of desire. This is captured in a respondent's statement that health is "being able to do what you want to do when you want to do it" (Crawford, 1984, p. 81). In this view, "releases" such as food, drink, or various "excesses" are seen as an adaptation to the stresses and demands of life. Concerns about excess, lifestyle change, and health promotion are criticized as themselves stressful and are rejected in favor of "feeling good."

The same person might view health as representing simultaneously both control and release. Crawford (1984) suggests that the apparent opposition is the outcome of structural contradictions in capitalist societies. The culture of consumption conflicts with the requirement for disciplined workers. This conflict is embodied in a literal sense in the demands to consume but be disciplined. " 'Eat!' is countered by the moral imperative to control eating" (Crawford, 1984, p. 93). As Crawford notes, the new health consciousness raises difficult questions about the balance of control and release, which coexist in an uneasy tension.

As discussed above, the reconceptualization of physical activity for fitness and productivity serves the interests of the state and capital: The emphasis on self-reliance and lifestyle management shifts responsibility to the individual, while the emphasis on appearance supports the expansion of the leisure industry and other commercial activities. These developments should not blind us to the *possibilities* of active living that are pleasurable and empowering as well as healthy. The reappropriation of physical activity for extrinsic concerns is a historical condition, not an essential feature of bodily practice.

A specific aspect of the rationalization of physical activity is the fragmentation of the human body and its subordination to processes of mechanization. This is one way in which the continuing dominance of medical models of health and well-being persist in the consideration of physical activity. Within this model, the body is viewed as a set of parts and systems; malfunctions are to be treated by technical intervention. Thus, in exercise programs we concentrate on flexibility, strength, or endurance, on parts of the body (legs, arms, abdomen, etc.), and even on specific muscles (quadriceps, biceps, etc.).

The means of intervention are professional and technical. The proliferation of body experts includes dietitians, trainers, physiotherapists, biomechanists, psychologists, and others. Technical intervention is achieved through an expanding array of equipment, an increasingly important aspect of the fitness industry. Couzens (1988, p. 23) quotes one successful fitness entrepreneur on this development: "Fitness centers are no different from an amusement park. You've got to bring in a new ride every year in order to entice the people back. If you stay static too long with your equipment then you'll lose your members." The metaphor of the body as a set of parts, to be manipulated through increasingly technical intervention employing the latest mechanical equipment, is an additional challenge to the ideal of active living.

THE KINESIOLOGICAL AND HEALTH SCIENCES AND THE RATIONALIZATION OF PHYSICAL ACTIVITY

The initial section of this chapter identified some trends in the sociological study of physical activity that moved away from the mechanism and ahistoricism which had characterized early work in the field. These advances exist alongside a traditional view of the discipline and professional practices that remains firmly fixed in a scientific perspective based in the natural sciences, which takes medicine as its exemplar. Speaking specifically of physical education, Demers (1988, p. 162) writes that "there is a strong tendency to regard physical education as a biological science, a science of the efficiency and rationality of human movement." In turn, the education and professional preparation of students in physical education and its successor disciplines, such as kinesiology, maintains the emphasis on a biophysical approach to the analysis of the human body and technical intervention to achieve mastery and control. In her study of an undergraduate physical education program in Canada, Dewar (1987) found that students viewed the content of courses in the biological and behavioral sciences to be "really useful knowledge" because they offered information directly applicable to analyzing and improving performance, not only in sport but in relation to health and fitness. Courses in the sociocultural areas that considered sport and physical activity as socially produced and shaped by historical circumstances and exposed students to alternate views of active living were considered neither interesting nor useful.

According to Demers (1988), the explanations for the maintenance of the biophysical approach can be traced to the institutional dynamics of universities and to broader social conditions. The growth and special-ization of knowledge led to fragmented fields of study, including the study of human movement and physical activity. Within this process, the natural sciences, because they conform more closely to the model of "real science" and offer greater promise of control and mastery of the human body, assumed a dominant position; the social sciences and humanities were relegated to a secondary status. While maintaining some representation of the social sciences in their curriculum, most departments of physical education and kinesiology have firmly adopted the biophysical approach and "a high percentage of graduates receive predominantly biological training and are taught to have a mechanistic view of the body in their work" (Demers, 1988, p. 167). These views are carried into their professional practice in sport, recreation, health pro-motion, and related fields.

An additional feature of this process is the evolution of the social and behavioral sciences within kinesiology and physical education. The dominance of the natural science model has had a profound effect on the entire range of disciplinary studies of human movement. Alan Ingham (1985, p. 51) argues that the "kinesiological and health sciences" are characterized by the triple tendencies of "behaviorism, empiricism, and voluntarism [which] combine to produce discrete responses to holistic health problems. We tinker with the biological and psychodynamic individual rather than the socioeconomic and political structures."

One example of tinkering is the contemporary concern with lifestyle. Ingham (1985) suggests that the emergence of the lifestyle solution to problems of health and well-being has been encouraged by the pre-occupation of researchers with the analysis of individual factors and behavioral change in the absence of a critique of broader social and political conditions. By favoring "discrete empiricist studies" (p. 53), which have the appearance of scientific validity and "value freedom," researchers have fostered a kind of "intellectual apartheid" (p. 51) with little regard for larger issues of political economy and culture. In this respect, kinesiological and health scientists "can be accused of wittingly and unwittingly aiding and abetting" (p. 52) efforts to relocate the responsibility for health and well-being away from the community and more squarely on the individual.

The complicity that Ingham (1985) criticizes arises from the material and ideological context of contemporary research and scholarship. In addition to the dominance of the natural science model of investigation, favoring quantitative methodologies and statistical analyses, researchers face increasing pressures to obtain funding from sources outside the university. Support from the private sector, government ministries, and public agencies does not come without a cost. The agendas of these concerns come increasingly to influence, and at times dominate, the work of university researchers. In a political and economic climate favoring the privatization of health and welfare services and the re-definition of individual responsibility for well-being, reliance on private and quasi-public agencies for research support often results in researchers' complicity in the agendas of these agencies. It is a particular irony that this is occurring at the same time that a critical, historical sociology of physical activity and active living is reaching a stage of maturity.

Rationalization and Domination

The study of physical activity has been especially advanced by the work of Michel Foucault and others who have elaborated and developed his formulations on the rationalization of bodily practices. Several aspects of this work are significant for understanding active living. Central among them is Foucault's conceptualization of power and his under-standing of the body as a site of power and domination. "When I think of the mechanics of power, I think of its capillary form of existence, of the extent to which power seeps into the very grain of individuals, reaches right into their bodies, permeates their gestures, their posture, what they say, how they learn to live and work with other people" (quoted in Sheridan, 1980, p. 217).

Foucault's insistence on the body as the central object of political struggle is particularly relevant to a consideration of active living today. That struggle goes on in many arenas: physical education, the fitness movement, sport and physical activity, exercise, and health.

An understanding of active living is also advanced by the emphasis in postmodern thought on discourse and the constitution of subjectivities. "Discursive fields consist of competing ways of giving meaning to the world and of organizing social institutions and processes. They offer the individual a range of modes of subjectivity" (Weedon, 1987, p. 35). For Foucault, "discourses are more than ways of thinking and producing meaning. They constitute the 'nature' of the body, unconscious and conscious mind and emotional life of the subjects which they seek to govern" (Weedon, 1987, p. 108).

Sandra Bartky (1988, p. 61) has argued that Foucault "treats the body throughout as if it were one, as if bodily experiences of men and women did not differ and as if men and women bore the same relationship to the characteristic institutions of modern life." Feminist studies of Foucault have shown the centrality of gender to an analysis of disciplinary practices. These practices, Bartky argues, "must be understood in the light of the modernization of patriarchal domination" (1988, p. 64). Bryan Turner makes a similar point in establishing the centrality of gender to the sociology of the body: "Any sociology of the body involves a discussion of social control and any discussion of social control must consider the control of women's bodies under patriarchy" (1984, pp. 2-3).

In an analysis of "Foucault, Femininity and the Modernization of Patriarchal Power," Bartky takes up the project of developing a feminist analysis of disciplinary subjugation. She argues that one category of these practices involves the contemporary emphasis on female body size and shape. In the current fashion, the female body is "taut, small-breasted, narrow-hipped, and of a slimness bordering on emaciation" (1988, p. 64). The disciplinary practices that enforce this regime are dieting and exercise; both of these, of course, figure prominently in the contemporary discourse of fitness and lifestyle management.

Foucault's stress on local operations of power and its discursive nature opens important lines of inquiry about bodily practices. We are led to an analysis not only of institutionalized forms of physical activity, perhaps most notably organized sport and physical education, but also disciplinary forms that are institutionally unbound (Bartky, 1988). The regulation of bodies in exercise and fitness programs, dietary concerns, and other forms of lifestyle management are not imposed by particular officials and institutional agents, yet these practices have a power and strength as formidable as that of formal structures of authority. In the contemporary discourse, the media are important agents in this process. Media constructions of health and fitness, along with media efforts to sell the "good life" of consumer culture, constitute a particularly modern version of disciplinary subjugation.

Further Comments on the Media and Active Living

At several points in this chapter, the media have been identified as an important influence on physical activity and active living. We return to this topic now to stress the significance of the media to active living: Their influence is wide-ranging and cuts across a number of issues. Earlier, we discussed media accounts that favor particular images of physical activity (e.g., organized sport and commercialized forms of physical recreation) and active persons (e.g., male, young, able-bodied, heterosexual); the role of the media in defining values and perceptions of physical activity and constructing an ideology of gender; the utilization of the media by state and commercial interests to advance their interests; and the role of the media in advancing processes of disciplinary subjugation.

The point that unites all these observations is that media presentations help to shape our ideas about what active living is and who active people are. These accounts generally support and serve to legitimize existing social relations, say between men and women and social classes, and to further the interests of dominant groups (Hall, Slack, Smith, & Whitson, 1991, p. 141). The power of the media is enhanced by a sense of immediacy and reality, leading to the perception that viewers have a "true" account of the events that are happening. As Gruneau (1989, p. 134) notes, however, this sense of immediacy and actuality are mythical; what is presented is always the outcome of complex processes of selection and representation.

CONSIDERING DIVERSITY

One of the most important criticisms of scholarship on active living in recent years is that it inadequately considers diversity, frequently assuming that physical activity is experienced similarly among otherwise diverse groups. The most fully developed critiques of this homogenization have been in response to compulsory heterosexuality (Rich, 1980) and racial relations.

Heterosexism poses a challenge to the thinking on physical activity and active living, both in regard to naming the problem and to identifying the forces that sustain heterosexual privilege. The struggle to name the problem is evident in the denial of the presence of lesbians and gays in sport. Boutilier and SanGiovanni (1983, p. 120) note that "lesbians are present in every type, level and degree of sport participation. While this point may be laughingly obvious to some, it is apparently vigorously denied by others." Recent attempts to correct this deficiency include Cahn's (1994) study of gender and sexuality in 20th century women's sport, which documents a history of homophobia and discrimination against lesbians; Schulze's (1990) analysis of lesbians' experience of bodybuilding as disruptions to conventional notions of gender, subjectivity, and bodily practice; and Theberge's (1995) discussion of relations between lesbian and heterosexual women in an analysis of the construction of community on a women's ice hockey team.

There is also little information and discussion of gay men in sport and physical activity. The work of Brian Pronger (1990) is an exception and possibly indicates a lifting of the veil on this topic. Additional contributions to the literature on gays and lesbians have been made by Griffin (1992), Griffin and Genasci (1990), and (on homophobia in physical education and sport), Lenskyj (1991).

Compulsory heterosexuality is an important aspect of the contemporary ideology of active living. Media portrayals of the active society, including health promotion campaigns, often rely on imagery that stresses appearance, sexuality, and heterosexual relations. In some instances, these portrayals rely on the conventions of soft pornography to accomplish this effect (Birrell & Theberge, 1989).

In contrast to the scarce literature on homosexuality and physical activity, there exists an extensive literature on race and sport; however, the volume of material is not an index of the depth of analysis. Birrell (1989, p. 214) has critiqued this work as "generally superficial." It includes well-intentioned but theoretically limited critiques of sport as a racist institution (Edwards, 1969; Hoch, 1972); personal accounts of the exploitation of black athletes (e.g., Wolf, 1972), and superficial studies, generally quantitative, that reduce race to a variable.

Moreover, as Birrell (1989, p. 213) notes, this literature is marked by a distressingly narrow scope: "To date, our focus on race has been, in reality, a focus on black male athletes." Speaking of the American context, Birrell notes that "completely absent from our samples, our analyses, and our theories is any consciousness of Chicanos, Asian Americans, Jews and Native Americans. Hispanics are studied only to the extent that they exist in Major League Baseball." A similar comment applies to research outside the United States. In Canada, Vicky Paraschak's work on sport in native Canadian communities (1991) is an exception.

In addition to obscuring other racial identities, this preoccupation with black male athletes obscures important features of the dynamics of racial relations. The interrelationships between race, gender, and sexuality have not been well explored, and class is almost completely eclipsed through the tendency to read race as race/class (Birrell, 1989; see also Smith, 1992).

There is also a need to admit diversity into the concept of physical ability. Physical activity was long viewed as the domain of the able-bodied (Theberge & Birrell, 1994b), a misconception fueled in recent years by the glorification of the body in consumer culture and the association of activity, appearance, and performance. However, a focus on the concerns and rights of the physically challenged is changing this. A 1987 survey of Canadian women with physical disabilities gathered data on their interests and the barriers to their involvement in physical activity (Fitness Canada, n.d.). Such projects are important to developing awareness and understanding of various experiences of active living.

The effort to represent marginalized groups offers important possibilities for the study of active living, two of which are particularly relevant. First, it represents an important campaign to "bring bodies back" into social theory. As Birrell (1989, p. 222) notes, ideologies of gender and race are grounded in commonsense understandings of "natural" differences. Because it is grounded in some basic way in physical practice, sport has been an important factor in the construction and affirmation of these ideologies. Analysis of diversity in experiences of physicality and bodily practice is important to the larger goal of theorizing active living.

Second, this effort has the potential to contribute to a political transformation, especially in respect to racial relations. In *Black Feminist Thought,* Patricia Hill Collins (1990) offers a compelling argument for reclaiming the suppressed voices of black women. This recovery is a process of discovering, reinterpreting, and analyzing the ideas of black women intellectuals and others such as musicians, writers, and members of black churches and other community groups. These materials are the basis for a black women's standpoint, a necessary component of a politics of empowerment. Collins (1990, p. 221) suggests that a distinguishing feature of black feminist thought is its insistence that "both the changed consciousness of individuals and the social transformation of political and economic institutions constitute essential ingredients for social change."

Yvonne Smith (1992), developing this point in respect to sport, argues that there is a particular need for approaches that empower marginalized groups, including African American, Hispanic, Native American, and Asian American women.

Accounts of the experience of physical activity among gay men (Pronger, 1990) and lesbians (Cahn, 1994) are important to this discourse on diversity. There is also a need to involve physically challenged people. The effort to more adequately consider diversity is an important aspect of active living.

FUTURE DIRECTIONS FOR THEORY AND RESEARCH

This chapter's examination of the contributions of a number of theoretical traditions to the sociological perspective of active living differs from

the standard discussion of active living in different institutional settings, such as the family and educational system, and general social
processes, such as stratification and socialization, and their relevance to
active living. It argues that the key issue of active living (and indeed all
social life) is how society and culture influence the structure and practice
of activities. Developments in political economy, cultural studies, and
feminism, as well as contributions from the sociology of the body, have
greatly advanced our understanding of active living; they inform the
analysis of processes central to the experience of active living in modern
societies.

The analysis suggests several challenges for further research and
theory. One of these, discussed in the previous section, is the need to
more adequately consider diversity. There is a need not only for more
information about patterns of physical activity among minority groups,
but also for an analysis of ways in which minority status and identity
condition the experience of active living in respect to both limitations
and resistance. These efforts must attend to the interrelationships of
race, gender, and class and the significance of systems of privilege based
on age, sexual orientation, and physical ability (Andersen & Hill Collins,
1992). Peiss' (1986) historical study of leisure patterns of working-class
women in turn-of-the-century New York suggests the possibility of this
type of analysis.

The discussion in this chapter has also stressed the importance of
"bringing bodies back in" to sociology and the relevance of this for
understanding active living. In *The Body and Society*, Bryan Turner (1984,
pp. 245-246) suggests that an adequate sociology of the body must
address some notion of agency, consider the nature-culture dichotomy,
and be social and not individualistic. Turner's agenda may be considered in light of the conception of active living that informs this volume
and is discussed in this chapter on sociological perspectives. Both
emphasize a holistic approach that rejects a mind/body dualism and
historical analysis that considers the social and cultural influences on
active living.

Turner's third point, the attention to human agency, has relevance for
active living and quality of life. This connection, however, is less clearly
developed in work to date and provides another important challenge to
future studies of active living. That challenge is to better theorize the
conditions and possibilities for human agency in the interests of an
enabling, empowering experience of active living.

As Turner writes:

> Although the body is an environmental limit over which human
> beings do not have total control, it is also the case that, through

embodiment, they exercise some form of corporeal government. They practice in, on and through their bodies. This argument reject(s) an overly socialized conception of embodied persons. (1984, pp. 245-246)

Earlier discussions of commodification and consumerism, the media, political and economic influences, and the rationalization of bodily practices have indicated some major ways in which bodily practices are, as Turner puts it, "controlled." This control, however, is never complete or total. Rather, within the context of social and cultural pressures and limitations, individuals fashion and create beliefs and practices. The important challenge for social theory, including theories of active living, is to explicate the conditions under which these processes occur and the factors that encourage and enable social change and resistance.

We have considered two of the recent contributions of the feminist movement for theorizing resistance. First are the writings of black feminists who have shown the importance of giving voice to women of color and other marginalized groups. As Collins (1990) argues, the changed consciousness of individuals is an important aspect of the politics of empowerment.

Second is the emphasis in postmodern thought on the connections between discourse and subjectivity, an issue that has been a particular concern among feminist theorists attempting to identify the bases for challenges to the disciplinary subjugation of women. The philosopher Iris Young has researched women's experience of their bodies and bodily processes, such as pregnancy. In Young's terms, these pieces "resonate with descriptive work about women's embodied oppression" (1990, p. 12). Young indicates that her effort to describe women's bodily experience has a dual political function. By naming forms and meanings of oppression, the process brings to life the content of these practices. In addition, the attention to experiential description holds out the possibility of resistance and alternatives.

Further commentary on the connections between discourse, subjectivities, and resistance is offered by Sandra Bartky (1988, p. 83), who notes that in the current political climate there is little reason to expect widespread resistance to dominant forms of fashion and bodily practices. Moreover, she suggests, were they to emerge such developments would face significant opposition from "material and psychological sources" (p. 83) with important stakes in maintaining contemporary practices of disciplinary control. And yet, Bartky notes, in spite of this, opposition has emerged—for example, women who pump iron in violation of canons of femininity and women in radical lesbian communities who have rejected hegemonic images of femininity. In addition, there is a "popular literature of resistance" (p. 83) that supports these challenges. Bartky suggests that the ultimate source of the challenge may lie in the "incoherence" between the progress some women are experiencing in the political and economic spheres and the continuing domination of their bodies in the discourse of femininity. This incoherence is experienced as more than inconsistency; it penetrates to self-identity, self-knowledge, and social positioning. While the examples of challenge Bartky cites are limited pockets of resistance, they suggest the possibility of a base from which a broader movement may develop.

These examples also suggest parallels in a sociology of active living that more fully attend to human agency and quality of life. Research in this area should consider how active living, ranging from fitness programs to outdoor recreation to physical education and organized sport, offers the possibility of resistance and empowerment. For example:

1. How are some women, elderly people, and physically challenged persons experiencing exercise and other fitness activities in a way that is energizing and empowering?

2. What kinds of programs and activities enable this, how are they organized and structured, and how is a discourse of resistance enabled?

3. How, in a culture that glorifies consumerism, do less privileged groups enjoy and benefit from physical activity not contingent on expensive equipment and facilities?

4. What is the meaning of this activity for their self-image and consciousness?

5. How can active living practices integrate notions of health as control and release so that these are complementary, not coexisting in an uneasy tension as in the experience of the Chicago adults interviewed by Crawford (1984)?

6. How may kinesiologists and health scientists foster a less fragmented and specialized understanding and practice of active living so that we can better realize a vision of active living that is holistic and empowering?

The ability of discourses of resistance to penetrate and challenge prevailing notions is contingent on their relation to broader sets of interests (Weedon, 1987, pp. 110-111). The political, economic, and ideological interests discussed in this chapter will not be easily dislodged. It is clear, however, that in the developing literature on critical perspectives on physical activity there are grounds for challenge and resistance. The task at hand is to extend the reach of this work to an inclusive analysis of active living in all its manifestations.

_____

Notes

[1] The subtlety of the construction of gender difference in the photos Duncan (1990) examined was the subject of a heated discussion among students in an undergraduate seminar that I teach. The initial reaction to the article among the majority of students was on the order of "Give me a break, these are just pictures of athletes, some men and some women. There's nothing more there." These students initially rejected Duncan's interpretation of the construction of meaning in photographs as a fanciful invention. Over the course of the class period, however, as discussion progressed a transition occurred: A number of students came to "see" the meanings embedded in the message and to appreciate the power of cultural texts.

[2] The extent to which physical activity has been reconceptualized in the popular mind as fitness activity and imbued with a moral dimension is often brought home to me in two settings. For many of the kinesiology students at the university where I teach, fitness is the *raison d'être* of physical activity. As an illustration of this, students commonly distinguish between organized sport and fitness activities, as though anything that is not competitive and skill-oriented is, by definition, for fitness. The moral dimension is evident at the local YMCA I frequent. In casual conversation and locker room chat, one often hears that a person has been "bad" for missing workouts or "deserves" a reward for having been "good" and faithful to an exercise program.

REFERENCES

Allard, J. (1987). Sex roles, social change and cultural ideals of fitness. *Leisure Information Quarterly, 12*(4), 1, 3-5.

Amateur Athletic Foundation. (1991). *Coverage of women's sports in four daily newspapers.* Los Angeles: Amateur Athletic Foundation.

Amateur Athletic Foundation. (1994). *Gender stereotyping in televised sports: A follow-up to the 1989 study.* Los Angeles: Amateur Athletic Foundation.

Andersen, M. & Hill Collins, P. (Eds.). (1992). *Race, class, and gender: An anthology.* Belmont, CA: Wadsworth.

Andrews, D.L. & Loy, J.W. (1993). British cultural studies and sport: Past encounters and future possibilities. *Quest, 45,* 255-276.

Bartky, S. (1988). Foucault, femininity, and the modernization of patriarchal power. In I. Diamond & L. Quinby (Eds.), *Foucault & feminism: Reflections on resistance* (pp. 61-86). Boston: Northeastern University Press.

Birrell, S. (1984). Studying gender in sport: A feminist perspective. In N. Theberge & P. Donnelly (Eds.), *Sport and the sociological imagination* (pp. 125-135). Ft. Worth: Texas Christian University Press.

Birrell, S. (1989). Racial relations theories and sport: Suggestions for a more critical analysis. *Sociology of Sport Journal, 6,* 212-227.

Birrell, S. & Theberge, N. (1989, June). *The fitness boom and the fragmentation of women's bodies*. Paper presented at the meetings of the National Women's Studies Association, Towson, MD.

Birrell, S. & Theberge, N. (1994). Ideological control of women in sport. In M. Costa & S. Guthrie (Eds.), *Women and sport: Interdisciplinary perspectives* (pp. 341-359). Champaign, IL.: Human Kinetics.

Boutilier, M. & SanGiovanni, L. (1983). *The sporting woman*. Champaign, IL: Human Kinetics.

British cultural studies (Special issue). (1992). *Sociology of Sport Journal, 9*(2).

Cahn, S. (1994). *Coming on strong: Gender and sexuality in twentieth-century women's sport*. New York: Free Press.

Canadian Association for Advancement of Women and Sport. (1989). *Action*. Ottawa: CAAWS.

Canadian Association for Advancement of Women and Sport. (1994). *Expanded survey reveals a modest upsurge in coverage of women's sports*. Ottawa: CAAWS (News release, February).

Canadian guidelines for healthy weights. (1988). Ottawa: Ministry of National Health and Welfare.

Cantelon, H. & Gruneau, R. (Eds.). (1982). *Sport, culture and the modern state*. Toronto: University of Toronto Press.

Collins, P. Hill. (1990). *Black feminist thought*. London: Unwin Hyman.

Couzens, G.S. (1988, June). Getting into the fitness business. *Sports, Inc., 6*, 22-23.

Crawford, R. (1984). A cultural account of "health": control, release, and the social body. In J. McKinlay (Ed.), *Issues in the political economy of health care* (pp. 60-103). New York: Tavistock.

Demers, P.J. (1988). University training of physical educators. In J. Harvey & H. Cantelon (Eds.), *Not just a game: Essays in Canadian sport sociology* (pp. 159-172). Ottawa: University of Ottawa Press.

Dewar, A. (1987). The social construction of gender in physical education. *Women's Studies International Forum, 10*(4), 453-465.

Donnelly, P. (1988). Sport as a site for popular resistance. In R. Gruneau (Ed.), *Popular cultures and political practices* (pp. 69-82). Toronto: Garamond.

Duncan, M.C. (1990). Sports photographs and sexual difference: Images of women and men in the 1984 and 1988 Olympic Games. *Sociology of Sport Journal, 7*, 22-43.

Edwards, H. (1969). *The revolt of the black athlete*. New York: Free Press.

Endel, B. (1991). *Working out: The dialectic of strength and sexuality in* Women's Sport and Fitness Magazine. Unpublished doctoral dissertation, University of Iowa, Iowa City.

Fitness Canada. (1991). *Active living: A conceptual overview*. Ottawa: Author.

Fitness Canada. (n.d.). *Physical activity and women with disabilities*. Ottawa: Fitness and Amateur Sport.

Frank, A. (1990). Bringing bodies back in: A decade review. *Theory, Culture, and Society, 7*, 131-162.

Giddens, A. (1991). *Introduction to sociology*. New York: Norton.

Griffin, P. (1992). Changing the game: Homophobia, sexism and lesbians in sport. *Quest, 44*, 251-265.

Griffin, P. & Genasci, J. (1990). Addressing homophobia in physical education: Responsibilities for teachers and researchers. In M. Messner & D. Sabo (Eds.), *Sport, men, and the gender order* (pp. 211-220). Champaign, IL: Human Kinetics.

Gruneau, R. (1989). Making spectacle: A case study in television sports production. In L.A. Wenner (Ed.), *Media, sports & society* (pp. 134-154). Newbury Park, CA: Sage.

Hagedorn, R. (1990). *Sociology*. Toronto: Holt, Rinehart & Winston.

Hall, M.A., Slack, T., Smith, G., & Whitson, D. (1991). *Sport in Canadian society*. Toronto: McClelland & Stewart.

Hargreaves, J. (1986). *Sport, power and culture*. Cambridge: Polity Press.

Hargreaves, J. (1987). The body, sport and power relations. In J. Horne, D. Jary, & A. Tomlinson (Eds.), *Sport, leisure and social relations* (pp. 139-159). London: Routledge & Kegan Paul.

Harvey, J. (1983). *Le corps programme ou la rhetoric de Kino-Quebec*. Montreal: Albert Saint-Martin.

Harvey, J. (1988). Sport policy and the welfare state: An outline of the Canadian case. *Sociology of Sport Journal, 5*, 315-329.

Hoch, P. (1972). *Rip off the big game*. New York: Anchor Books.

Ingham, A. (1985). From public issue to personal trouble: Well being and the fiscal crisis of the state. *Sociology of Sport Journal, 2*, 43-55.

Ingham, A.G. & Loy, J.W. (Eds.). (1993). *Sport in social development: Traditions, transitions and transformations*. Champaign, IL: Human Kinetics.

Kidd, B. (1988). The elite athlete. In J. Harvey & H. Cantelon (Eds.), *Not just a game* (pp. 287-307). Ottawa: University of Ottawa Press.

Kidd, B. (1990). The men's cultural centre: Sports and the dynamics of women's oppression/men's repression. In M. Messner & D. Sabo (Eds.), *Sport, men and the gender order* (pp. 31-43). Champaign, IL: Human Kinetics.

Kidd, B., Corner, F., & Stewart, B. (1983). *For amateur boxing*. Toronto: Government of Ontario.

Labonte, R. (1982). Half-truths about health. *Policy Options, 3*(1), 54-55.

Landry, F., Landry, M., & Yerles, M. (Eds.). (1991). *Sport . . . the third millennium: Proceedings of the International Symposium*. Quebec City, Canada: May 21-25, 1990. Quebec: University of Laval Press.

Lenskyj, H. (1991). Combatting homophobia in sport and physical education. *Sociology of Sport Journal, 8*(1), 61-69.

MacNeill, M. (1988). Active women, media representations, and ideology. In J. Harvey & H. Cantelon (Eds.), *Not just a game: Essays in Canadian sport sociology* (pp. 195-211). Ottawa: University of Ottawa Press.

Mangan, J. (1981). *Athleticism in the Victorian and Edwardian public schools: The emergence and consolidation of an educational ideology*. Cambridge: Cambridge University Press.

Messner, M.A. (1988). Sports and male domination: The female athlete as contested ideological terrain. *Sociology of Sport Journal, 5*(3), 197-211.

Messner, M. (1992). *Power at play: Sports and the problem of masculinity*. Boston: Beacon Press.

Olympian. (1990, November). 1992 Olympic Games Program, 58-59.

Paraschak, V. (1991). *Variations in race relations for native Canadians in sport.* Paper presented at 1991 meetings of the Canadian Sociology and Anthropology Association. Kingston, ON.

Peiss, K. (1986). *Cheap amusements: Working women and leisure in turn-of-the-century New York.* Philadelphia: Temple University Press.

Pronger, B. (1990). *The arena of masculinity: Sport, homosexuality and the meaning of sex.* New York: St. Martin's Press.

Rich, A. (1980). Compulsory heterosexuality and lesbian existence. *Signs, 5*(4), 631-660.

Schulze, L. (1990). On the muscle. In J. Gaines & C. Herzog (Eds.), *Fabrications: Costume and the female body* (pp. 59-78). New York: Routledge.

Shaw, S.M. (1991). Body image among adolescent women: The role of sports and physically active leisure. *Journal of Applied Recreation Research, 16*(4), 349-367.

Shaw, S.M. & Kemany, L. (1989). Fitness promotion for adolescent girls: the impact and effectiveness of promotional material which emphasizes the slim ideal. *Adolescence, 24,* 677-687.

Sheridan, A. (1980). *Michel Foucault: The will to truth.* London: Tavistock.

Smith, Y. (1992). Women of color in society and sport. *Quest, 44,* 228-250.

Stephens, T. & Craig, C.L. (1990). *The well-being of Canadians: Highlights of the 1988 Campbell's survey.* Ottawa: Canadian Fitness and Lifestyle Research Institute.

Theberge, N. (1985). Toward a feminist alternative to sport as a male preserve. *Quest, 37,* 193-202.

Theberge, N. (1989). Women's athletics and the myth of female frailty. In J. Freeman (Ed.), *Women: A feminist perspective* (pp. 507-522). Mountain View, CA: Mayfield.

Theberge, N. (1995). Gender, sport and the construction of community: A case study from women's ice hockey. *Sociology of Sport Journal, 12*(4), 389-402.

Theberge, N. & Birrell, S. (1994a). The sociological study of women and sport. In M. Costa & S. Guthrie (Eds.), *Women and sport: Interdisciplinary perspectives* (pp. 323-330). Champaign, IL: Human Kinetics.

Theberge, N. & Birrell, S. (1994b). Structural constraints facing women in sport. In M. Costa & S. Guthrie (Eds.), *Women and sport: Interdisciplinary perspectives* (pp. 331-340). Champaign, IL: Human Kinetics.

Turner, B. (1984). *The body and society.* Oxford: Blackwell.

Weedon, C. (1987). *Feminist practice and poststructuralist theory.* Oxford: Blackwell.

Whitson, D. (1987). Leisure, the state and collective consumption. In J. Horne, D. Jary, & A. Tomlinson (Eds.), *Sport, leisure and social relations* (pp. 229-253). London: Routledge & Kegan Paul.

Whitson, D. & Macintosh, D. (1993). Becoming a world-class city: Hallmark events and sport franchises in the growth strategies of western Canadian cities. *Sociology of Sport Journal, 3,* 221-240.

Willis, P. (1982). Women in sport and ideology. In. J.A. Hargreaves (Ed.), *Sport, culture and ideology* (pp. 117-135). London: Routledge & Kegan Paul.

Wolf, D. (1972). *Foul: The Connie Hawkins story.* New York: Warner Books.

Young, I. (1990). *Throwing like a girl and other essays.* Bloomington: Indiana University Press.

In Perspective

ECONOMIC APPROACHES FOR EVALUATING ACTIVE LIVING

Louise B. Russell

The application of cost-effectiveness analysis to health is a richly rewarding process. It addresses a fundamental issue: How can we best use our scarce resources—time, money, and energy—to get the most out of life, both individually and collectively? How can we apply limited resources to yield as much life and good health as possible? In the economist's jargon, how can we best maximize utility? To answer these questions requires knowledge of epidemiology, clinical medicine, demography, statistics, and other subjects, as well as economics. That is partly what makes cost-effectiveness analysis so interesting—there is always something new to learn.

I was drawn to cost effectiveness in health by the intrinsic interest of the subject, the wide range of information and methods it requires, and the broad overview it permits of decisions in medicine. Cost effectiveness is a methodology for reflection and the attainment of a balanced life. The nature of the analysis forces us to ask, is this the best way to spend our effort? Should we perhaps spend more of it there and less of it here? Are we getting the most we can out of life? Indeed, is it cost effective even to ask these questions, or are the costs and benefits of some decisions too small to be worth detailed analysis?

Even my early work was clearly leading toward cost-effectiveness analysis. I examined the diffusion of several major inpatient technologies—intensive care, open-heart surgery, and the like—and, in tracing the reasons for their diffusion, considered their costs and health benefits from a more qualitative perspective.

Cost effectiveness was a natural next step. The field of prevention offered fascinating topics, ranging from clinical preventive services to behavioral changes (like active living) to community programs aimed at environmental threats to health. Clinical preventive services have received considerable attention from analysts, but behavioral or lifestyle changes have been evaluated less often and less carefully. In my first book on the subject, *Is Prevention Better Than Cure?*, I used exercise to demonstrate how one should do a cost-effectiveness analysis of behavioral change, but there was no study available at that time. In *Evaluating Preventive Care: Report on a Workshop*, experts in the various fields assessed the evidence on effectiveness for exercise and four other kinds of lifestyle change as a first step toward conducting cost-effectiveness analyses. The article by Hatziandreu and colleagues discussed in this chapter reports an actual cost-effectiveness analysis, but it focuses solely on jogging.

Many interesting issues remain to be examined, especially involving programs and interventions that change the way we live. Cost-effectiveness studies are regularly published in the medical and health services research literature. Panels in the United States, Canada, and elsewhere are considering how to make the methodology more useful and more accessible for actual decision making. It is clear that cost effectiveness has much to contribute to a better allocation of resources for health. Studies show that current investments in health range, in terms of cost effectiveness, all the way from a few thousand dollars per life-year gained for pneumococcal pneumonia vaccine to hundreds of thousands of dollars per life-year for the use of lovastatin to reduce blood cholesterol and more than $1 million per life-year to screen women for cervical cancer annually rather than every two years.

Active living deserves careful evaluation. In this chapter, I suggest that active living differs from other interventions in ways that must be taken into account in an analysis. The books and articles cited in the chapter should serve as a good introduction to the subject of cost-effectiveness analysis.

Chapter 5

ECONOMIC APPROACHES FOR EVALUATING ACTIVE LIVING

Louise B. Russell

Persuading and enabling people to adopt active lifestyles requires the use of some of society's scarce resources to build or adapt facilities and provide the proper encouragement and services. Since these resources could be used for other worthwhile purposes, an economist would urge that their use for active living be evaluated in order to determine whether and under what circumstances it is the best use of those resources.

This chapter describes economic evaluation. The first section outlines the economic approach to modeling decisions. The second describes the fundamentals of cost-effectiveness analysis—the estimation and valuation of effects, side effects, and resources and the aggregation and presentation of results. The third section discusses a study of exercise, illustrating how economic analyses are done and the kinds of results they produce. The final section offers an agenda for future research on active living.

THE ECONOMIC APPROACH
TO MODELING DECISIONS

In their simplest models, economists think of individuals as making choices in the following way. The individual derives satisfaction, or "utility," from a variety of goods and services and has some amount of income with which to purchase those goods and services. Within the constraint imposed by income, the individual weighs the satisfaction provided by each good or service against its cost and buys the ones that provide the most satisfaction for the money. In economic jargon, the individual maximizes utility subject to the income constraint.

Even this simple depiction illustrates several important characteristics of economic decisions. An economic decision is based on a comparison of the satisfaction to be gained from a choice (the benefits) with the cost of that choice (and, by implication, with the benefits of alternative choices). The balance between benefits and costs—not either one alone—determines the better choice. Benefits and costs are measured from the perspective of the individual making the decision and may differ from one decision maker to another.

More realistic models recognize that, ultimately, time is the constraint on the consumer (Dunn, 1979; Gronau, 1977; Kiker & Mendes de Oliveira, 1990). Time is devoted to various activities—jobs, housework, school, leisure, sleep, and so on. Everyone has only 24 hours each day and only 365 days each year. Given that allotment, an individual chooses to engage in each of the possible activities until the marginal benefit from the last hour equals the cost of that hour, and cost is measured in terms of the benefits foregone by not spending the hour in some other activity. An individual's nonparticipation in an activity is a signal that the marginal benefit, as perceived by the individual, of an hour spent in that activity is less than the marginal cost. The general idea is the same—benefits are weighed against costs from the perspective of the individual—but the focus on time proves particularly appropriate for an analysis of active living, because regular physical activity requires a relatively large amount of time.

At the governmental level, the analogs to the individual's comparison of benefits and costs are cost-effectiveness analysis and cost-benefit analysis. Both methods evaluate the costs and benefits of alternative choices, such as whether to promote active living over more conventional approaches to physical activity. Both give the government the information necessary to choose the alternative that maximizes benefits subject to the available resources, where resources are usually measured in terms of budget allocations. The difference is that cost-benefit analysis values benefits as well as costs in dollar terms, which makes them easier to compare but raises issues about whether the valuation of benefits accurately reflects the values of the people who will make, and live with, the decision. Cost-effectiveness analysis, by contrast, presents benefits in terms such as years of life saved, cases of disease avoided, or recreational opportunities provided, leaving the final valuation to the decision maker(s). (The disadvantage is that the decision maker may find it difficult to value benefits consistently across alternatives and thus difficult to compare them.) This chapter focuses on cost effectiveness, with brief mention of some subjects special to cost-benefit analysis.

In the following discussion of cost effectiveness, the decision maker is the government, which is assumed to take the social or national point of view. The social perspective accounts for all costs and benefits, no matter who pays or receives them (except for any that may fall outside the country). It is broader than the perspective of a government program, which would count only costs paid and benefits received by the program and its beneficiaries, ignoring any that fell to other individuals, organizations, or government programs.

Cost-effectiveness analysis can be applied to various choices relevant to active living: the costs and effects of building bicycle paths and hiking trails, or of running folk-dancing programs; or the costs and effects of advertising campaigns or educational programs in schools to encourage people to take up active living. Because active living should be proven to be cost effective before promotional policies are considered, this chapter will consider methods of economic evaluation from the perspective of activities themselves rather than from the perspective of promotional programs. The distinction is not, however, hard and fast: Some types of physical activity will be more appealing than others and will serve, in themselves, to promote the lifestyle more effectively.

It is important to define at the outset what we mean by a cost-effective choice. Although the term is often used to mean that something *saves money*, this is not its meaning among cost-effectiveness experts in health (or, indeed, in other fields of applied economics). Instead, its meaning follows from the simple economic models discussed above: *A choice is cost effective if its benefits are worth its costs.* The costs of the choice may be substantial, but if the benefits are valuable enough to the decision maker, he or she will consider it cost effective.

FUNDAMENTALS OF COST-EFFECTIVENESS ANALYSIS

The discussion of cost-effectiveness analysis and its application to physical activity in this section, including the material on the evidence for the health effects of exercise, is based on my two earlier books (Russell, 1986, 1987).

In the analysis of interventions or policies aimed at improving health, costs include providing the intervention and treating its side effects minus medical and other savings because disease and disability are prevented. Health effects are defined as the years of life added by the intervention minus those lost to side effects.

Years of life can be adjusted for the state of health during years added by the intervention and for any improvement or deterioration in health during years that would have been lived anyway, using methods that will be discussed later.

Typically, costs are divided by health effects to produce a cost-effectiveness ratio. When effects are measured in years of life, the cost-effectiveness ratio is the cost for a year of life added by the intervention.

Several aspects of these definitions need to be adapted and expanded for an intervention that is not purely, or even primarily, a medical intervention, as is the case with active living. The first two items of costs are the intervention and its side effects, which apply whether the intervention is medical or not, but the third item may also include savings beyond the medical sphere. More important, health effects, while a major reason for the interest in active living, are not the only effects worth considering; there are others, such as opportunities for family and social time together, transportation to work or other activities (by walking or bicycling, for example, rather than driving), enjoyment of the activity itself, greater physical attractiveness, and so on.

Every cost-effectiveness analysis involves a comparison between the intervention or policy being analyzed (i.e., active living) and something else. Costs are calculated as the difference between the costs of the intervention and those of the alternative; effects are calculated as the difference between the effects of the intervention and those of the alternative. The alternative may be doing nothing (more accurately, doing whatever people would do in the absence of the intervention), or it may be another specific policy. In the case of active living, two alternatives seem reasonable: "doing nothing," which, in this case, means the current mix of activity and inactivity people engage in; or the "20-to-30-minutes-at-least-three-times-a-week" guideline that for many years was treated as a standard for exercise (American College of Sports

Medicine, 1978). Because there is a published cost-effectiveness analysis of the second alternative, which will be discussed later in this chapter, it will serve as the comparison in much of the discussion.

The discussion throughout will consider how each element of cost effectiveness would differ depending on whether the usual approach to exercise, or active living, is being considered.

Effects

The effects of an intervention or policy—that is, its benefits net of any undesirable side effects—can cover as wide or as narrow a range of possibilities as the decision maker's interests. Government interest in promoting exercise has traditionally focused on the benefits to health— longer life and less illness. Individuals' reasons for being interested in exercise include not only health, but also the more immediate benefits of weight control, physical attractiveness, physical fitness, and a sense of well-being. Some individuals, but not all, derive enjoyment and a sense of accomplishment from the exercise itself and enjoy the companionship (or solitude) it makes possible.

Concepts such as active living suggest that a wider range of benefits is relevant. They suggest even more focus on benefits that can be provided by some forms of physical activity but not others, such as time with family and friends, alternative ways of getting to work, going to school, and running errands that may reduce pollution, and so on.

To be complete and accurate, the estimation of effects must be an interdisciplinary exercise (Russell, 1987). Economics provides the framework for cost-effectiveness analysis and some essential methodological tools. The tools include the concept and measurement of the utility (satisfaction) derived from effects such as better health, time with family and friends, and any pleasure from the exercise itself. The notion of measuring benefits and costs at the margin in order to arrive at the right allocation of time across activities is also important, but unless the effects are economic, such as unemployment, their measurement depends fundamentally and critically on the knowledge and techniques of other disciplines. The cost-effectiveness analyst who does not work with an interdisciplinary team must develop a thorough understanding of the relevant research. Even when working with experts from other disciplines, the analyst needs a good grasp of that research to ensure that the right issues are analyzed and analyzed correctly.

The effects of physical activity on life expectancy provide a good example. Ideally, a cost-effectiveness analysis is based on a mathematical description of these effects—a model—which specifies the dose-response relationship between physical activity and life expectancy.

Such models make it possible to estimate the gains in life expectancy from different amounts (different doses) of physical activity for people with different characteristics, and they can only be derived from medical and epidemiological studies that show the outcomes when people exercise and when they do not.

The data used for the model should meet several criteria. The criteria listed below reflect the fact that there are no large, controlled studies of exercise. The major studies have measured exercise and other factors that influence health at one baseline point and then related health outcomes some years later to those baseline measurements.

• The data should measure changes in deaths from all causes, not from a single disease, such as heart disease. While the major effect of physical activity is thought to be reductions in heart disease, its effects on life expectancy will be understated if it also reduces deaths from other causes, or overstated if it increases deaths from other causes.

• The studies should correct for baseline factors in addition to exercise that may influence the outcome, such as blood pressure, weight, and family history. These adjustments present a special problem when they involve factors relevant to exercise. For example, exercise helps control weight, reduce blood pressure, and so on, and people who exercise more at baseline may thus have lower blood pressure and weight as well. When these factors are controlled, the effect of exercise may be understated, yet if they are not, its effect is likely to be overstated, because exercise is not the only determinant of blood pressure or weight.

• Studies should be designed to avoid the problem of "self-selection," in which people who feel well tend to exercise more than those who do not, with the result that exercise gets credit for some benefits it does not cause.

• The total amount of exercise individuals get should be measured carefully and accurately—calories of effort is the most precise measure available in the literature. Many studies make only crude distinctions, such as the individual's assessment of whether he or she is sedentary, engages in regular moderate exercise, or engages in regular vigorous exercise. In addition, studies often measure individuals' exercise on the job or during leisure time, but not both.

A more complete discussion of the characteristics of the medical and epidemiological data needed for a good model can be found in two books by Russell (1986, chapter 4, and 1987, chapter 5). The study discussed later in this chapter offers a real-life example of the process. As that study demonstrates, even the most carefully developed models involve compromises made necessary by incomplete and imperfect information. This is not a criticism of models; indeed, it is one of their strengths that these compromises are made explicitly and thus are more likely to encourage attempts to improve on them.

The range of other possible effects presents opportunities and challenges for the study of active living. While research on such outcomes as mood changes exists, the social, environmental, family, and other benefits of various kinds of physical activity remain to be explored.

If, however, reductions in pollution are a substantial benefit of more active living—say, because more people walk or bicycle to get around— available research on the pollution produced by cars may be sufficient to provide an estimate of the reduction. This opportunity arises because available research on pollution is probably adequate to support an estimate of the benefits from its reduction.

These outcomes may create benefits or costs for individuals other than those making the decision to adopt an active lifestyle. Economists call these *externalities*. Because externalities do not affect the individual making the decision, his or her choices may not be optimal from the point of view of society. But when the government evaluates a decision, it can include externalities in the analysis and consider them as part of the societal decision-making process.

Side effects. Any negative effects must be subtracted from positive ones, so that the final result is the net gain from physical activity. Some effects come naturally in this form. For example, data showing the difference in death rates between people who exercise and those who do not automatically include any negative influence exercise may have on death rates and show only the net gain. However, some of the negative (or side) effects, such as injuries from physical activity, must be estimated separately.

Careful thought will be required to determine whether the wider range of benefits that may be relevant in an evaluation of active living has related side effects and whether those side effects need separate consideration. For example, opportunities for more family time together might also produce more family friction if some members of the family want to participate as a group and others don't, perhaps because they do not like the activity as well. Surveys might identify the potential for family activities, but not for family fights.

Valuing effects. For the most part, cost-effectiveness analysis simply presents the effects and lets the decision maker evaluate and compare them with the costs. Thus it serves much the same purpose as an evaluation of cars or refrigerators by *Consumer Reports*, which provides detailed information on the characteristics and costs of each choice. The decision maker considers the characteristics of each alternative, weighs them against costs, and makes a choice—to maximize utility, in economic terminology.

When a single effect is of interest, such as changes in life expectancy, it is easy to compare alternative interventions or policies. But when there are several different kinds of effects, especially when the effects differ in type as well as amount across alternatives, drawing accurate conclusions can be very difficult. Methods that allow different kinds of health effects—years of additional life and improvement or deterioration in health or function—to be valued in common terms and added together to yield the number of "quality-adjusted life-years" (QALYs), "well years," or "years of healthy life" (Kaplan, 1985; Office of Technology Assessment, 1979) offer some help. These methods, however, do not allow nonhealth benefits to be combined with health benefits.

In one school of thought, a QALY or well year is made operational by equating a certain condition or set of symptoms to an appropriate fraction of a year of good health. For example, a year with a torn knee ligament might be valued at 0.95 of a perfectly healthy year. Improvements in the condition can then be valued in terms of healthy years. An operation that repaired the ligament, for example, would be credited with a gain of 0.05 healthy years for each year of relief; 10 years of relief would equal 0.5 healthy years (10 × 0.05) and could be added together with years of increased life expectancy as well as years due to other improvements in health.

Another school of thought argues that the weights applied to various states of health should be proper utilities; that is, they should meet certain general criteria for sensible preferences (Torrance & Feeny, 1989). This requires a somewhat different method—the standard gamble technique—for eliciting an individual's preferences for different states of health. The standard gamble technique requires the respondent to compare a particular outcome (say a chronic illness) with a gamble between two more extreme outcomes (for example, perfect health and death) and state the probabilities for the gamble that would make it equivalent, in the respondent's judgment, to the first outcome. When utility-weighted QALYs are used in cost-effectiveness analysis, Torrance and Feeny have termed the method *cost-utility* analysis.

Although the approach has intuitive appeal, it is important to note that, except under very special circumstances, the result is not a measure of utility as defined by economists—the QALY index does not always reflect the way the individual really feels about the whole package of outcomes, as opposed to the various elements included in it (Mehrez & Gafni, 1989).

The problem applies, of course, to any variation of the QALY approach. However the weights are derived, the result is not a measure of utility, and the alternative that maximizes QALYs will not necessarily be the one that maximizes utility (Torrance & Feeny, 1989). Mehrez and Gafni (1989) have proposed methods that attempt to develop true measures of an individual's utility for each alternative.

However, an additional stumbling block remains. Cost effectiveness is used to aid decisions that will apply to groups of people, even entire nations, and economists generally believe that there is no way to derive a consistent set of preferences for a group from the preferences for the individuals in the group. But decisions that affect groups are made all the time and, as Torrance and Feeny (1989) note, individual preferences must be compared in the process so that the question becomes not whether to make such comparisons but how to make them. QALYs offer one well-developed approach, but the field is open for challengers.

Cost-benefit analysis goes further and values all effects, of whatever kind, in dollars; therefore it is easy to add them and compare them with costs. Wage rates and "willingness-to-pay" are the principal measures proposed for valuing benefits in dollar terms. Hodgson and Meiners (1982) discuss the use of wage rates for valuing benefits in some detail, while Coursey, Hovis, and Schulze (1987), Gregory (1986), and Knetsch and Sinden (1984) provide excellent discussions of the willingness-to-pay method. As noted in the next section, the use of wage rates to value health tends to creep into cost-effectiveness analysis as well, where it is inappropriate.

Costs

The costs of active living include the resources necessary to make it possible: additional facilities, such as halls for square dancing, athletic fields, or new walkways; equipment or clothing needed to engage in the activities; transportation necessary to use the facilities; and informational or persuasive activities devoted to encouraging active living. The costs of side effects, such as the costs of caring for injuries, are added to the costs of producing active living. As these items suggest, a set of activities must be specified before costs can be identified.

A potential advantage of the active living concept is that it may be able to piggyback appropriate activities onto existing facilities. Thus, the marginal cost of the activity—the additional cost necessary to adapt it to support active living, as well as its other uses—is the only cost that is appropriately charged to active living. If people use the fire stairs instead of elevators, the cost of the stairs, which already exist, is not a cost to active living, but those costs necessary to make them appealing to use, such as air conditioning in summer or heating in winter. In other cases, however, the facilities required for active living might be quite expensive to add to existing arrangements, but much less expensive to plan from the beginning. For example, bicycle paths are often difficult to add to existing roadways because there remains no room to do so; it is much easier to add to new ones.

The costs of active living include all resources necessary to produce the specified activities, whether or not the resources come with a clearly recognizable price attached. In particular, people's time is a resource, a very scarce one, and the traditional approach to exercise requires a lot of it. Clearly, physical activity cannot be produced without it, and, equally clearly, competing demands on their time often keep people from exercising. Here again, holistic approaches such as active living may be better able to take advantage of existing activities than the more conventional approach to exercise can. If someone decides to walk rather than drive to work, the time cost of walking is not the entire time spent walking, only the additional time it takes as compared to commuting by car or bus.

Volunteer time and donated facilities are also costs, even though they are donated. Volunteer time could be spent in other productive or pleasant pursuits, and donated facilities could usually be put to some other use. When this is the case, their use for active living involves a cost—the loss of the benefits they could have produced in those alternative uses.

Valuing resources. The appropriate valuation for each resource is its opportunity cost, an economic term which is defined in several alternative ways: as the payment the resource would receive in its next best use, as the benefits it would produce in its next best use, or as the payment necessary to draw the resource into the use under consideration.

For a marketed commodity, like concrete, which is sold under reasonably competitive conditions, these definitions all come down to the same thing—the market price. If the commodity is not bought for one use, some other buyer will pay the market price for it and put it to some other use. The price of the commodity is equal to the (marginal) benefit it can produce in that use. And the commodity could be drawn into the use under consideration at the same market price. Thus resources are generally valued at their market prices.

For nonmarketed resources, appropriate valuation is more difficult. The valuation of time is particularly difficult. Because many adults market some of their time in the form of paid work, the wage rate is often used to measure the opportunity cost of time on the assumption that workers can adjust their hours spent on work and other activities until the marginal benefit is the same in each, and therefore the same as the marginal benefit of work, which is the wage. The standardization of the workweek suggests that this condition is unlikely to be met for all workers. More important, the opportunity cost of time for unpaid work—that is, by housewives, children, and retired people—must be measured by some other means. A voluntary decision to stay out of the paid work force indicates that an individual values the time spent in other pursuits at some level higher than his or her market wage. When the choice is not voluntary, the value of time can be less than the relevant market wage. The appropriate valuation of time spent in exercise represents an important area for future research.

Savings.   Costs are calculated net of any savings. The costs of anything that would have been provided in the absence of active living and anything that is saved because of active living is subtracted from the total. The most common example is the medical care costs saved because people do not become ill as often. When the effects are as wide-ranging as those of active living, other savings are possible, although they may be difficult to identify and measure. As a simple example, if active living persuades people to spend more time walking to work and less going to movies, the cost of movie tickets and popcorn would be a saving attributable to active living.

Sometimes the wages people could earn on account of their extra good health are treated as savings and subtracted from the costs of providing the intervention. This practice, although fairly common, is incorrect and amounts to a double-counting of the health effects. Health is intrinsically valuable, and the health benefits of the intervention are already estimated and valued in the form of life expectancy or QALYs gained. Health benefits are valuable partly because healthier people add more to the output of the economy, but health that enables more or better time to be spent on school, child care, volunteer work, or at leisure is also valuable. Subtracting gains in earnings from costs thus amounts to counting health effects that are used for paid work twice—once as a gain in years of life and again as a saving to be subtracted from program costs. This practice is subject to criticisms similar to those leveled at the use of wage rates to value health effects in cost-benefit analysis. In that context, the use of wage rates values *only* the health gains used for paid work. The subtraction of wages from costs is not that extreme, but it does value health gains used for productive work much more highly than other health gains by valuing them twice, while the others are valued only once.

Presenting the Results

Physical activity and active living involve repeated costs over many years—and produce benefits over many years, as well. The pattern of costs and benefits can differ greatly: Costs are likely to be higher in the beginning, and benefits to grow larger as the activities produce effects over time. Moreover, alternative policies may yield very different patterns of costs and benefits, making it difficult to compare them and decide which is best. Discounting is used to summarize costs and benefits that occur in different years. Once costs and benefits have been discounted and summed, they should be presented in ways that help the user understand the most important results of the evaluation and decide how much confidence to place in them.

Discounting. Discounting derives from the observation that money and services that are available today are usually valued more highly than the same money and services several years from now. It is easy to see how this applies to money: Today's money can be invested in productive uses and earn a return, so that several years from now it will be worth even more; how much more depends on the real interest rate, that is, the interest rate net of inflation. For example, $100 invested today at a real interest rate of 5 percent will be worth $105 a year from now, $110.25 two years from now, and $115.76 three years from now. Thus, $100 today is worth more than $100 three years from now because of the opportunity to invest.

To make dollars that will be spent in different years comparable, economists calculate their *present value*, the number of dollars today that is equivalent in each case to the dollars in some future year. The present value of an amount depends on how much the money could earn if invested and, thus, on the real interest rate. At an interest rate of 5 percent, $115.76 three years from now is worth $100 today; that is, its present value is $100. Why? Exactly because $100 today could be invested and would, in three years' time, be worth $115.76. Similarly, the present value of $110.25 two years from now is, at a 5 percent rate of interest, also $100.

The general formula for the present value of a stream of costs applies this calculation to each year. If the interest rate is denoted by r, costs by C, and each year is measured from the present, with today equal to 0, one year from now equal to 1, and so on, the formula for present value is:

$$\text{Present value} = C_0 + \frac{C_1}{(1+r)} + \frac{C_2}{(1+r)^2} + \ldots + \frac{C_t}{(1+r)^t}.$$

This process of dividing each year's costs by $(1 + r)$ raised to the same power as the year is known as discounting.

The discounting process is simplified by the fact that there is no need to allow for future inflation in the estimates of costs. All costs should be, and usually are, expressed in "real" terms, that is, in the dollars of a given year. The discount rate used should then also be a real rate, net of inflation. Most published analyses use 4, 5, or 6 percent, so that 5 percent is a good choice for comparability with other studies. Because discounting can make a significant difference to the ranking of alternatives (Berwick, Cretin, & Keeler, 1980), and insofar as there is no exactly "correct" discount rate, it is also a good idea to show the results for other rates, including zero (which is the same as no discounting).

Calculating the present value of costs is a widely accepted practice, but many people have difficulty with the idea that it is necessary to discount effects, including health effects, as well as costs in order to compare different alternatives correctly. Some analysts, in fact, do not discount health effects. Keeler and Cretin (1983) have shown that this practice leads to the illogical result that it is always worthwhile to delay a project because it always is more cost effective next year than this year.

Tables and ratios. When costs and effects have been summarized as present values, they are presented in tabular form and as cost-effectiveness ratios. Tables reveal the details—the component costs and effects as well as the costs and effects for important subgroups. Cost-effectiveness ratios make it easier to see beyond the detail to compare alternatives. Cost-effectiveness ratios are only possible, of course, when all the effects can be summarized in terms of a single measure, say years of life. When the range of important effects covers outcomes that cannot be so summarized, it may be impossible or unhelpful to use ratios.

Costs or effects that differ significantly among groups of people should be calculated separately for each group. The costs of active living may differ greatly, for example, for the elderly, the poor, city dwellers, or inhabitants of very hot or cold climates, because of their different activities or the facilities available to them. Studies indicate that the health effects of physical activity differ significantly, with the greatest benefit accruing to people over 60 years of age, those with high blood pressure, and those who are overweight, and little or no benefit for men with very high cholesterol levels—265 milligrams per deciliter or higher (Russell, 1987). Other benefits—enjoyment, social time, and so on—are also likely to differ significantly across population groups. Active living may, as a result, be a more worthwhile investment for some groups than for others.

Sensitivity analyses. Estimates of costs and effects are inexact because they are based on inexact information. In cost-effectiveness analyses, the usual way of handling this problem is to present a base case, which incorporates what is thought to be the most reasonable information on each point, then do "sensitivity analyses" and make estimates that incorporate alternative assumptions. Standard practice is to change one assumption at a time, showing, for example, what happens when a different discount rate is used or when health effects are assumed to be larger or smaller than in the base case. The impact of the compromises required by the data on health effects can be tested in this way.

An alternative procedure, used by the Office of Technology Assessment in the U.S. Congress (1981), is to change several assumptions at a time to indicate "best-case" or "worst-case" results. A variant of this approach, proposed by Mishan (1976), builds on the notion of a statistical distribution by asking experts to indicate the range of possibilities around the assumption used in the base case and, more specifically, to guess at the values that would mark off one standard deviation from that assumption. Estimates can then be made for the case in which several critical assumptions are one standard deviation better or worse than the base case assumption.

COST-EFFECTIVENESS ANALYSIS APPLIED TO EXERCISE: AN EXAMPLE

Hatziandreu and colleagues (1988) have published a cost-effectiveness analysis of jogging, which provides a good example of many of the points just discussed. The study considers not only the health benefits of exercise, but also tries to incorporate enjoyment or dislike of the activity as well. Thus it encounters some of the problems that would confront an analysis of active living which tried to include benefits beyond those strictly related to physical health.

Cost effectiveness always involves a comparison between the intervention of interest and something else. In this study, jogging is the former, and the latter is the more or less sedentary living that characterizes men who do not exercise regularly. The authors analyze two hypothetical cohorts of 1,000 35-year-old men and follow them for 30 years. All the men in the intervention cohort jog; those in the control, or comparison, cohort do not exercise regularly.

Modeling Effects

The jogging study illustrates how data are pieced together to model health effects. It focuses on reductions in heart disease as the potential benefit from exercise and makes the assumption that deaths from other causes are the same in both cohorts. Data from a study of Harvard alumni, one of the major studies of exercise in the literature, suggest that this is a reasonable assumption (Paffenbarger, Hyde, Wing, & Hsieh, 1986). These data show that deaths from all causes were lower among men who exercised in their leisure time and that the beneficial effects of exercise on heart disease were not offset by harmful effects on other diseases.

To calculate differences in rates of heart disease between joggers and sedentary men, the authors began with age-specific rates of heart disease events (death, myocardial infarction, angina, or coronary insufficiency) taken from the Framingham Study, a longitudinal study of the population of Framingham, Massachusetts. These rates include both exercisers and nonexercisers. The authors then assumed that 10 percent of the men in the Framingham sample engaged in vigorous exercise (like jogging) and that exercise reduces the risk of heart disease by 50 percent. Thus, if the rate of heart disease for sedentary men is denoted HD, the rate for men who jog is 0.5HD. Using these assumptions, they calculated separate rates from the fact that the overall Framingham rate is the weighted average of the rates for the two separate groups:

$$\text{Framingham rate} = 0.9(\text{HD}) + 0.1(0.5\text{HD}).$$

The authors further assumed that joggers expend 2,000 calories weekly while running.

The assumption that the heart disease rate for exercisers is half that for sedentary men is supported by three major studies of exercise in men, as well as several smaller studies (see David Siscovick's review in Russell, 1987, chapter 5). Although the authors do not discuss the evidence for the assumption that only 10 percent of the men in Framingham engaged in vigorous exercise, they test an alternative assumption—20 percent—in their sensitivity analyses.

The health effects of jogging were calculated in terms of increases in life expectancy, reductions in disease, and injuries from jogging. They were presented two ways: first, simply as the increase in life expectancy from jogging; second, as the sum of increased life expectancy and changes in the quality of life (quality-adjusted life-years) from heart disease avoided and injuries sustained. To calculate quality-adjusted life-years, the authors chose weights for the different health states that seemed reasonable. They assumed that a year with heart disease was valued at 0.8 of a healthy year, so that prevention of heart disease caused a gain of 0.2 QALYs for every year of disease prevented. They also assumed that each year with an injury was valued at 0.9 of a healthy year, so that an injury sustained for a year caused a loss of 0.1 QALY. (An injury sustained for less than a year would be correspondingly less of a loss, e.g., three months with an injury would be a loss of 0.25×0.1, or 0.025 of a QALY.)

The estimation of health effects took into account that men who were injured while jogging might give up the activity. The authors calculated that 5 percent of the men who jogged would be injured annually and that 17 percent of those injured would quit as a result. It was further assumed that the men who quit would not take up any other form of aerobic activity and would suffer the same rates of heart disease as sedentary men.

The analysis treated enjoyment as a possible additional benefit from jogging. This benefit is difficult to estimate because enjoyment is a personal and subjective benefit, which varies greatly from one person to the next. It is clearly related to the amount of time spent jogging. But time is also a resource required to produce jogging and, therefore, appropriately valued, it produces an entry on the cost side of the analysis as well. The authors chose to tackle both valuation problems simultaneously by estimating the *net* cost of time, that is, the cost of each hour of jogging minus its enjoyment benefit, with due allowance for the fact that this net cost would not be the same for everyone. Since the result was a net cost, the method for arriving at this valuation will be discussed in the next subsection.

Modeling Costs

The costs of jogging include the costs of clothing and shoes, medical counseling, time, and injuries due to jogging, less the medical expenses saved because the risk of heart disease is diminished. All costs and savings were estimated in terms of 1985 dollars.

The authors estimated the cost of clothing and shoes at $100 per year for each man. They implicitly assumed that facilities—sidewalks, tracks, or something else—were available and that the marginal cost of using them for jogging was zero. It was assumed that a physician counseled each man about exercise during a periodic examination scheduled for some other reason; at a cost of $75 for the exam, the counseling took one tenth of the allotted time and thus cost $7.50 per man.

The amount of time involved in jogging was estimated at five hours each week—five sessions of one hour each, with 36 minutes spent running four miles and the remaining time for preparation and cleanup. As noted, time was valued in terms of its net cost—the cost of the time less its enjoyment value. To give them a basis for making this calculation, the authors asked six experts to estimate the percentages of men who like, dislike, or are neutral about jogging. The averages they got in response were that 55 percent liked jogging, 35 percent disliked it, and 10 percent were neutral.

Time was valued at its opportunity cost, which was assumed to be the same for all men and equal to the hourly wage of $9.00 in 1985. This implicitly assumed that the men were able to vary their allocation of time between paid work and leisure until the marginal benefit from the last hour was the same in each activity. The assumption is not unreasonable for working-age people, but it does ignore the standardization of the workweek, which makes it impossible for at least some people to arrive at that point of equality. It would not provide much help for an analysis focusing on children or retirees. (Use of the full wage rate also implicitly assumes that taxes on wages are matched, in the individual's view, by the benefits received from governmental services.)

It was then assumed arbitrarily that men who enjoyed jogging would value their enjoyment at $9.00 an hour, so that the net cost of their time would be zero. Those who were neutral were assumed to value the enjoyment of jogging at $4.50 per hour, less the opportunity cost of the time, so that their net cost of time was $4.50. Finally, the men who disliked jogging were assumed to derive no enjoyment from it, so that the net cost of their time was the full $9.00. Note that, in the latter two cases, assumptions less favorable to jogging could have been made. It would have been reasonable to assume that those who were neutral were truly neutral—that is, they received no enjoyment, so their net cost of time was $9.00 an hour—while those who disliked jogging actually registered something stronger than zero enjoyment (i.e., a negative number for enjoyment) and thus had a net cost of time higher than $9.00 an hour.

The costs of injury were calculated as the costs of the medical care required by the injuries. The reduction in heart disease produced savings in the form of the medical care costs that were rendered necessary.

Results

The study used a real discount rate of 3 percent in calculating the present values of health effects and costs.

The first bank of Table 5.1 shows the health effects of jogging as estimated by the study: years of life expectancy added because death is postponed; quality-adjusted life-years gained because of less disease; and quality-adjusted life-years lost because of injury. The effects attributed to jogging are the *differences*, shown in the last column, between the life expectancies and quality-adjusted life-years calculated for the jogging cohort and those for the sedentary cohort.

Table 5.1

Costs and Effects of Exercise for Cohorts of 1,000 35-Year-Old Men, Followed for 30 Years

	No exercise	Exercise	Difference
Effects in years of life lost[a,b]			
Death	492.1	276.9	215.2
Disease	778.2	449.8	328.4
Injury	0	13.8	–13.8
Total effects	1,270.3	740.5	529.8
Costs in thousands of dollars[b,c]			
Clothing	0	1,670	1,670
Time	0	15,450	15,450
Injury	0	52	52
Disease	2,390	1,410	–980
Total costs	2,390	18,582	16,192

Cost per year of life expectancy: $16,192,000/215.2 = $75,242
Cost per quality-adjusted life-year: $16,192,000/529.8 = $30,562

[a]Effects for disease and injury were derived using the quality-adjusted life-year method. See text.
[b]Effects and costs are discounted at a real rate of 3 percent.
[c]1985 dollars.
Data from Hatziandreu et al. 1988.

The second bank of Table 5.1 shows the costs associated with jogging. The presentation differs from that of the original study in two ways. First, the cost of time is included in what the study's authors would call the "direct" costs of exercise. The authors' classification of time as an indirect cost in the original article is incorrect. Because jogging or any other exercise cannot possibly be produced without time, it is a direct resource cost, just like clothing and shoes. Traditionally, wages lost because of illness and death have been referred to as the "indirect costs" of disease, and the authors may have thought time belonged in that category because it too is valued at the wage rate.

Estimations of the wages that could be earned if the added life and health were used for paid work are valid as an example of one of the possible consequences of the health effects. However, the authors went further and subtracted these potential gains from the costs of jogging in some of their results. As discussed earlier, this amounts to double-counting the health effects.

Second, the authors' estimates of potential wages lost due to illness and injury have been omitted. Like the time and health gained from exercise, the time and health lost because of injuries due to exercise is already included in the QALYs, and adding the wages for that time to costs amounts again to double-counting.

The results show that time is the major resource cost in jogging, as in most physical activity. It accounts for 95 percent of total costs—in spite of the fact that for the 55 percent who enjoy jogging the net cost of time is estimated to be zero. This result agrees with common sense. People often react to recommendations to exercise by exclaiming that they just cannot find the time; rarely is the cost of clothing or anything else a major concern. If the cost of time were omitted, the cost-effectiveness ratios would fall to about $3,500 per year of life expectancy and $1,400 per quality-adjusted life-year.

The major role of time gives active living a potential advantage over more traditional approaches to exercise in terms of benefits and costs alike. On the cost side, as noted earlier, active living may be able to piggyback onto existing activities, thus incurring only the marginal time cost. On the benefit side, the more benefits in addition to better health that can be combined in a single activity, the larger the number of people who will find that the cost of time is outweighed by the benefits.

In their sensitivity analyses, the authors examined an interesting alternative to the case in which every man in the exercise cohort continues jogging unless forced to quit by injury. The alternative assumed that every man jogged for a year and that only those who liked it or were neutral continued after the first year. Because the time cost is highest for those who dislike jogging, this alternative is predictably much more cost effective than the base case.

Comparisons of the results for jogging with cost-effectiveness results for other interventions to improve health must be made cautiously because the authors used a discount rate of 3 percent, and most studies use 5 percent. Because the health gains from jogging occur later, whereas costs are incurred from the beginning, the lower discount rate probably means that the costs per year of life are lower than they would be if calculated at a 5 percent rate and are thus understated compared with other interventions. With this caveat, it seems likely that jogging is in the middle range of medical interventions—not as good a use of resources as some, but a better use than others (see, for example, the interventions in Russell, 1989, all of which are discounted at 5 percent). If the net cost of time could be substantially reduced, it would rank among the most cost-effective interventions.

RESEARCH AGENDA
FOR EVALUATING ACTIVE LIVING

The models developed by economists stress that, in choosing among alternative courses of action, individuals weigh the benefits of each alternative against its costs. An individual tries to maximize overall satisfaction, or utility, within the boundaries set by his or her resources. The fundamental resource constraint is time, which can be used for schooling, various kinds of paid and unpaid work, and recreational activities. Maximum utility is achieved by increasing each activity until the benefit from the last hour spent in that activity equals its cost. Cost-effectiveness analysis parallels this decision-making process for governmental decisions. The method identifies the alternatives that will produce the maximum effect, or benefit, subject to the government's resource constraint, usually a budget.

Economic models thus point to the importance of accurately measuring benefits and costs. Both jobs represent a challenge for active living that must be met with new research. Consider the dose-response relationship, which is necessary to estimate the effects of active living. Recall that when the only effect of interest is that of physical activity on longevity, the units which measure dose and response are relatively straightforward. In studies of exercise, the dose has been measured most precisely as calories of effort expended in physical activity, and the response as the change in life expectancy.

Correct definitions of active living are neither straightforward nor likely to be captured by a single dimension of the activity. Calories of effort will be only one dimension of the dose; others might be the opportunity to socialize, the skills required, the setting in which the activity takes place (running through a beautiful park will have benefits different from those of running along a busy street), and so on. The response goes beyond changes in life expectancy to encompass effects such as physical attractiveness, mental well-being, socializing with family or friends, and a sense of accomplishment, among others. The first challenge, then, is to identify, if not all, at least the most important effects of active living and develop ways to measure them so specific activities that contribute to active living can be compared.

A survey of a sample of the population could be conducted to address these issues. Its purpose would be to learn more about the types of physical activity that appeal to different groups of people—the elderly, the poor, those who live in either urban or rural settings, families with children, and so on. The survey could identify specific activities, search for those that involve clusters of desired benefits (rather than only one or two), and describe how subgroups of the population differ in terms of the likely effects and costs of active living. Cost-effectiveness analysis should be applied separately to these distinctive groups in order not to average out important differences.

With so many dimensions to consider, it is obvious that some means of summarizing effects will be useful for comparing alternatives. The concept of utility, which represents the satisfaction derived from an activity—the overall effect—is particularly appropriate for the cost-effectiveness analysis of active living because it emphasizes the broad range of benefits active living proposes to provide the individual. Torrance and Feeny (1989) outline the use of multi-attribute utility theory for developing utility weights for QALYs. Mehrez and Gafni (1989) propose a method for measuring utility itself. Further research is required to apply these methods to active living.

The major cost of active living seems to be time, but specific activities differ in terms of other costs involved. The same survey proposed above could study the differences in activities in terms of cost, the types of activities currently available or most easily provided, and those that can be added most easily to everyday schedules of different groups.

Since time is a major cost, its valuation is an important issue for active living. Economists are agreed in principle that time should be valued at its opportunity cost for the individual. For people who engage in paid work, the wage rate may be a sufficiently accurate value, but for those who do not, more research is needed to identify methods for measuring the opportunity cost of time.

In general, the collection and analysis of data for active living should focus, in Maguire's term (1991), on studying people "in the round." It must recognize that many people engage in a great deal of activity in their daily lives. Past studies of physical activity tended to look either at activity on the job or at leisure activity, not at both, which clearly leads to a distorted view of what people actually do. Further, data collection and analysis must be conducted keeping in mind that some of the potential benefits from active living, such as family time together, are also available through other means (such as reading bedtime stories or visiting relatives for Sunday dinner).

Studies that evaluate the potential role of active living thus face a tall order. They must look at what people want in their lives and what they already do. They must identify activities that emphasize physical activity and best supplement the benefits people derive from their usual activities. That is, studies need to identify marginal changes in activity that will add the most to people's satisfaction compared with the marginal cost of engaging in those activities. Measuring the changes in both benefits and costs, and valuing them correctly so that possible policies can be evaluated on their merits, are challenging tasks, but they present a variety of interesting research questions.

ACKNOWLEDGMENTS

I am grateful to Jim Curtis, Storm Russell, and an anonymous reviewer for their comments on an earlier draft of this chapter.

REFERENCES

American College of Sports Medicine. (1978). *Position statement on the recommended quantity and quality of exercise for developing and maintaining fitness in healthy adults.* Indianapolis: ACSM.

Berwick, D.M., Cretin, S., & Keeler, E. (1980). *Cholesterol, children, and heart disease: An analysis of alternatives.* New York: Oxford University Press.

Coursey, D.L., Hovis, J.L., & Schulze, W.D. (1987). The disparity between willingness to accept and willingness to pay measures of value. *Quarterly Journal of Economics, 8,* 679-690.

Dunn, L.F. (1979). Measurement of internal income-leisure tradeoffs. *Quarterly Journal of Economics, 8,* 373-393.

Gregory, R. (1986). Interpreting measures of economic loss: Evidence from contingent valuation and experimental studies. *Journal of Environmental Economics and Management, 13,* 325-337.

Gronau, R. (1977). Leisure, home production, and work—the theory of the allocation of time revisited. *Journal of Political Economy, 85,* 1099-1123.

Hatziandreu, E.L., Koplan, J.P., Weinstein, M.C., Caspersen, C.J.L., & Warner, K.E. (1988). A cost-effectiveness analysis of exercise as a health promotion activity. *American Journal of Public Health, 78,* 1417-1421.

Hodgson, T.A. & Meiners, M.R. (1982). Cost-of-illness methodology: A guide to current practices and procedures. *Milbank Memorial Fund Quarterly, 60,* 429-461.

Kaplan, R.M. (1985). Quality of life measurement. In P. Karoly (Ed.), *Measurement strategies in health psychology.* New York: Wiley.

Keeler, E.B. & Cretin, S. (1983). Discounting of life-saving and other nonmonetary effects. *Management Science, 29,* 300-306.

Kiker, B.F. & Mendes de Oliveira, M. (1990). Estimation and valuation of non-leisure time. *Oxford Bulletin of Economics and Statistics, 52,* 115-141.

Knetsch, J.L. & Sinden, J.A. (1984). Willingness to pay and compensation demanded: Experimental evidence of an unexpected disparity in measures of value. *Quarterly Journal of Economics, 8,* 507-521.

Maguire, J. (1991). Human sciences, sport sciences, and the need to study people "in the round." *Quest, 43,* 190-206.

Mehrez, A. & Gafni, A. (1989). Quality-adjusted life years, utility theory, and healthy-years equivalents. *Medical Decision Making, 9,* 142-149.

Mishan, E.J. (1976). *Cost-benefit analysis.* New York: Praeger.

Office of Technology Assessment, U.S. Congress. (1979). *A review of selected federal vaccine and immunization policies based on case studies of pneumococcal vaccine.* Washington, DC: OTA.

Office of Technology Assessment, U.S. Congress. (1981). *Cost effectiveness of influenza vaccination.* Washington, DC: OTA.

Paffenbarger, R.S., Jr., Hyde, R.T., Wing, A.L., & Hsieh, C.C. (1986). Physical activity, all-cause mortality, and longevity of college alumni. *New England Journal of Medicine, 314,* 605-613.

Russell, L.B. (1986). *Is prevention better than cure?* Washington, DC: The Brookings Institution.

Russell, L.B. (1987). *Evaluating preventive care: Report on a workshop.* Washington, DC: The Brookings Institution.

Russell, L.B. (1989). Some of the tough decisions required by a national health plan. *Science, 246,* 892-896.

Seppanen, P. (1991). Values in sport for all. In P. Oja & R. Telama (Eds.), *Sport for all.* Amsterdam: Elsevier Science Publishers, B.V.

Thomas, G.S., Lee, P.R., Franks, P., & Paffenbarger, R.S., Jr. (1981). *Exercise and health: The evidence and the implications.* Cambridge, MA: Oelgeschlager, Gunn, and Hain.

Torrance, G.W. & Feeny, D. (1989). Utilities and quality-adjusted life years. *International Journal of Technology Assessment in Health Care, 5,* 559-575.

In Perspective

THE POLITICS AND IDEOLOGY OF ACTIVE LIVING IN HISTORICAL PERSPECTIVE

Richard Gruneau

My father worked in market research, and there were occasions in my childhood when the whole family coded questionnaires around the breakfast table. I dabbled in market research as an undergraduate student, gravitating toward sociology, not least because I felt I had a head start in social research methods. I was also obsessed with sport, but for most of my undergraduate training it never occurred to me to think about sport in sociological terms. Then, in my final year, I discovered John Loy and Gerald Kenyon's (1969) book *Sport, Culture and Society*. Here was an exciting new field—the sociology of sport—that was right up my alley. Even better, the field had just enough published material to define a coherent set of core readings, but not so much that it couldn't be easily managed by an undergraduate student. I was hooked and began to search for graduate programs where I could combine the study of sociology with my sporting obsession.

In the early 1970s, when I entered graduate school, North American sociology was going through an identity crisis. Much of the work in the field tacitly accepted the major organizing assumptions of postwar suburban life. At the same time, many sociologists believed that the discipline should emulate the methods of the natural sciences, with a view to hypothesis testing and the pursuit of law-like, deductive theories. But there was also a new generation of critical sociologists whose inspiration lay in philosophy, history, and critical political theory rather than empirical science. Perhaps it was simply a matter of youthful rebellion, but before long I began to identify far more with the critical, philosophical, and historical side of sociology than with the discipline's mainstream theories or its "scientific," empirical traditions.

I soon realized that "sport sociology" was going through an even greater identity crisis than sociology at large. Many of the early leaders in North American sport sociology had backgrounds in physical education, and this influenced many of the early debates in the field as well as the types of problems being studied. In addition, the sociology of sport was theoretically underdeveloped; preference was given to isolated, empirical studies rather than theoretically inclined discussions or broad historical and interpretive works. To make matters worse, while the sociological discipline at large showed a passing interest in popular culture, sport had long been virtually ignored, with the result there were few classic sociological studies to guide work in the area.

My book, *Class, Sports and Social Development* (1983), was written both as a sustained critique of the tendencies noted above and as an attempt to map out new theoretical ground for the sociological study of sport. It was published at a time when more and more people were beginning to realize that sport ought not to be studied in a vacuum and that sociological research on sport necessarily required engagement with other sociological studies—for example, the sociology of culture, the sociology of the body, the sociology of leisure, and the sociology of power and inequality. By the same token, there was a growing awareness of the need for new, interdisciplinary, theoretically sophisticated perspectives.

Much of this awareness was rooted in a more widespread challenge to established research agendas in Western intellectual life and to the boundaries that had traditionally divided the humanities and social sciences. A withering attack on traditional canons of Western art, literature, philosophy, and social science through the 1980s created opportunities for formerly marginalized academic research areas to achieve unprecedented importance and legitimacy. Notably, there was an upsurge in scholarly interest in contemporary cultural studies: in comic books, sit-coms, grunge, rap, Elvis, and Madonna. Within cultural studies, the lines between history, sociology, philosophy, literary theory, and political economy were blurring beyond recognition.

By the mid-1980s, I had become caught up in the general project of contemporary cultural studies. I began to study media, took a job in a communications department, and immersed myself in the debates about the politics of leisure and popular culture in a media-dominated age (e.g., my *Popular Cultures and Political Practices* [1988]). I also kept up my interest in sport, but now with a heightened critical emphasis on new themes such as modernity, identities, and the politics of the body in Western popular cultures (e.g., see "The Critique of Sport in Modernity: Theorizing Power, Culture, and the Politics of the Body" [1993]; and [with Dave Whitson] *Hockey Night in Canada: Sport, Identities, and Cultural Politics* [1993]). In the chapter that follows, I try to extend these themes to an analysis of the changing meanings and politics of health, fitness, and active living in Western life. When I first agreed to write the chapter, I saw the emphasis on active living as something of a departure from the work I usually do. But I soon realized that a consideration of the notion of active living in the broadest possible sense was highly compatible with my background and interests in political economy; the social analysis of leisure, sport, and the body; the history of popular culture; and theories of cultural politics.

Chapter 6

THE POLITICS AND IDEOLOGY OF ACTIVE LIVING IN HISTORICAL PERSPECTIVE

Richard Gruneau

Academic research and government policies in the areas of health, fitness, and lifestyle have long been influenced by biomedical conceptions of the human body and scientific approaches to the improvement of physical performance. Health and physical activity professionals have campaigned for a definition of the good life based in a philosophy of "biological self-betterment" (Vertinsky, 1990, p. 78). If people committed themselves to this philosophy, the argument ran, they could look forward to a wide range of positive outcomes including longer life, more productive work, new levels of sporting achievement, and, above all, greater personal happiness. In this context, contemporary discourses on health, fitness, and physical performance typically assumed an individualistic and behaviorist cant. Exercise, fitness, and physically active lifestyles were studied and promoted in isolation from the analysis of culture, economics, and politics (cf. Ingham, 1985; Maguire, 1991). Even when health and physical activity professionals began to champion more holistic approaches to health and promote the broader concept of "wellness," they rarely demonstrated much sensitivity to the social structural and cultural constraints that limited the opportunities of men and women in different social classes and racial and ethnic groups to live physically active lifestyles (cf. Crawford, 1980). There appeared to be even less understanding of the inherent cultural paternalism implicit in exhortations to eat right, exercise regularly, and become trim (cf. Harvey, 1983). But above all, there was almost no attention paid to the political and economic vested interests associated with the selling of health, fitness, and active lifestyles.

Over the last 15 years, these tendencies and omissions have been challenged by a growing number of critical studies in the history and sociology of health, medicine, leisure, popular culture, and the body (Whorton, 1982; Hoberman, 1984; Turner, 1984; Featherstone, 1991; Green, 1986; Grover, 1989; Navarro, 1986; Bolaria, 1988). This chapter draws on this critical tradition to construct a broad historical outline of the changing political, economic, and cultural dimensions of active living in modern Western societies. I argue that images and ideals of human activity in Western societies—along with attitudes to the shape, smell, and look of the human body—are distinctly social and cultural products grounded in relations of power. The definition and promotion of good activity, good health, the good body, and the good life have always been (and continue to be) a matter of negotiation and struggle between powerful and less-powerful social groups, often with markedly different understandings of how life should be lived.

For this reason it is useful to explore the social and cultural roots of the belief that biomedical, behavioral, or social science can objectively determine the ideal pathway to physical or mental well-being. In my view, this belief is a uniquely modern and Western cultural conceit. Indeed, I argue that no definition of good activity, good health, the good body, or the good life has ever become influential in Western societies simply because of its inherent logic or truthfulness; rather, the influence of particular definitions has largely been secured because of the differential capacity of some social groups to promote their preferred ideals, skills, and activities as more fulfilling, legitimate, and prestigious than others. Privileged groups have never been universally successful in this regard, but to the extent that their preferences have become institutionalized at any given time, competing ideals, skills, and activities have often been pushed to the cultural periphery.

My discussion begins with a brief examination of changing definitions and ideals of active living in Western history from classical antiquity to the emergence of self-consciously modern societies in Europe and North America after the eighteenth century. This is followed by a consideration of new organizations and tactics for regulating and disciplining the body, and new meanings of the value of physical activity, that arose in conjunction with Protestantism, industrial capitalism, and the institutions of the modern liberal state. The changing meaning of active living is then set against the background of nineteenth and early twentieth century conceptions of "civilization" and the body politic. At this point, the argument shifts to consider the impact of a burgeoning consumer culture in the early twentieth century on health, conceptions of the body, images of well-being, and the values of the active life. I conclude with a brief discussion of changes in popular culture, social structure, economic, and state policy from the time of the early, postwar, welfare state in North America to the present day.

MODERNITY AND THE CHANGING IDEAL OF THE ACTIVE LIFE

The Active Life of the Mind

Between the sixteenth and late nineteenth centuries, Western societies experienced a series of immense upheavals. Population increases in Europe and the affluence generated from colonial empires after the fifteenth century, the scientific and philosophical innovations that led to the Enlightenment, the Protestant Reformation in the sixteenth century, the revolutionary political movements of the 1790s and 1840s, and the growth and international expansion of wage labor and industrial technology in the nineteenth century, all combined to undermine existing traditional cultures and economic and political structures. By the early nineteenth century, social commentators were beginning to argue that Western societies were in the throes of a social transformation so far-reaching that it threatened to destroy everything that people in Western societies had, everything they knew, everything they were (Berman, 1983, p. 15). The preferred term that emerged to describe this transformation was *modern*. Throughout the nineteenth and early twentieth centuries, Western artists and intellectuals wrestled continually with the tensions, ambiguities, and contradictions of modernity, sharing the sense that they were living through a revolutionary age (cf. Berman, 1983; Harvey, 1989).

New conceptions of health and the body, and of the relationships between body, mind, and the concepts of energy, motion, and activity, were an important part of life in this revolutionary age. We can map the emergence of these new conceptions by comparing and contrasting them with earlier perspectives, beginning initially with the traditional Christian concern for mental and spiritual "activity." Cultural leadership throughout much of Europe before the eighteenth century was rooted in Christian ideals. The dominant Christian view of life drew on selected ideas from classical Greek philosophy that emphasized the importance of spirituality and contemplation. Aristotle had noted that human life can never be anything other than "active" insofar as it was necessary for people to be involved in productive activities necessary to ensure survival (de Grazia, 1964, p. 11). Training the body was an important part of a well-rounded life. But Aristotle argued that thought can also be said to move, even pure speculation and contemplation involves a sense of activity. Indeed, thoughts are actually active in the fullest measure because it is thoughts that move people and things "to the outward, visible kind of activity" (de Grazia, 1964, p. 12). For that reason, Aristotle argued, the activity of contemplation is of a higher form than activities undertaken out of social necessity or for simple amusement.

In this classic formulation the ideals of freedom and creative development were closely tied to a nonutiltarian conception of human well-being wherein contemplation is the highest form of the active life. When understood in a secular manner, this conception of idealized human creativity, defined as the activity of mind, greatly influenced Western traditions of the arts and humanities as they were to develop from the end of the Roman Empire through the early twentieth century. More notably still, the emphasis on contemplative activity found in Aristotle also represented a powerful line of thought that ran from classical Greece through certain strands of Roman philosophy into medieval Christianity and monasticism. Contemplation became widely viewed as the pathway to divine revelation and, through the frequently close relations between church, state, and community, the contemplative ideal was institutionalized as a socially desirable feature of personal development and well-being.

While medieval high theology viewed contemplative activity as necessary to piety and self-betterment, this ideal had to be reconciled continually with more secular forms of *physical* activity associated with craft, commerce, amusement, and military prowess. Traditional pagan festivals often blended with Christian teachings and new religious holidays at the local community level and were celebrated with gaming and public displays of strength and agility. At the same time, the medieval Church was necessarily interested in trade, and religious leaders had to continually negotiate power-sharing arrangements with secular leaders who valued the development of martial prowess and the advancement of sovereign power over the activity of contemplation. Throughout the history of medieval Europe, the priority that the Church gave to the active life of the mind necessarily coexisted with more secular and bodily centered understandings of valued activity.

Physical Activity, Discipline, and Indulgence

Most of the secular forms of active living evident in the history of medieval Europe shared an important dimension with the religious emphasis on contemplation: Each was widely incorporated into formal and informal systems of social regulation and control. From the time of the breakdown of the Roman Empire to the sixteenth century, social life in Europe was governed by a diverse patchwork of systems of political organization. On the one hand, Mediterranean city states had independent charters and acted as quasi-autonomous political bodies (Hall, 1984, p. 4). Outside these city states, the vestiges of Roman law and the late Roman labor system of "free" tenants under the patronage of great agrarian landlords, and a peasantry tied in tenancy to the estate, provided much of the inspiration for feudalism. Simultaneously, much of Europe was also dominated by Germanic clan societies—kinship groupings, often tracing their membership matrilineally—owning and working land in common, with little private property. These clan societies were governed rather loosely "through aristocratic-based councils with, below them, powerful assemblies of free warriors and, attached to them, retinues of soldiers in bands, often with their own chiefs" (Hall, 1984, p. 4). The legacies of the martial emphasis and bonds of personal loyalty and mutual obligation among these settler/warrior communities contributed a second major element to feudalism.

After 800 AD, an attempt was made to recreate the legacy of the Roman imperial system under the patronage of the Catholic Church in order to centralize and unify the fragmented nature of European political life. Despite this initiative, the legacy of secular clan organization and of powerful warrior classes ensured conflicting levels of authority and a high level of autonomy from Church domination. Moreover, the power of local lords was such that they could frequently block trends toward the centralization of power in the hands of any one monarch. The incursions of Mongol invaders in eastern Europe in the 14th century introduced further divisions and cultural variations in types and modes of political organization. As a result, life in Europe before the sixteenth century was continually torn by internal tensions between different and overlapping sources of power (Hall, 1984, p. 6). The most visible form of power, sovereign power over a territory and population, was necessarily connected closely to martial prowess and military discipline. The territorial claims of clans, lords, kings, and merchant princes was something that could best be secured and protected by force. However, that force could only be generated effectively through high levels of internal social controls and discipline within the warrior classes.

Much of that discipline was centered on the human body and its utility as a force that could be deployed in the defense of sovereign power. Formal military training is one of the oldest examples of the calculated use of bodily exercises of various types—including physical strength and fitness training, weapons instruction, drills, and the practice of strategies—to train the individual body to the perceived maximum of its powers and then to integrate it as a moving part into a larger social composite (Giddens, 1984, pp. 148-151). Warrior traditions in Europe before the sixteenth century also embraced the ideal of free-roaming, adventurist military activity as a defining component of masculine honor and prowess. These masculine warrior traditions celebrated the restless activity of military adventurism while simultaneously embracing an ethos of bodily asceticism and mysticism that loosely paralleled monastic practices. But in contrast to the orthodox Church's emphasis on disciplining body and mind to promote piety and contemplation, warrior cultures emphasized discipline for the purpose of instilling loyalty while building physical prowess. The drills, habits, ceremonies, and rituals associated with techniques and practices of physical training helped to solidify a sense of social attachment that facilitated the integration of individuals into the larger social group (Connerton, 1989).

Throughout medieval Europe, bodily indulgence and unrestricted consumption seemed the obvious antithesis to the bodily discipline associated with the life of the military campaign, the monastery, or the convent. Traditions of bodily indulgence in drink, sexuality, food, and, frequently, violent sport, were integrated into people's lives as part of the seasonal rituals of agrarian production and village life. These popular traditions tended momentarily to create a temporary freedom from the restrictions of local authority; they opened up access to a sensuous and hedonistic world of pleasures often denied in day-to-day living (Bakhtin, 1968; Stallybrass & White, 1986). Yet, because these festival activities and bodily indulgences were so heavily bound by ritual and local custom, they were rarely threatening to local structures of authority. On the contrary, the heads of clans, lords, priests, and monarchs frequently shared in these activities and indulgences. In some instances, festival indulgence even took on the character of a kind of gift exchange: Festivals could be offered as a dramatization of a ruler's power and generosity.

Understandings of bodily indulgence as a manifestation of the good life, as well as a key symbolic marker of power and social ranking, had deep roots in Western history. The late Roman Empire provides the most widely cited example of the link between power and indulgence in Western history. There were important strands in Roman culture that emphasized the importance of living an active life centered around work, politics, and military service. Similarly, early Roman culture was influenced by the Greek idea that health could be maintained by obeying natural laws pertaining to diet, exercise, sleep, and sanguinity. But the economic surplus that was generated through military conquest, trade, and slavery began to support a Roman nobility that adopted the hedonistic pursuit of bodily pleasures both as a right and symbol of privilege. Ultimately, as the size and complexity of the Roman Empire grew, and in the face of growing unemployment and civic unrest, the Roman nobility popularized and institutionalized a culture of indulgence through the provision of "bread and circuses" (Brantlinger, 1983, pp. 68-80).

Late Roman culture was not alone in granting a high degree of social legitimacy to the "undisciplined" pursuit of bodily pleasures and sensations. The pursuit of indulgence as a manifestation of aristocratic privilege and as a signifier of rank can be found throughout "premodern" European history in examples as varied as the consumptive excesses of the court of Louis IV in France to the obsessions of England's Henry VIII. Bodily indulgence also became a notable feature of symbolic representations of affluence in modernity. This was particularly evident in late nineteenth century consumer capitalism: Girth became a signifier of bourgeois prosperity—a feature clearly observed in American editorial cartoonists' designation of the capitalist entrepreneur as a "fat cat." This is an obvious hint of the degree to which bodily indulgence, both among the elite and the masses, has also carried lasting, negative connotations in Western social thought. Bodily indulgence was widely equated with a violation of "natural laws" and as a signifier of decadence and decline—something to be contrasted to the apparent virtues of self-discipline, religious denial, or physical preparedness for war. Indeed, many late nineteenth and early twentieth century critics of modernity argued forcefully that modern Western societies were entering a cycle of decadence and decline that paralleled ancient Rome (Brantlinger, 1983). This concern brought some conservative thinkers, particularly in early twentieth century Germany, to yearn for the return of a culture of "barbarian" energy, vigor, and bodily discipline to "cleanse" the apparent decadence of modernity, just as earlier barbarian invaders had supposedly cleansed the decadence of the Roman Empire.

Power, Morality, and Bodily Activity

Both the argument that bodily indulgence was an indelible human characteristic, a right of privilege, or a popular entitlement, and the opposite view that such indulgence was a sign of immorality, irrationality, decadence, and weakness, left indelible marks on modern European and American cultures. Still, throughout the development of Western cultures and societies in the nineteenth and early twentieth centuries, it was the latter idea that emerged to define much of the political and institutional culture of modernity. If modern civilization was to survive, the argument ran, it was necessary to meet the challenges of immorality, irrationality, decadence, and weakness with new forms and strategies of education and discipline. Many of the new strategies of education and discipline that emerged had origins in much older traditions. For example, the Church had long maintained an interest in morality and education, and monastic traditions had always promoted high levels of self-discipline. Michel Foucault (1977) has argued that the medieval Catholic Church's concern for discipline can be traced back to the ideas of self-examination and the guidance of conscience in Greek philosophy. Building on these ideas, the Church promoted obedience and bodily asceticism through a unique system of pastoral regulation that combined record keeping about members of individual parishes with monopolistic control over education in moral and religious matters. That education included a complex set of strictures about bodily propriety regarding diet, sex, defecation, and dress. When these strictures were combined with the Church's self-defined powers of hearing confessions and offering absolution, the pastoral system can be understood as a remarkably broad-scale deployment of power through the use of discipline in the government of individuals in Western life (cf. Harvey & Sparks, 1991, p. 167).

It is useful to adapt another of Foucault's ideas here in a slightly modified form. Foucault's work (1977) leads one to recognize that a key aspect of such disciplinary power was its dependence on surveillance. Foucault argues that while "technologies" of power centered around discipline and surveillance have a long history they do not really develop fully in Western societies until the nineteenth century. However, I am persuaded by Zygmunt Bauman's argument (1983, p. 34) that forms of power somewhat similar to the kind described by Foucault were a major dimension of social control, integration, and reproduction of society well before the dawn of modernity. Indeed, throughout a medieval world characterized by overlapping centers of authority and a wide variety of autonomous microsystems of power, local customs governing attitudes and bodily propriety were surely the primary source of social stability on a day-to-day basis. Social historians of medieval Europe have noted that there was very little formal separation between the worlds of public and private life, and, while the ruling classes tended to be generally uninterested in the day-to-day activities of common people, the level of surveillance by kinfolk, neighbors, pastors, and local leaders was extremely high. Community control, nonetheless, operated in a matter-of-fact, largely unobtrusive manner. It had a diffused and totalizing character, with few specialized agencies devoted to maintaining the orderly reproduction of social life.

Slowly, between the twelfth and fifteenth centuries, the overlapping sources of power and authority in medieval Europe began to coalesce, although unevenly, around more centralized "national" churches linked with more unified national monarchies. And, after the sixteenth century, a new form of state rooted in increasingly unified monarchies, supported by but not dependent upon the Church, began to develop in France, Spain, and England. Perry Anderson (1974) has called this new form of state *Absolutist* because it undermined many of the dense local structures of earlier feudalism through such initiatives as the commutation of feudal dues into money rents; the supplanting of feudal military obligations by the growth of new, professional, standing armies; the implementation of taxation by the centralized state authority (often promoting rebellions by the poor); and the creation of more unified national economies.

With these initiatives, the territorial boundaries of the Absolutist state "increasingly coincided with the limits within which the state could effectively impose a uniform system of law, order and administration" (Hall, 1984, p. 7). In addition, mercantilism—the dominant economic doctrine under Absolutism—united state and crown in new, national-commercial enterprises that effectively linked the interests of bureaucrats, imperially supported merchants, and monarchs. This is not to say that the strength of traditional community control and custom was completely transformed with the emergence of Absolutism; on the contrary, much of the European countryside was still dominated by regressive local custom, and while the Absolutist state challenged communal control with new centers of "national" authority, this often had the effect of simply layering another level of surveillance onto daily life.

The Modernist Ideal of the Active Life

The self-conscious cultural modernism that slowly developed in Europe from the sixteenth through the nineteenth centuries was centered on the related ideas of expanding individual rights against Absolutist power, perceived aristocratic parasitism and indulgence, and the religious domination of literate culture. It also expressed a desire to break free from the static, backward-looking, and highly conformist character of European communal life. The revolt against tradition and conformity became a particularly significant dimension of cultural modernism in art and literature by the early years of the nineteenth century. On this point, Marshall Berman (1983) singles out Goethe's *Faust* as a classic example of a literary work that dramatizes the emergence of a uniquely modernist sensibility at the turn of the nineteenth century.

Berman suggests (pp. 39-49) that *Faust*'s early pages are largely a rumination on three powerfully interwoven features of traditional European cultures: the value given to the contemplative tradition in Western religions; the deeply rooted character of pastoral romanticism, which idealized the passive life lived in Gothic villages; and the strength of Christian ideas about predestination and fate. Faust begins to feel suffocated by the ways in which these traditions had worked to prevent people from actively changing their world. He finds the contemplative ideal especially problematic because it has the effect of separating mind from body and detaching culture from the totality of life. The legacy of contemplative vision handed down from Aristotle, adapted through Christian monastic traditions, and incorporated into science and philosophy was inherently passive because it kept the visionary individual in place as a mere spectator rather than an active participant in the making of the world.

By contrast, Faust comes to believe that the human body and the human mind "are there to be *used*, either as tools for immediate application or as resources for long-range development. Body and soul are to be exploited for maximum return—not, however, in money, but in experience, intensely felt life, action, creativity" (Berman, 1983, p. 49). He then makes his famous "Faustian" pact with the Devil and embarks on a mammoth program of economic and social development. However, while this program is both creative in intent and progressive in consequence, it nonetheless requires the tragic destruction of older ways of life and the people committed to them. Berman emphasizes how Goethe's rendering of the Faustian myth integrated two great historical traditions that had hitherto been separate: the romantic quest for self- and spiritual development merged subtly with a new form of romance for large-scale social, economic, and political projects. For Goethe this merger represents both the promise and the tragedy of modernity. Nevertheless, there can be no turning back to passive, backward-looking ways of life. The modern life is necessarily an active life, and the active life is devoted to self-realization, autonomy, and freedom through the ongoing transformation of the world.

It is important to note that Goethe's self-conscious modernism was open to a variety of interpretations. In this sense it was similar to modern bourgeois cultures themselves. On the one hand, like many progressive modernist thinkers in the late eighteenth and nineteenth centuries, Goethe struggled to articulate an implicitly emancipatory conception of active living that had progressive, perhaps even socialist, overtones. Being modern meant using one's energies and powers to remake the world rather than living in it passively. Communities that thrived on the repression of free individuality in the defense of a closed system had to be remade into communities whose collective resources would enable individuals to become autonomous and freely creative for the first time in human history. From this standpoint, the active life came to be seen as the relentless and ongoing pursuit of freedom to act; the only true pathway to the affirmation of self was to engage in a struggle to create forms of political organization that would both reflect and enhance this freedom. However, on the other hand, Goethe's emphasis on the centrality of intensely felt experience, on will, sensation, and authenticity, ironically provided opportunities for later antimodernist thinkers to link the new ideal of active living to a romanticism of physical vitality, the irrational, and the primitive (Mosse, 1975). That romanticism eventually became an important part of the fascination for nationalist spiritual authenticity and bodily perfectibility that became increasingly popular in Germany by the late nineteenth century—an issue I return to later in this chapter.

THE REGULATION OF "FREE ACTIVITY" IN MODERNITY

Protestantism and the Ideology of the Market

Modernist ideals of individual autonomy and free activity in Western life were framed from the outset by corollary notions stressing the importance of self-help and individual responsibility. New classes of merchants and industrialists in Western societies typically understood the idea of exploiting body and soul for maximum return far more narrowly than modernist intellectuals. Building on the mercantile and imperial traditions of the great European monarchies, members of these new classes tended to view the practical use of body and soul in monetary terms. On the one hand, that often meant forming alliances of expedience with the old ruling classes of the Absolutist/mercantilist state; on the other, it meant struggling for free markets and broader political rights of representation. There was increasing support for the idea that people ought to be free to enter the exchange process as artisans, farmers, laborers, merchants, or factory owners unimpeded by the traditional legacies of serfdom and aristocratic privilege. By the same token it was argued that competition in the market should also be freed from the unfairness of legally sanctioned aristocratic preference or state monopolies. As more and more of these freedoms appeared to be won, it became more possible to understand success or failure in the marketplace as a clear reflection of personal worth and ability. Even though the image of market freedom in Western societies was at odds with continuing privileges attached to class, race, and gender, the emerging ideology of free market individualism implied that the responsibility for success or failure in worldly matters had to be borne by individuals (Lukes, 1973, pp. 88-93).

The spread of Protestantism throughout Western societies from the sixteenth to the twentieth centuries also promoted the ideals of self-help and personal responsibility. However, Protestantism added a decisive moral twist to the notion of individual responsibility by linking the idea of worldly success to the very meaning of spirituality. In the sixteenth century, the Protestant Reformation came largely in response to rapid population growth in Europe, great increases in the volume and circulation of money due to imported colonial bullion, a long-term rise in grain prices, naval and military innovations, and a global broadening of trade. All of this benefited groups of merchants, city magistrates, and territorial princes in northern Europe, many of whom were able to take advantage of the expanding trade between "the Baltic and the Mediterranean through the Rhineland corridor, along the Atlantic coast, and through the Danish Sound" (Wuthnow, 1987, p. 238). By the middle of the sixteenth century, the core of the European economy began to shift northward, ironically benefiting both Protestant and Catholic political communities that occupied Europe's northern periphery.

In those communities most influenced by Protestantism, however, economic expansion received an ideological boost by Protestantism's unique acceptance of worldly activity as a pathway to salvation. According to Harvey Green (1989, p. 7), the Protestant tradition suggested that while God made decisions about the fate of a person or the human future more generally, there was nonetheless "a close relationship between visible deeds and signs of what the Divine had decided. So too the idea of personal culpability and reward was blended into the more humanistic and optimistic world view that characterized the gradual (and in many cases grudging) acceptance of Enlightenment ideology that ultimately overtook the free-will-predestination arguments of the older faith."

Liberty and responsibility, called by Green a "double edged sword" (p. 7) had combined throughout Western societies in a powerful new way by the early nineteenth century. The greatest problem for political philosophy in a modern liberal society composed of freely creative individuals was to determine the basis on which such a society would cohere. What would prevent it from degenerating into sheer egoism and endless struggle as everyone pursued their own conceptions of free creativity? Prominent liberal theorists like Adam Smith, John Locke, and John Stuart Mill had argued for solutions in the invisible hand of the market and the political structures of a centralized yet more democratized form of state system. Enlightenment philosophy, in particular, was optimistic about the power of human reason and rational calculation to create political structures that would reconcile the well-being of society as a whole with a recognition of broader rights to property and the freedom of individual action (Berlin, 1956; Macpherson, 1963).

This view gradually combined with alterations in religious theory in countries heavily influenced by Protestantism to form a millenarian ethos based on hope for the advent of Christ on earth. Earlier ideas of predestination were adapted to the modernist ideal of free creative practice by suggesting that the human spirit was perfectible only by means of individual and social action. One could do God's work on earth by striving for perfection at work, at home, and, indeed, through all of one's creative activities. But more important, this striving took on the character of moral duty. It was a necessary element in the process of realizing human salvation. Yet the duty to strive for perfection also carried with it the need to find a modicum of success or else face "the reality that life's reverses—economic, social political, even medical— were one's own fault" (Green, 1989, p. 7).

In the wake of these developments it is not surprising in largely Protestant countries that growing numbers of social thinkers became concerned about social pressures and breaches of responsibility that seemed to threaten social progress and eventual salvation. In so doing, many thinkers made the obvious connections between the health of the spirit and that of the body. For example, in the United States in the second quarter of the nineteenth century, fears were frequently expressed about alleged declines in bodily vigor, strength, diet, and health as an effect of the transition to an increasingly industrial and urban culture. Middle-class reformers influenced by the dual legacies of Calvinism and the Enlightenment faith in science began to express concern about a wide range of apparent ills such as increasingly rich diets, too much time spent indoors, the prospect of urban vice and disease, and the growth of sedentary occupations focused on clerical or intellectual tasks (Betts, 1975; Green, 1986; Park, 1989; Whorton, 1989).

These concerns took on special importance in the face of arguments that the health of the body could not only be linked to that of the spirit but to the overall health of the body politic as well. New adherents of dietary reform and physical exercise often understood health and fitness as a moral and patriotic responsibility and promoted their cause with evangelical fervor.

State Formation and the "Dangerous Classes"

The idea that health and fitness ought to be part of one's moral and patriotic duty dimly echoed earlier traditions of masculine adventurism and martial prowess in Western life. But by the early nineteenth century, the primary patriotic attachment in Britain, France, and the United States had shifted from local lord or Absolutist monarch to the modern, national society and its attachment to the territories of the *liberal state*. The liberal state differed from its Absolutist antecedents by virtue of a more expansive sharing of sovereign power within the state structure. The mercantile and commercial classes—and those sections of the landed classes increasingly treating their property as "fixed capital"— grew in strength and struggled successfully for a larger share of power within the emergent system of modern nation-states (Hall, 1984, p. 9). The wealth and growing influence of these classes was rooted to contractual legal principles, and this provided a "metaphor for a new conception of state: a contractual state where power was shared, the rights of the upper and middle ranks of society to participate in power along with the ruler was guaranteed by law and formalized in a constitutional system" (Hall, 1984, p. 9).

The idea of the contractual/liberal state developed unevenly in Europe and North America. It is also important to underscore the fact that the liberal state was initially *not* a democracy. The majority of men could not vote, women could neither vote nor dispose of property, freedom of speech and of assembly was limited, and political representation was limited in scope (Macpherson, 1965). Yet once the contractual form of state was in place, the *possibility* existed that excluded groups might win expanded terms for the social contract. And, indeed, struggles by the majority of ordinary men and women to extend the range of political and civil rights provided the basis of many of the reform movements of the nineteenth and early twentieth centuries. Such struggles grafted a higher degree of "democracy" onto the liberal state to create a new hybrid form of political-economic organization, the liberal-democratic state (Hall, 1984, p. 11; Macpherson, 1965).

The nature and scope of political, economic, and cultural change in Europe and North America from the late eighteenth century to the end of the nineteenth century created immense problems of control for the new blocs of class and political power that had coalesced around the emerging liberal state and the industrial capitalist economies of Western nations. Increasing population growth in the eighteenth century, the gradual breakup of Absolutist authority, the spread of individualist philosophies, and the expansion and mobility of classes of "free" wage laborers severely challenged traditional communal controls. Viewed from the perspective of dominant groups, this created significant problems of labor force discipline and law and order. Concern increased that idleness and fatigue posed threats to the newly required industrial labor force. Concern was also expressed about the emergence of new "dangerous classes" that existed beyond any form of community control or surveillance: the rabble, the mob, and the great unwashed (Bauman, 1983).

These threatening groups appeared to have no loyalty to any readily identifiable organic, social community. Moreover, they often resisted abandoning their traditional ways of living and working in order to accommodate the emerging structures of wage work and factory production. Growing industrialization in Western capitalist economies meant subjecting workers to new forms of organization in the factory and the office, the technical requirements of machinery, and the competitive pressures of a system of production designed to extract maximum productivity from human labor power. In order for the increasing numbers of factories and workshops to be productive and profitable, traditional work habits based on the natural rhythms of the days and seasons had to be replaced with something new. Work was becoming routine, repetitive, and inflexible in its use of time and space. In workshops and mills, people had to work at specified times, work specified hours, and stay in specified places in order to accomplish their designated tasks. All of this required powerful new forms of labor discipline and surveillance in order for owners to get a maximum return on their investment in labor. The problem was that many new urban workers were stubbornly resisting the emerging forms of industrial work discipline and surveillance.

Large numbers of the new, "dangerous" classes also appeared to engage in ways of living that, from the perspective of dominant conceptions of public morality, often seemed immoral and showed little deference to centralized authority. The popular traditions of carnival, bodily indulgence, and often rough recreation inherited from medieval Europe became extremely worrisome in their new social context. Above all, they appeared to have the capacity to mobilize into a protopolitical force capable of great violence and destruction. To cite just one example, the perceived role of the mob in supporting the destruction of Absolutism in France by Jacobin reformers during the French Revolution, and the subsequent horrors of the guillotine, were terrifying to political leaders across Europe. These concerns were particularly acute in England and strengthened the beliefs that idleness was something to be feared and that unruly recreation and "moral levity" led potentially to political sedition (Thompson, 1968, p. 442).

Regulating the Social Body

There is an important point to be made here about violence and its newly threatening character to the liberal state and the bloc of masculine, racial, and class interests which it supported. Social analysts have noted the comparatively high levels of casual violence that existed throughout medieval Europe (Elias, 1978). Physical violence to children, women, and "outsiders," and violence in popular recreations, had a notable presence in many areas of medieval life. In the long tradition of communal control there had been a wide variety of censures that could be put in place at the local level for people who expressed "different" ideas or somehow breached community expectations. Most of all, in a world of highly localized communities, many of which were engaged in ongoing struggles over territory, the fear of being ejected from the protection of one's community and potentially subjected to violence from outsiders was a powerful incentive to maintain popular allegiance to the group. And, if this was insufficient, violent censures within the community would readily follow. The patriarchal, familial model upon which many of these groups were initially secured lent itself to a xenophobic understanding of people outside the community as "the other," a condition which effectively dehumanized them and opened up the possibility of normalizing extremely violent acts.

In addition, the normalization of violence in medieval life was sustained symbolically by a metaphorical attachment between the understanding of individual bodies and collective bodies. Priests, monarchs, and local leaders promoted an organic conception of the world—complete with complex hierarchies, interdependencies and distinctions between rulers and ruled—as part of the natural order of things. In this context, social disruptions could be interpreted as a symbolic violation, a kind of mutilation, of the body of the monarch himself and, indirectly perhaps, even of Christ. For that reason, as Foucault (1977, 1981) has noted, public mutilation and bodily humiliation by inquisitors or royal torturers seemed necessary in response. However, with the advent of the Enlightenment, the gradual spread of the liberal values of universal liberty and equality, and the formation of the liberal state, the idea of the *social* body began to emerge as the dominant sign of social solidarity in

Western life. Intellectuals and cultural leaders began to argue that it was the body of society that now needed to be protected. This protection was increasingly understood, Foucault argues (1981, p. 55), "in a quasi-medical sense. In the place of rituals that served to restore the corporal integrity of the monarch, remedies and therapeutic devices are employed such as the segregation of the sick, the monitoring of contagion, the exclusions of delinquents."

So, for Foucault, by the nineteenth century the consequences of modernity can be measured largely by a widespread shift in the understanding both of relations between the individual body and the body politic and of strategies and tactics of the administration of individual bodies. The body of the sovereign as a sign of social authority was replaced with an emergent belief in the need to defend the integrity of the social body—now seen to be comprised by the idea of "society" in the abstract—and the preferred method of social administration shifted from violent punishment to discipline on its own terms. The age of inquisitors, torturers, and dungeons passed over into an era of new regulatory organizations that operated first and foremost through the deployment of disciplinary power: the prison, the poor house, the asylum, the factory, the hospital, and the school. In these organizations the "health" of the social body could be defended metaphorically against infection from such seemingly virulent social disorders as crime, poverty, madness, laziness, disease, and ignorance. In keeping with this transformation, the idea that there are important moral and political connections between individual health, necessary bodily (self-) discipline, and the health of "society" was additionally reinforced.

Foucault wants to view this transformation as a broad paradigm shift in "technologies" of power associated with the advent of modernity. However, I find it more useful to consider the emergence of state agencies such as the asylum, the poor house, the prison, and the school as an attempt by newly dominant groups to apply in more developed form some of the traditions of discipline and surveillance that had long been associated with local communal controls in Europe. The apparent inadequacy of traditional controls in emerging, industrial, capitalist societies created a sense of urgency about the necessary reintegration of social life. Leaders in the new liberal states in Europe and North America increasingly felt it necessary to articulate a new form of collectivism, to build a new sense of national community, and to promote a competitive national economy, now composed of "free" individuals unencumbered by the kinds of traditional allegiances and obligations that had bound lord to serf and ruler to vassal. They sought to do this with the redeployment of discipline in state institutions geared toward the kind of socialization perceived to be necessary to create a newly harmonious social body integrated around the emerging demands of industrial production and international economic competition between modern nation states. In addition to this, people within the power blocs that controlled the liberal state in various countries also sought to consolidate a monopoly on violence (see Elias, 1978). The orderly workings of the market and the state could not be guaranteed if faced with threats of violent political protest or Luddism. For that reason, forms of violence that threatened the market or the state had to be excised from daily life. The legitimate use of violence, in theory at least, was to be limited only to state agencies, such as the military and the police.

ACTIVE BODIES, CIVILIZED BODIES, AND THE BODY POLITIC

Civilizing and Engineering the Body

I do not want to imply that the developments previously described were necessarily undertaken as an automatic, systemic response to the erosion of traditional community authority, or as a clear and conscious conspiracy of control. There is little doubt that people within the complex blocs of power that dominated various liberal states in Europe and North America in the nineteenth century had a sense of their own (sometimes internally conflicting) interests, but it is unlikely that they were able to knowingly transform this sense of self-interest into a set of consistent strategies of regulation. On the contrary, the emergence of organizations involved in constructing the new collectivism was not due to any single set of elite or ruling-class initiatives. Rather, these organizations and initiatives emerged out of a diverse array of struggles involving relations between dominant and popular forces. For example, people living in the new urban squalor of industrial cities *wanted* better diets, protection from disease and random violence, relief from poverty, literacy, and job training. In pushing for these things they often secured reluctant concessions from dominant groups unwilling to make substantial public investments in the maintenance of "society."

Still, dominant groups were also not prepared simply to stand by and entertain popular protests or reform initiatives without putting their own cultural and political stamp on them. More notably, they became increasingly interested in the cultures and everyday lives of the broad masses of people living within the boundaries of modern national societies. The dominant classes in medieval Europe had *ruled* but, with the exception of the activities of the Church, they tended not to teach or proselytize (Bauman, 1983, p. 36). But by the early part of the nineteenth century in certain parts of Europe and North America, the new dominant classes were beginning to step into the role of collective teacher. As Bauman (p. 36) suggests, the subordinate classes—"the people"—were increasingly cast in the roles of pupils, and certain members of the dominant classes felt the need to teach, through voluntary and state agencies, a way of life they considered properly human or "civilized." The medieval imagery of the "continuous chain of being," in which for everybody there is an interconnected, but nevertheless separate and different type, was gradually replaced by the image of a single "truly human, or civilized, or rational pattern of life" (p. 36).

This emergent vision of ideal human life linked a belief in the values of human reason with the liberal conception of progress and the artistic and cultural achievements of an emergent bourgeois civilization. Throughout much of Europe and North America, the task of civilization became viewed as the necessary expansion of rationality over the body and the emotions, coupled with cultivating a discerning taste for the high-culture products of bourgeois reason. It is important to note that there was always considerable debate about the extent to which certain groups could ever aspire to "civilization"—for instance, aboriginals, blacks, women, and the male working classes—and the implications of such perceived differences on the disciplining of the body and the mind. But, with this caveat in mind, it is clear that reform movements in areas like health and education throughout much of western Europe and North America in the nineteenth century were largely swept up in an evangelical zeal to promote the rational, civilized life. As Bauman points out, the (primarily bourgeois and masculine) vision of the civilized life existed in contrast to "less perfect" forms of life, which it was now called on to banish or amend: "the ignorant, the superstitious, the emotion-ridden, the beastly" (p. 36). The vision also carried with it an emerging, idealized sense of what the rationalized human body ought to look like and how it ought to function. Being human, both in mental and physical terms, was no longer seen as a "natural condition enjoyed by all though in many alternative forms"; it now became "a skill to be learned"—a skill which everyone had the duty to undertake but few were able to accomplish unassisted (p. 36).

Assistance was provided by a growing collection of professionals, experts, and entrepreneurs targeting various areas of emotional, intellectual, and physical development. Much was made by professional educators about the importance of recovering classical Greek ideals of balance and harmony, including the idea that body and mind are closely connected. This theme had been evident in much of the thought of the Enlightenment, arguably receiving its most popular expression in John

Locke's widely-cited reference in "Some Thoughts Concerning Education" to the importance of a "sound mind in a sound body." Thus, in early nineteenth century North America, for example, health reformers and early specialists in physical education stressed how knowledge of one's body was crucial to the well-educated and healthy individual. Physical education, in this context, emerged as part of a broad hygienist movement embracing "everything that by bearing in any way on the human body, might injure or benefit in its health, vigor and fitness of action" (Berryman, cited in Vertinsky, 1990, p. 73).

However, simple knowledge of the body was not enough. By the second decade of the nineteenth century it is possible to see the forward edge of an increasingly popular belief that the performance and the look of the natural body can and ought to be improved through "scientific" interventions in diet and programs of exercise. Exhaustion and fatigue had increasingly come to be recognized in Western cultures as the constant nemeses of modern progress (Rabinbach, 1990, pp. 6-10). The key was to fight against these nemeses through new strategies that deployed, conserved, and expanded the energies of the human body. In this context the body came to be seen as something that could be increasingly *engineered* along the lines of an industrial machine. Bodily engineering became yet another set of "skills to be learned."

In the highly commercial world of American popular culture, entrepreneurs sought to sell these skills through a growing number of health and exercise programs and products. The engineering of bodily improvement was also taught in more formal educational settings. And, indeed, in the modern school, developing the body beyond its natural state through formal exercise increasingly became a disciplinary obligation. Physical training for young citizens was important for very pragmatic reasons. North American educators believed there was a lesson to be learned from Calvinism's gradual embrace of educational gymnastics as a form of discipline that might stave off the urges for revelry, gluttony, sexual license, intemperance, and gaming. Not surprisingly, gymnastic exercise was also understood to be important by educational, civilian, and military leaders in the modern state for its role in developing a fit population for the defense of national interests. Military drills in voluntary associations and schools also promised to promote the idea of patriotism and blur the interests of the military with those of the "nation" as a whole.

The Political Organization of Exercise

The history of organized exercise in the military and the schools and broad movements for hygienist reform in different Western societies is far too complex to discuss in detail here. I shall only remark on a few of the most notable themes and issues relevant to my earlier discussion of the political and cultural history of active living. Developed systems of gymnastics could be found in northern European countries like Prussia, Denmark, and Sweden well prior to the expansion of organized gymnastics in France, Britain, Canada, or the United States. Moreover, the social meanings and uses of gymnastics, and the degree to which they became dominated by the state, also differed in various Western countries at varying points throughout the nineteenth century. For example, Harvey and Sparks (1991, p. 178) note how the early formation of gymnastics associations in France were seen to be politically suspect during the Bourbon Restoration (1814-1830) because they constituted potential sites for the diffusion of republican ideology. Similarly, it was understood that gymnastics developed the physical powers of individuals, powers that might someday be turned against the state. In addition, there was a tradition in the popular culture of the underclass of associating the individual virtuosity and strength associated with acrobatics with the morally and politically alarming traditions of carnival, drinking, and masculine bravado.

For these reasons, the French state sought to preserve its monopoly over the legitimate use of force by strictly controlling the development of gymnastics associations and school programs. After the Franco-Prussian war in the late nineteenth century, gymnastics became part of national mobilization in France and the defense of republican ideals. Military influences over gymnastics increased significantly, exercise was made compulsory in schools, and gymnastic festivals and fairs, complete with flags and other national symbols, were organized for the diffusion of nationalistic sentiment and political myth-making. Outside the military, gymnastics also became used for rather different purposes by the "catholicized vision of the Christian Order." Religious involvement in gymnastics was designed to help defend the Church by protecting participants from militant republicanism and other secular influences (Harvey & Sparks, 1991, pp. 182-183).

In Germany, the associations between exercise, the military, and national political imagery were also strongly developed throughout the nineteenth century. Most notably, Friedrich Ludwig Jahn had founded a gymnastics movement which would prepare the bodies of German youth to wage war against Napoleon early in the century. Jahn was also a seminal figure in the "Volkish" tradition, which sought to define a spiritual nationalism founded on the racial doctrine of a transcendental German essence (Hoberman, 1984, p. 100). German social thought had long been gripped by a deep interest both in understanding the unfolding of human consciousness in history and in searching for the underlying essences of societies and cultures. However, throughout the nineteenth century, increasing numbers of German intellectuals became influenced by the idea that Germany either possessed, or ought to possess, a national/social essence that could be understood in physiological terms.

While Jahn provided much of the early inspiration for this view, additional validation was evident in Friedrich Nietzsche's celebration of sheer instinctive physicality. Nietzsche saw the male body as the quintessential seat of human vitality, the primary source of an animal energy that expresses human will through a dominating instinct (Hoberman, 1984, p. 90). He suggested that this energy is on display historically in the powerful physicality demonstrated through the actions and judgments of "knightly-aristocratic" peoples. Moreover, he argued, it is precisely this physicality that "links the noble races" to the "beast of prey, the splendid blond beast prowling about avidly in search of spoil and victory" (cited in Hoberman, p. 90). In contrast to priestly asceticism or the organization of social life and "civilization" around contractual-legal principles, Nietzsche saw the ideal expression of the individual and general will in adventure, war, hunting, dancing, and games—all masculinizing practices that celebrated "vigorous, free, joyful activity" (Hoberman, p. 90).

Throughout the nineteenth and early twentieth centuries, Marxism provided the most dramatic counterpoint to the emerging racial nationalism that ultimately swept across Germany. Marx had been interested in physiology, but he paid little attention to the importance of the body in Western history and its possible metaphorical connections to the social or political body of capitalist societies. More notably, Marx rejected "idealist" philosophies that identified the essences of societies with an abstract spirit or national will. In their place, Marx emphasized the *socially* determinate character of human life. Organic and mystical conceptions of Western nations and societies, he argued, had to be superseded by analyses that stressed the class-divided character of capitalist societies as distinctive social formations. For Marx and his later followers, the struggle for human freedom and autonomy was subverted by misleading abstractions like "the general will," "the nation," or "the people." These abstractions merely confused the interests and the will of ruling classes and their state agents with the general interest. However, despite Marx's influence in nineteenth century Germany, there was an upsurge of nationalism following Germany's unification and Prussia's wars with France. This upsurge of nationalism became an effective vehicle for linking conservative ideas about German sovereignty with the idea of advancing popular interests. The German people, the argument ran, needed to celebrate their emerging sovereignty and express their will as a modern nation. This required new politics designed to draw people into active participation in the national mystique through rites, festivals, myths, and symbols designed to give the popular will a concrete expression (Mosse, 1975, p. 2).

Through these ideas, modernist conceptions of free citizenship and popular sovereignty in Germany were not only pushed away from Marxism but also from the Enlightenment-inspired ideal of the contractual state. Similarly, much of the potentially oppositional character of traditional popular festivals and recreations was yoked to a mystical romanticism. Attendant to this, the ideal of active living in late nineteenth century Germany increasingly became oriented toward the "primitive" appeal of bodily vigor. Early in the nineteenth century, Friedrich Jahn saw himself as a pedagogue in possession of a "healing doctrine" required by the body politic (Hoberman, 1984, p. 101). Later German apologists for the Volkish tradition viewed that "healing doctrine" as the necessary recovery of the mythical vital energies and physical prowess of earlier Germanic peoples. The memorable content of history, Jahn had claimed, required "the spectacle of masculine power." By the late nineteenth century, that image of masculine power was understood to involve a commitment to the active pursuit of sensation and the exercise of will, defined primarily through sheer physicality and the perfectibility of the body. Visions of perceived bodily "perfectibility" were supplied through the athleticized imagery available through Greek art. Necessary political imagery was supplied through grand festivals of exercise rich in the symbolism of flames, flags, and monumentalist architecture (Mosse, 1975).

Thus, in Germany, organized gymnastics in the schools, in the military, and in voluntary associations—in addition to the growing German interest in competitive sport—were ultimately drawn into a powerful, antimodern, anti-urban bias that provided a foundation for the later Fascist cult of the body. German primitivism and the celebration of bodily vigor were responses to the supposedly inauthentic rationalism, empiricism, and utility that defined modern "civilization" elsewhere in Europe, especially as demonstrated in Anglo-French culture (Eksteins, 1989, pp. 76-77). It was argued that German vigor and primitivism had the capability of stripping off the artificial veneer of modern civilization. Only in Germany, the argument continued, had the technical, the national, and the artistic fused into a single national spirit reflective of a healthy and strong body politic. Europe could be cleansed of its overly mannered, decadent civilization, its modernist agitation, and hypocrisy by German physical and moral superiority. As John Hoberman wryly notes (p. 101), all of this provided the developing rationale for a "spectacle of masculine power" in the twentieth century, the likes of which Jahn and his early followers could scarcely have dreamed.

In Britain and North America, the state became involved in the organization of gymnastic exercise through the nineteenth century far less directly, even though gymnastic exercises quickly found a place in the military and in state-supported schools. American state involvement in the organization of exercise was mediated by a history of strong voluntary associations and a heavy reliance on the market as a provider of satisfactions and social goods. In addition, both Britain and North America had strong, popular traditions of competitive sports and games, which effectively rivaled the influences of formal gymnastic exercises. This tradition provided a parallel, sometimes alternative, vehicle for pursuing individual health, manliness, bodily strength, and vigor. For example, by the late nineteenth century, physicians and physical educators in North America frequently extolled the virtues of "scientific" gymnastic and calisthenics programs designed in accordance with the structures and functions of the body. But other specialists in exercise maintained that games and sports offered the added dimension of being social in nature and called for such qualities as courage, cooperation, and self-reliance (Park, 1989, p. 124).

There was far more indigenous popular interest in games and sports in Britain and North America in any case, and the majority of non-professional commentators became convinced that sport offered the superior form of exercise. Dominant groups, especially, were attracted to the apparent values of sport as a vehicle for moral training. The development of movements for "muscular Christianity" and amateur sports soon integrated popular sporting traditions into the prevailing climate of moral entrepreneurship. It is now widely understood that amateur sports were first constituted in Britain and North America as an attempt by dominant groups to contour popular sporting traditions to prevailing systems of class, racial, and gender privilege. In this formulation, amateurism was dominated by a logic of exclusion—it operated to prevent certain groups from entering the field of "gentlemanly" sporting competition. However, it was not long before amateurism became more widely understood as a way of teaching large sections of national populations the apparent values of Anglo-bourgeois civilization through the bodily disciplines of team games. Many commentators, educators, and sporting enthusiasts in Britain, Canada, and the United States were also drawn to the idea of civilizing amateur sport as a vehicle for refrigerating "animal passions," both men's and women's, in favor of the virtues of reason, fairness, temperance, and modesty. Moreover, for many male opinion leaders, the "civilized" form of organized sport, and especially those sporting contests which featured physical contact, were understood as especially dramatic and powerful vehicles for the promotion of manly prowess and strength.

Just as in Europe, many proponents of sport and exercise in North America were influenced by the racial nationalism of the nineteenth century, which invidiously compared the "health" of the social bodies of particular groups and nations (Park, 1989). Natural or cultural differences in strength and vigor were regularly attributed to men and women, to different races, social classes, ethnic groups, and nations. After mid-century, the idea of racial nationalism was given a new urgency by the popularization of Darwinian thought. In the evolutionary struggle between groups within nations, and between the social and political bodies of modern nations, a "healthy" social body and a fit body politic were increasingly viewed as social necessities. In the United States, for example, there was growing concern throughout the nineteenth century that the restless energy and modern inventiveness that had seemingly brought about American wealth was, ironically, threatened by growing prosperity because fewer people worked with their hands (Green, 1986; Mrozek, 1989; Park, 1989). Similarly, waves of immigration threatened to import "alien" and subversive ideas, which dominant groups feared might undermine American values and traditions. A renewed commitment to a robust physicality that would draw on Anglo-Saxon and Teutonic virtues in order to invigorate the health of the American social body seemed necessary.

I want to summarize this brief overview of movements for exercise, hygiene, physical activity, and sport in different Western societies by highlighting a single point: Despite all the differences between France, Britain, Germany, Canada, and the United States, the dominant classes in these societies during the nineteenth and early twentieth centuries demonstrated increasing concern over the production of "ideal citizens"—or at least docile ones—and corresponding degrees of bodily discipline and health. There was a widespread modernist acceptance of the value of restless and vigorous activity—physical, intellectual, economic, political, creative—that could be directed toward human and societal growth and improvement. However, in order to consolidate their hegemony, dominant groups had to struggle to channel that restless sense of vigorous activity into preferred social and cultural practices that were consonant with imperial ambition and did not threaten the emerging economic and political structures of industrial production, wage labor, and the state. Most importantly, the ideal of active living as a form of self-conscious political practice—as the necessary transformation of self through the transformation of the world—had to be defined in ways that precluded any symbolic connections to a revolutionary politics that challenged the structures of nineteenth century capitalism. In the ensuing struggle over common sense, the potentially radical dimensions of the modernist ideal of active living were continually challenged by the introduction of new forms of bodily discipline in the workplace and in state institutions and by the reworking of old secular traditions which defined the active life in largely physical terms. Dominant conceptions of active living in Western societies became increasingly centered upon the physical activities of military adventurism, organized physical exercise, and male sporting prowess.

LEISURE, CONSUMER CULTURE, AND THE POLITICS OF THE ACTIVE LIFE

Moral Regulation and the Commodification of Leisure

Many owners and managers of industrial enterprises in the nineteenth and early twentieth centuries believed strongly that the need to impose rational work discipline required an equally rational leisure discipline. Traditional patterns of release, riot, and indulgence had to be subordinated to the timed needs of the industrial labor process, and this required the tutelage of "the masses" in the healthy and "civilized" uses of leisure time. The drinking, merrymaking, and sometimes disorderly recreations still popular among the urban underclass were widely seen as activities that disrupted the daily routine of business and encouraged absenteeism and low productivity, debt, and insubordination. As a result, play in the streets was made illegal in the business centers of most Western societies, tavern locations and hours became heavily regulated, alcohol consumption at public events was controlled, traditional sporting activities likely to encourage violence or drunkenness were banned, and more "rational" forms of recreation and amusement were promoted in their stead.

Despite these regulatory pressures, a great many of the older popular recreational traditions adapted to new conditions and flourished across Europe and North America, especially in the growing industrial cities and towns (Cunningham, 1980). While the dominant classes of most Western societies struggled to introduce increased levels of discipline and rationality to the lives of everyday citizens, traditional popular cultures centered on drink, song, and spectacle continued to attract a widespread following. In countries whose economies and cultures were becoming increasingly influenced by market-led priorities, the market, ironically, provided additional challenges to industrialists' desires for a docile workforce, as well as dominant class tutelage in the acquisition of "civilized" tastes and attitudes. Modern popular cultures increasingly became centered around the consumption of commercial recreations that seemed to offer relief from the emerging disciplinary orientations of the military, state and private schools, and middle-class organizations and clubs devoted to self-improvement.

Market pressures on popular recreations were arguably most influential during the nineteenth century in the Unites States and Canada. After the 1860s, a great many traditional home- and community-centered forms of popular entertainment were becoming more widely available as consumer items. A growing urban population of wage earners created new markets for products and services that had hitherto been provided in nonmarket form through more traditional family and community relations. In addition, the increasingly clear delineation of work and leisure created a situation in which large groups of people were available for consumption at regular and predictable times. The emergence of wage labor and mass production in North America thus created the conditions for mass audiences, and these audiences in turn began to develop an exchange value of their own. Audience attention not only began to take on a monetary value for entrepreneurs selling various forms of commercial entertainment; it also began to be marketed to advertisers through the newspapers, specialist magazines, and trade publications, which proliferated throughout the latter years of the century. The 1890s, in particular, witnessed the beginnings of a new age of consumer advertising in North America. A new style of advertising tended to emphasize product performance over product character, thereby stimulating the desire to consume rather than merely informing the public about what wares were available and how much they cost (Leiss, Kline, & Jhally, 1990). This self-conscious promotion of consumption flew in the face of established middle-class and Protestant values of thrift and self-restraint.

The important point is that, throughout the nineteenth century in North America, more and more areas of human experience were becoming transformed into relationships governed by economic exchange. As a result, the moral regulation of leisure and its correlative disciplining of the body in state and private organizations became profoundly contradictory. The first problem for moral entrepreneurs— people committed to the selling of rational recreation and rational bodily discipline—was that the very idea of rational or "civilized" leisure was an apparent paradox. The popular concept of leisure was something done, almost by definition, after and indeed in contrast to work, duty, and routine. Most people understood leisure as the setting for deeply personal experiences of sociability and pleasure and as a sphere of their lives where they could indulge their free creativity, personal whims, and choices. The challenge for the dominant classes and their middle-class allies was how to encourage habits of discipline and self-improvement in leisure while acknowledging popular rights to the "free" use of leisure time.

This challenge turned on a key tension that lay at the core of relations between work, leisure, and culture in late nineteenth century North America. Religious, cultural, business, and political leaders were committed to the control of leisure and the body on the one hand and yet, on the other, to a grudging acceptance of the ideological importance of free time as a reward for work and membership in a liberal-democratic society. The attempted resolution of this tension was manifest in the dual process of banning or regulating activities deemed to be irrational, immoral, undisciplined, or uncivilized while promoting more suitable, more disciplined, and more rational forms of living. People were supposed to learn that the pursuit of pleasure ought to be balanced against the higher earnestness of the Protestant work ethic and the ideals of patriotic duty. The hope was that, if given proper exposure through schools, religious and military organizations, parks, libraries, theaters, gymnasia, and sporting clubs, people would learn to choose a "self-improving" form of active living over idleness, hedonism, or bodily indulgence. Yet, the moment the ideal of truly free time was accepted, it became possible for people to legitimately elect to use that time in wasteful or irrational ways no matter how strenuous the effort to prevent it. That being the case, all that dominant groups could hope for was to regulate wasteful or indulgent activities to the best degree possible and restrict their existence to specified areas, classes, races, or ethnic groups.

By the last two decades of the nineteenth century, the pace of commodification in North America and of conflicting views about the nature of popular rights provided additional complications to these tensions. If the majority of business owners and managers sought to extend the working day and defined workers' needs only as simple physical survival, there were nonetheless some who believed that happy workers were more efficient and who were prepared therefore to offer tacit support for workers' attempts to carve out more free time from the workweek. With this came the growing realization that workers were consumers, too, that they provided a valuable market for new entertainment commodities. These commodities were sold with very little reference to the concerns of moral entrepreneurs. For every moral entrepreneur selling rational recreation and biological or spiritual self-improvement in late nineteenth century North America, an economic entrepreneur emerged ready to market anything that was potentially profitable—drink, sex, or spectacle—whatever its alleged effects on morality and individual or public health. The competitive drive for profit that lay at the core of the burgeoning American and Canadian economies was becoming *dependent* upon the stimulation of collective needs and capacities to consume. Ironically, many businesses began to have a vested interest in cultivating excess and indulgence and feeding imaginary appetites to the point where the very idea of individual needs and pleasures became fueled by consumptive fantasies (Harvey, 1989, p. 102).

Attendant to this, more and more leisure choices, opportunities, and forms of personal satisfaction, bodily expression, and identity also began to depend upon the market. Market transactions had begun to act as a concentrated field of personal satisfaction as far back as the sixteenth century (Mukerji, 1983). However, by the early twentieth century, the goods and consumption styles made available by mass production began to exercise a powerful new kind of authority. In response to the weakening of the distinctive and relatively stable forms of satisfaction and identity created by traditional cultures, the dominant classes and their state agents had sought to substitute new models of authority centered around bodily discipline and moral regulation. But the marketplace also developed as a parallel agency for constructing models of collectivism in capitalist modernity—an agency which sometimes usurped the authority of moral entrepreneurs by assuming "the tasks of instructing individuals how to match their needs and wants with the available stock of consumption styles" (Leiss, Kline, and Jhally, 1990, p. 65).

Self-Expression Through Consumer Activity

By the 1920s, leisure and popular entertainment in North America were already highly commodified. At the turn of the century, North American business and political leaders successfully embarked on a wide-scale campaign to expand the realms of consumption in North American life (Ewan, 1976). One manifestation of this campaign was that Americans and Canadians were regularly being exhorted by advertisers to spend more and more of their paychecks on newly mass-produced automobiles, clothing fashions, household goods, and recreational equipment, in addition to regularly scheduled commercial entertainment. For most worker-consumers, making money to spend during one's leisure time became a makeshift power substituted for the limited power that workers exercised in the sphere of production (Bauman, 1983, p. 38). The act of consuming seemed to equalize people through the apparent (but highly limited) "democracy" of the market. Yet, the extent to which this emerging culture of consumerism drew its lifeblood from an intense preoccupation with the human body—what to eat; how to dress; how to look good; how to find the most pleasure and the most excitement; how to be healthy, fit, energetic, and strong—is remarkable (cf. Bauman, 1983; Featherstone, 1991).

Early twentieth century consumerism in the United States brought this preoccupation with the body into a unique relationship with the modernist ideals of free creativity and self-development. By the end of the nineteenth century, the power of the post–Civil War American dominant classes had begun to wane. The climate of moral utility, self-discipline, and gentility that had surrounded much of the nineteenth century concern for health, exercise, and sport was challenged by the increasing visibility and power of ultrarich industrialists and financiers. Drawing on the new authority of the market, the ultrarich began to displace the genteel as the exemplars of moral influence and discipline. Donald Mrozek (1989, p. 19) has noted how this increasingly powerful group within the American dominant class made material success "the test of a new version of character—tested by the accumulation of possessions and the prompt service of one's desires." In point of fact, however, this test of character was hardly new at all. It simply recycled deep-rooted traditions in Western culture which linked indulgence to wealth and power. The emergent dominant culture of American industrial wealth celebrated what Thorstein Veblen (1899/1953) called "conspicuous consumption" as a mark of success and self-worth, but it did this, Veblen argued, in ways that echoed an earlier predatory temperament in Western history.

Thus, in the early years of twentieth century American capitalism one can perceive an emerging cult of self-gratification and personal pleasure that drew on two distant traditional sources and integrated them around the new structures and practices of consumer capitalism. The echoes of older popular traditions of carnival and rough recreations from preindustrial times were brought into a new harmony with the residues of the timeless tradition that connected indulgence to class privilege. However, at the same time, the powerful nineteenth century discourses of health, bodily and moral discipline, and self-improvement were far from extinguished. They stayed alive in schools and governments, the medical and social service professions, physical education, and amateur athletics. They also drew on a large market of people captured by the pleasures and the disciplinary mastery offered by sports and organized exercise.

Still, even this market was increasingly drawn to search for self-discipline and self-discovery through the pursuit of what Jackson Lears (1981) has called "intense experience." Whereas the modernist emphasis on activity and the accompanying quest for sensation ultimately led Germany to a fascist body culture by the early twentieth century, in the United States these features of cultural modernism became inextricably connected to the pleasures of individual consumption. For the "high cultured" intellectual who continued to enjoy the privilege of the active life of the mind, the discipline entailed in seeking such intense experience sanctioned the pleasures found in the process of exploring oneself by developing one's intellect (Mrozek, 1989, p. 20). But for the vast majority of American consumers, the lure of "intense experience" promised a future defined through new possibilities for self-expression, personal taste, and "the implicit sense that the pursuit of happiness was the essence of liberty and the purpose of life" (Mrozek, p. 20). By the 1920s, the pursuit of enjoyment and the quest for satisfaction through fun were emerging as legitimate goals to which one might commit the body and the mind.

Donald Mrozek (p. 20) even goes so far as to argue that by the early 1930s fun itself came to be understood as having a measure of social utility, even to the point of carrying a sense of social duty. In this context, the dominant nineteenth century focus on individual and national health and well-being as the purpose of an individual's pursuit of fitness and athletic accomplishment were gradually surpassed in American popular culture by a new turn toward health, fitness, and sportive engagement as their own reward. In previous decades, Mrozek continues, virtue was the reward of athletic bodily discipline, but by the 1920s and 1930s "the athletic quest and the cultivation of the body were themselves increasingly taken as virtuous" (p. 20). In other words, exercise and sports could be understood as offering extremely exciting, challenging, and intense experiences on their own terms.

The popular obsession with sport as the quintessential form of the active life in early twentieth century America was aptly reflected in the emerging iconography of twentieth century advertising. The celebration of youthful male exuberance, health, and athleticism became increasingly evident in advertising codes that equated bodily imagery, and the expenditure of energy through sport, with happiness and success in a modern, market-driven society. The popularization of this imagery correlated with a growing revulsion in American popular culture toward body odor, stained teeth, bad breath, and other alleged manifestations of undisciplined living and ill health. Jackson Lears (1989) makes the case that such views were typically created by affluent male advertising executives and were a harbinger of the impact that a new generation of upward-striving middle-class males would have over the culture of consumption that would continue to expand throughout the twentieth century.

Early twentieth century advertising was just beginning to exploit desires to "fit in" that had become palpable in a more mobile, more individualistic, and rapidly changing industrial society. For both men and women, bodily propriety emerged as one of the key dimensions of appropriate conformity—something that had to be weighed continually against the pursuit of fun in exclusively hedonistic terms. In this way, long-standing middle-class concerns about the importance of health, bodily discipline, and self-improvement became connected to a deepening anxiety about the body in its natural state, thereby creating markets for a legion of health, beauty, fitness, and self-improvement products (Lears, 1989). Early twentieth century marketing in the United States promised popularity and success, but only if one mediated the natural body with the right consumer choices. Young men, in particular, were instructed that commodities pertaining to sport, exercise, bodily vigor, strength, and muscularity were extremely appropriate ways to exercise the power of their paychecks.

CONCLUSION

I have argued that the culture of capitalist consumption in North America has always been shot through with contradictions. Throughout the twentieth century, it has readily supported an understanding of active living that connects the ideal of activity to self-gratification and pleasure-seeking in ways that have potentially threatened, and continue to threaten, moral entrepreneurship and labor discipline. Whatever one thinks of that tradition, it is kept alive today in consumer entertainment ranging from beer to whiskey and from Madonna to Snoop Doggy Dogg. But this potentially disruptive consumerism, which appears to have no obligations to anything but the purchase of intense experience, only exists in societies governed by economic systems characterized by wage labor and continually evolving forms of capitalist work discipline. The full-scale pursuit of indulgence by everyday consumers is limited both by the size of their wages and the necessity of turning up for work the next day. Similarly, in order to consume more one has to work harder and focus one's energies more tightly on the necessity of earning a living.

It is not my intention to romanticize popular traditions of hedonism, excessive indulgence, or rough recreation. On the contrary, in contemporary Western societies such things often strike me as manifestations of the lack of control people often feel in other parts of their lives. These things have always provided a very clear counterpoint and frequent source of opposition to the attempts of dominant groups to regulate the use of free time and discipline the body. Even some of the most comparatively innocent features of commercial popular culture have been depicted as problems for business, cultural, and political leaders throughout this century. During the 1920s in North America and, significantly, again in the 1950s and 1960s, serious concern was expressed about the apparent threat to industrial productivity and civilization made by commercial consumer cultures, which understood active living to be the pursuit of fun. Such cultures were typically said to develop at the apparent expense of health, work effort, and a commitment to self-improvement.

Even within the realm of commercial popular culture there have been powerful mediating factors to limit popular concepts of the active life as the pursuit of socially acceptable, intense experience. The centrality of the body in consumer culture, and the role that advertising has played in constructing idealized images of the body from the 1920s to the present day, have led to an ongoing pursuit of bodily images and ideals through consumption in ways that offer little threat to established relations of power. Most recently, the lifestyle advertising that first emerged during the 1960s and still dominates in the present day has helped to constitute yet another new vision of the active life. It is a vision organized around an obsession with youth, sexuality, sports, outdoor activities, and consumerism—a view that has played an important role in the restructuring of social and economic relations in countries competing in a media-dominated global capitalism (Harvey, 1989). In the 1990s, one vision of the active life is that of the affluent, global consumer continually searching out intense experience through the consumption of goods and activities distributed by a progressively narrower range of international retail outlets, celebrities, destinations, and events such as Benneton, Disneyland, Michael Jordan, and The Blue Jays (see Gruneau and Whitson, 1993).

Because other contributors to this collection have concentrated on the contemporary scene, my discussion has focused on the historical antecedents of current conceptions of active living. However, at the risk of excessive simplification, I want to make a few brief observations about current state initiatives in Western societies that now seem to be promoting active living as a dimension of personal empowerment rather than as disciplinary obligation to work effort, the production of modern nations, or biological self-betterment. For much of the twentieth century, traditions that value bodily discipline in the service of masculine adventurism and martial prowess have continued to dominate the military in Western societies. These traditions figured prominently during the two World Wars, prompting varying degrees of state involvement in fitness and exercise promotion in differing Western societies. After 1945, the Cold War led to renewed support for these traditions in the NATO countries. For example, in the United States and

Canada, fitness promotion by the Kennedy administration was heavily influenced by the belief that a postwar generation of suburban youth—made soft by television and a consumer society that overvalued self-indulgence—would not be up to the task of meeting the postwar challenge of new international economic competition and containment of the Soviet sphere of influence.

There was, of course, also the emergence of a discourse on health that was tied to the economic viability of the welfare state. From the 1920s through the 1970s, the contractual basis of Western liberal democracies was challenged by the struggles of disenfranchised and underprivileged groups. After the war, governments responded to these struggles with an expansion of the range of entitlements that accrued to individual citizens—and were funded by the state. It is in this context that many people suggest we can understand the transformation of liberal-democratic states into the postwar welfare states that we know today. In reality, however, the roots of the welfare state in different Western societies reach back to the first third of the twentieth century. Early welfare state programs were often created to link social reform with the deployment of discipline because of social and political concerns about high rates of unemployment. Early state-supported physical training and recreation programs were frequently directed to the attempted resolution of these concerns.

By the 1960s, informal, haphazard policies that used public funds for recreation and exercise in the service of reform and control became more formalized around newly emerging initiatives tied to international high-performance sport, public health, and recreation. Similar initiatives continued through the 1970s. But the growing fiscal crisis of many Western governments was also creating pressures for a new concentration of effort on the ways in which fitness and health might play a role in responding to the problem of public deficits while simultaneously increasing national productivity, health, and competitiveness. It was in this context of these multiple forces that biomedical and science-oriented approaches to health, exercise, and sport took off during the 1970s.

All this led to a growing constellation of vested interests around the promotion of physical activity defined in a very narrow physiological manner. The emphasis came to be placed on the promotion of physically active lifestyles. The corollary was that inactive lifestyles—as well as a host of other "unhealthy" cultural practices associated with indulgent consumerism, or even certain ethnic or class dietary or recreational habits—needed to be driven from the center of popular life. Using the status of medical expertise and the techniques of modern advertising, people were to be coaxed to live more physically active lives. The payoff would ostensibly come in the form of fewer costs incurred by the medical systems of Western societies, lower absenteeism, and an overall increase in public satisfaction. The problem was that in this formulation the promotion of physical activity often took on a victim-blaming character that sought to respond to social and health problems by the adjustment of individuals rather than by making structural changes in the factors influencing high levels of stress, environmental toxicity, poverty, unemployment, racism, and sexism. The prevailing tendency has been to limit the role of the welfare state simply to the social management of risks.

The 1980s have witnessed an important series of more holistic and self-consciously progressive attempts to broaden public initiatives in the definition and promotion of active living. There has been a shift away from the overemphasis on sports or aerobics, which have sometimes characterized public initiatives in the past, in favor of a much broader understanding of the values of activity. Attendant to this, active living is now increasingly represented as a right of citizenship rather than a public duty, and there is a growing recognition of the need to change existing "opportunity structures" in order to secure this right for all citizens. Government representatives and health professionals who promote active living today increasingly borrow terminology from broader social movements associated with struggles against poverty, imperialism, and racial and gender inequality. We are told that active living should be understood as part of a broad project of "empowerment."

All well and good, but I do not see much evidence that the promotion of this expanded, progressive idea of active living in countries like Canada and the United States has advanced significantly beyond the initiatives of the 1970s. For one thing, the initiatives still tend to come from state agencies and professionals with vested interests rather than from community groups, trade unions, or ethnic support organizations. Second, the new promotion of the right to active living still seems too narrowly focused on the idea of physical activity on its own terms. In this chapter I have argued that we have seen a continued reduction of the *ideal* of active living in the last century to discipline-oriented physical activity and bodily centered practices of consumption. The early modernist vision—which had conceived of active living more broadly as the pursuit of self-development while changing the world—has been lost.

I think some measure of a return to this vision is necessary even to achieve the more limited objectives of winning increased opportunities for people to live physically active lives if they choose. Can one broaden popular rights to health and recreational opportunities without struggling politically to change the factors influencing structured social inequality or the constraints of contemporary work, family, and consumer life? There has been a good deal of government rhetoric about such things in recent years, clamoring (ironically) about the need to change "opportunity structures" at the very moment that legislation is rolling back the welfare state at every turn while defining the pursuit of health and happiness as primarily a matter of individual discipline and responsibility. Surely, to be emancipatory at all, the promotion of active living has to be undertaken in the broadest sense of the term. That includes a necessary recognition of political issues. Throughout Western history, competing definitions and ideals of active living, and related conceptions of good health and good bodies, have always been about politics. The situation today is no different. The question is simply, what politics does one want to choose?

REFERENCES

Anderson, P. (1974). *Lineages of the absolutist state.* London: New Left Books.

Bakhtin, M. (1968). *Rabelais and his world.* Cambridge, MA: MIT Press.

Bauman, Z. (1983). Industrialism, consumerism and power. *Theory, Culture & Society*, 5(3), 32-43.

Berlin, I. (Ed.). (1956). *The age of enlightenment.* New York: Mentor Books.

Berman, M. (1983). *All that is solid melts into air: The experience of modernity.* London: Verso.

Betts, J. (1975). Mind and body in American thought during the age of Jackson. In E. Zeigler (Ed.), *A history of physical education and sport in the United States and Canada.* Champaign, IL: Stipes.

Bolaria, B.S. (1988). The politics and ideology of self-care and lifestyles. In B.S. Bolaria & H. Dickenson (Eds.), *Sociology of health care in Canada.* Toronto: Harcourt Brace Jovanovich.

Brantlinger, P. (1983). *Bread and circuses: Theories of mass culture as social decay.* Ithaca, NY: Cornell University Press.

Connerton, P. (1989). *How societies remember.* London: Cambridge University Press.

Crawford, R. (1980). Healthism and the medicalization of everyday life. *International Journal of Health Services*, 10(13), 365-388.

Cunningham, H. (1980). *Leisure in the Industrial Revolution, 1780-1880.* New York: St. Martin's Press.

de Grazia, S. (1964). *Of time, work and leisure.* New York: Anchor Books.

Dunning, E. (Ed.). (1993). *The sports process.* Champaign, IL: Human Kinetics.

Eksteins, M. (1989). *Rites of spring: The Great War and the modern age.* New York: Bantam Press.

Elias, N. (1978). *The civilizing process: Vol. 1. The history of manners.* Oxford: Blackwell. (Original work published 1939).

Ewan, S. (1976). *Captains of consciousness: Advertising and the social roots of the consumer culture.* New York: McGraw-Hill.

Featherstone, M. (1991). *Consumer culture and postmodernism*. London: Sage.

Foucault, M. (1977). *Discipline and punish*. New York: Vintage Books.

Foucault, M. (1981). *Power/knowledge: Selected interviews, 1972-1977*. Toronto: Random House.

Giddens, A. (1984). *The constitution of society*. Berkeley, CA: University of California Press.

Green, H. (1986). *Fit for America: Health, fitness, sport and American society*. New York: Pantheon Books.

Green, H. (1989). Introduction. In K. Grover (Ed.), *Fitness in American culture: Images of health, sport and the body, 1830-1940*. Amherst, MA: University of Massachusetts Press.

Grover, K. (Ed.). (1989). *Fitness in American culture: Images of health, sport and the body, 1830-1940*. Amherst, MA: University of Massachusetts Press.

Gruneau, R. (1983). *Class, sports and social development*. Amherst, MA: University of Massachusetts Press.

Gruneau, R. (1988). *Popular cultures and political practices*. Toronto: Garamond Press.

Gruneau, R. (1993). The critique of sport in modernity: Theorizing power, culture, and the politics of the body. In E.G. Dunning, J.A. Maguire, & R.E. Pearton (Eds.), *The sports process* (pp. 85-109). Champaign, IL: Human Kinetics.

Gruneau, R. & Whitson, D. (1993). *Hockey night in Canada: Sport, identities and cultural politics*. Toronto: Garamond Press.

Hall, S. (1984). The state in question. In G. McLennan, D. Held, & S. Hall (Eds.), *The idea of the modern state*. Milton Keynes: Open University Press.

Harvey, D. (1989). *The condition of postmodernity: An enquiry into the origins of cultural change*. Oxford: Blackwell.

Harvey, J. (1983). *Le corps programme ou la rhetorique de Kino-Quebec*. Montreal: Albert Saint-Martin.

Harvey, J. & Sparks, R. (1991). The politics of the body in the context of modernity. *Quest, 43*, 164-189.

Hoberman, J. (1984). *Sport and political ideology*. Austin, TX: University of Texas Press.

Ingham, A.G. (1985). From public issue to personal trouble: Well being and the fiscal crisis of the state. *Sociology of Sport Journal, 2*, 43-55.

Lears, J. (1981). *No place of grace: Antimodernism and the transformation of American culture*. New York: Pantheon Books.

Lears, J. (1989). American advertising and the reconstruction of the body, 1880-1930. In K. Grover (Ed.), *Fitness in American culture*. Amherst, MA: University of Massachusetts Press.

Leiss, W., Kline, S., & Jhally, S. (1990). *Social communication in advertising* (2nd ed.). Scarborough, ON: Nelson.

Lukes, S. (1973). *Individualism*. Oxford: Blackwell.

Macpherson, C.B. (1963). *The political theory of possessive individualism*. Oxford: Oxford University Press.

Macpherson, C.B. (1965). *The real world of democracy*. Toronto: Canadian Broadcasting Corporation.

Maguire, J. (1991). Human sciences, sport sciences, and the need to study people "in the round." *Quest, 43,* 190-206.

Mosse, G. (1975). *The nationalization of the masses: Political symbolism and mass movements in Germany from the Napoleonic wars through the Third Reich.* New York: Meridian Books.

Mrozek, D. (1989). Sport in American life: From national health to personal fulfillment. In K. Grover (Ed.), *Fitness in American culture.* Amherst, MA: University of Massachusetts Press.

Mukerji, C. (1983). *From graven images: Patterns of modern materialism.* New York: Columbia University Press.

Navarro, V. (1986). *Crisis, health, and medicine.* New York: Tavistock.

Park, R. (1989). Healthy, moral and strong: Educational views of exercise and athletics in nineteenth-century America. In K. Grover (Ed.), *Fitness in American culture.* Amherst, MA: University of Massachusetts Press.

Rabinbach, A. (1990). *The human motor: Energy, fatigue, and the origins of modernity.* New York: Basic Books.

Stallybrass, P. & White, A. (1986). *The politics & poetics of transgression.* Ithaca, NY: Cornell University Press.

Thompson, E.P. (1968). *The making of the English working class.* Harmondsworth, UK: Pelican Books.

Turner, B. (1984). *The body and society.* Oxford: Blackwell.

Veblen, T. (1953). *The theory of the leisure class.* New York: Mentor. (Original work published 1899).

Vertinsky, P. (1990). Science, social science, and the "hunger for wonders" in physical education: Moving toward a future healthy society. *The Academy Papers, 24.* Champaign, IL: Human Kinetics.

Whorton, J. (1982). *Crusaders for fitness: The history of American health reformers.* Princeton: Princeton University Press.

Whorton, J. (1989). Eating to win: Popular concepts of diet, strength, and energy in the early twentieth century. In K. Grover (Ed.), *Fitness in American culture.* Amherst, MA: University of Massachusetts Press.

In Perspective

THE ENVIRONMENT
AND PHYSICAL ACTIVITY

Thomas L. Burton

My research on active living and the environment began in 1963, when I joined the Department of Economics at Wye College, University of London, to research issues in recreational land use in Britain. Even at that time, there was concern about the conversion of first-class agricultural land to nonfarming uses and the consequent impact on the quality of Britain's rural environment. A political economist by training, I rapidly became involved in recreational planning and environmental issues of a much wider kind—at various ous times carrying out studies of New Town development, urban recreation planning, the quality of urban life, and parks planning and development. In 1968, I served as a consultant to the United Nations Economic Commission for Europe (UNECE) for an international seminar on the "Planning of Recreation Areas Including Development of the Natural Environment" in Geneva, Switzerland, an experience which coalesced my interests (in policy, recreation, environment, and planning) into a focused area of study.

During the past quarter century, research studies in leisure, recreation, and sport have shifted from an early emphasis on physical fitness, outdoor recreation, and organized sport to an interest in active living, health, and lifestyle. At the same time, environmental studies changed direction from a primary focus on preservation, conservation, and protection of resources to the current preoccupation with sustainable living. Significant milestones have been passed on the way: Muscular Christianity, the Playground Movement, PRO-REC, 5BX, and ParticipAction, on the one side, and the Conservation Movement, environmental impact analysis, public participation, and sustainable development on the other. The one common thread throughout the past 25 years is a clear evolution toward interdisciplinary and multi-disciplinary approaches and tools in both the study and the practice of active living and the environment. Both disciplinary specialists (physiologists, biologists, geographers, economists, and the like) and traditional professions (physical education, education, urban and regional planning, surveying, landscape architecture, and so on) have made important contributions throughout the period. And they have been joined by others: wildlife conservationists, psychologists, sociologists, parks and recreation practitioners, political scientists, historians, and many more. Models, methods, and approaches have been carried across disciplinary boundaries: For example, the Limits of Acceptable Change (LAC) approach to environmental management for active living and recreation emerged from the early carrying capacity models, which derived directly from biological studies of wildlife management.

Interdisciplinarity and multidisciplinarity are the keys to the future evolution of both the study and the practice of environmental management for active living and recreation. While the separate disciplines and professions will continue to contribute, the greatest advances are likely to come from the efforts of different disciplinary specialists and professionals working together. The natural environment and the human condition do not lend themselves easily to compartmentalization. As the saying goes: "Pick up something and you'll find it's attached to the universe." The development of new forms of recreation and sport, often through technological change, will invariably affect the management of the environment—as we have learned over the past quarter century of snowmobiling, mountain biking, and power boating. The environmental issues arising from the widespread adoption of new recreation and sport forms demand multidisciplinary and interdisciplinary treatment. As I remarked earlier, human well-being and the welfare of the natural environment are inextricably linked. Research and practice in both areas should be similarly integrated.

Chapter 7

THE ENVIRONMENT
AND PHYSICAL ACTIVITY

Thomas L. Burton

An understanding of the relationships between physical activity and the environment must begin with an appreciation of two opposing societal worldviews, or paradigms. The first, known variously as the Consumer Society, the Dominant Social Paradigm, or the Dominant Western Worldview, incorporates a set of values which originate in and draw their meaning from a perception of the biosphere as unlimited in its ability to meet human needs and wants. It also presumes a technology that makes possible continuous economic growth and rising human prosperity and measures human progress primarily in material and quantitative terms. In contrast, the Conserver Society (or New Ecological Paradigm, or New Environmental Paradigm) worldview perceives the biosphere as limited in its ability to satisfy human needs and wants, thereby imposing constraints upon the workings of technology and the practicality of continuous economic growth. This view measures human progress in spiritual and qualitative terms as well as material and quantitative ones. It has become a prominent area of research in the leisure studies field in recent years and is addressed particularly by those engaged in attempting to identify and measure the benefits of leisure (see, for example, Schreyer & Driver, 1989).

In the context of each of these worldviews, the relationships between physical activity and the environment can be explored through three themes: an examination of environmental attitudes and, especially, the ways in which these are expressed through participation in different kinds of (physical) recreation activities; an investigation of the impact such recreation activities have on the environment; and a consideration of alternative approaches to the management of the environment for recreation activity. Before conducting this exploration, however, it will be instructive to review briefly the origins and evolution of the concern in North America for fitness and active living as well as conservation and the natural environment. This will then enable links to be made between two modern social movements—active living and sustainable living.

FITNESS, PHYSICAL ACTIVITY, AND ACTIVE LIVING

While the active living concept is relatively new, first taking shape at the 1988 Canadian Summit on Fitness, its roots are over a century old. Meller (1976) has shown how, in the late Victorian period in Britain, a sustained effort was made by voluntary social and religious organizations to provide wholesome influences on the lives of the poor. Organizations such as the Young Men's Christian Association, the Women's Christian Temperance Union, and the Boys' Brigade set out to change the lives of the urban poor—morally and socially. An important component in this effort was physical activity, which was perceived as a means of instilling discipline, character, and moral rectitude into a rather degenerate and desperately poor urban population. The central theme in Britain's Civilizing Mission to the Poor and Muscular Christianity movements was the integration of physical recreation pursuits into everyday social activity. Life in the urban slums could (and would) be enhanced immeasurably by wholesome recreation. As the Rev. T.W. Harvey of Bristol noted at the time, it "was part of our ideal that the Church should provide, and be a center of social life, for all the parish, not for its congregations only; that all that is innocent and refreshing—in reading rooms and games, in music and the drama, in gymnastics and drill, in clubs and other associations—should find its headquarters in [church] buildings" (quoted in Meller, 1976, p. 144).

This concern for the integration of physical activity with ordinary social life found its way to Canada and was expressed in a variety of forms, perhaps the most significant of which was the Playground Movement. The National Council of Women launched the movement in Canada, at its Eighth Annual Meeting in 1901, with the overwhelming approval of the following motion: "Whereas the agitation for vacation schools and playgrounds where children may find organized recreation having become so widespread that it is now known as the playground movement, and whereas the establishment of such vacation schools and playgrounds is acknowledged by educators and philanthropists to be desired in every community, and whereas the necessity for such schools and playgrounds to improve the condition of children in the cities of Canada is obvious, therefore, be it resolved that this National Council of Women of Canada declare themselves in favor of the establishment of vacation schools and playgrounds, and pledge themselves to do all in their power to promote their organization" (quoted in McFarland, 1970, p. 19). The early vacation playgrounds were invariably staffed by teachers who were responsible not only for the management and operation of the playgrounds, but also for "protecting the children from evil, seeing that their language and conduct were proper, and for gathering them together during periods when they should rest to tell them appropriate stories to kindle their imagination and to store their minds with high ideals" (McFarland, 1970, p. 27). The physical activities and games on the playground were part and parcel of a much larger concern for developing a responsible and uplifting lifestyle among the children.

The Canadian government's involvement in physical activity and fitness can be traced to the PRO-REC programs in British Columbia during the Great Depression. On November 9, 1934, the Minister of Education for the province announced the initiation of classes in recreation and physical education to protect the youth of British Columbia from the degenerating effects of enforced idleness caused by unemployment and to develop morale and character (McFarland, 1970). The success of these classes attracted the attention of the federal Purvis Commission, which had been established in 1936 to investigate the needs of unemployed youth. Following the commission's report, the government of Canada began a program of assistance to the provinces for physical training and recreation projects through the Unemployment and Agricultural Assistance Act.

The passage of the National Physical Fitness Act in 1943 signaled the first direct federal involvement in the physical development of Canadians through sports, athletics, and fitness activities. A National Council on Physical Fitness was created, which interpreted its mandate broadly to include physical, recreational, and cultural activities. The Canadian approach to fitness would be by way of recreation. The Minister of National Health and Welfare, the Honorable Paul Martin, reinforced this view in a speech to the Annual Meeting of the Council in 1947:

> I think we should have a broader view of the concepts of fitness and what the program should entail. No narrow definition will be adequate. It should be broad enough to include mental and cultural fitness as well as the more narrowly physical. One of the aims should be the social integration of the various types of people who make up this nation. (quoted in McFarland, 1970, p. 53)

Here, again, is the idea that physical activity and fitness are essential components of a well-rounded lifestyle.

The repeal of the National Physical Fitness Act in 1954 signaled a federal withdrawal from the field, ostensibly because the perceived need for fitness as part of the daily regimen was now met adequately through the expanding provincial and municipal programs and the schools. It wasn't long, however, before the federal government re-entered the field—through the Fitness and Amateur Sport Act of 1961. The principal impetus for this new initiative was the poor showing of Canadian athletes in international competition in the preceding years. A second factor was the apparent decline in the levels of fitness and health of Canadians generally. But, paradoxically, while the new act excluded the word "physical" from its title—thereby suggesting a broad-based definition of fitness—the interpretation that was in fact employed was not nearly as broad as had been the case earlier. Music, dance, and cultural projects, which would have received support under the earlier legislation, were invariably rejected because they contained no physical activity component. Organized sport became the dominant interest. In fact, the years following the passage of the act saw a growing emphasis on the development of elite sport in Canada, made most evident in the creation of the carded athlete system. It was only in the early 1970s that much attention was again given to the fitness of the population at large, through the development of the ParticipAction program. But, while this indicated a greater disquiet about general fitness levels in Canada, the bulk of federal activity was still directed at the elite sport system. In fact, the recreation component of the Fitness and Amateur Sport Directorate was redefined in 1979 to emphasize its restriction to physical recreation (Minister of State for Fitness and Amateur Sport, 1979).

Not until the mid-1980s was a new initiative launched to address levels of physical fitness in the Canadian population as a whole. The 1988 Canadian Summit on Fitness set out to re-examine the concept of fitness. Delegates acknowledged the need to widen the meaning of fitness from a narrowly defined physiological condition to one that reflected personal well-being in an overarching sense. Furthermore, it was recognized that the notion of exercise should not be limited to separate, distinct, structured activities specifically intended to strengthen fitness and enhance health. The concept of active living was developed to describe a situation in which physical activity experiences are integrated into everyday life (Fitness Canada, 1988).

Active living broadens, extends, and reaches beyond the traditional idea of fitness. It broadens the notion to include unstructured and unregulated activities, such as gardening, walking, and flying a kite. It extends it to connect fitness to other aspects of lifestyle, including such things as healthy eating and stress management. And it reaches beyond fitness to emphasize physical activity as part of the social domain of life, through the family, workplace, school, and other social institutions.

It seems, then, that there is at least a partial sense of *deja vu* in holistic approaches such as active living. The inclusion of unstructured and unregulated activities reiterates one of the principal themes of the Playground Movement: that the supervision of play activities on playgrounds did not mean that all activities would be chosen for the children by adults. Opportunities for play were to be structured and regulated, not the play activities themselves. The emphasis upon physical activity as part of the wider social domain of life echoes the tenets of the Civilizing Mission to the Poor and Muscular Christianity Movements. It is, perhaps, only in its focus upon a holistic lifestyle and, in particular, on the linkages between fitness and such things as nutrition and stress management that the active living concept explores wholly new ground.

CONSERVATION AND SUSTAINABLE LIVING

Concern for the natural environment in Canada and the United States has gone through three distinct phases during the twentieth century: conservation, particularly as reflected in the Conservation Movement; environmental concern, expressed in the Environmental Movement; and what may be called sustainable living. The first phase was a direct outcome of the late nineteenth century Conservation Movement, whose origins are to be found in two main streams: the naturalists and the resource professionals. The naturalists epitomized the emotive and aesthetic desire for preservation of the natural environment. Their primary concern was for the spiritual, even mystical, qualities of nature. Often described as transcendentalists, they believed that the natural world transcended its physical dimensions and reflected spiritual truth and moral law. But while the naturalists' sentiments were noble, the preservation that they advocated was simply unacceptable in the expansionist climate of late nineteenth century North America. They succeeded in formulating and developing the concept of the national park, and even managed to have several parks established. Still, something more pragmatic was needed in the climate of the times—and it came from the resource professionals, especially the foresters (Burton, 1972).

The principles of the Conservation Movement first took tangible form in Canada in the activities of the federal Commission of Conservation from 1909 to 1921. The Commission's philosophy was unashamedly utilitarian and reflected the views of resource professionals. Emphasis was given to the essential complementarity of development and conservation. At the Commission's first annual meeting, the Chairman, Clifford Sifton, set out the boundaries of its jurisdiction as he saw them. In so doing, he indicated clearly that conservation was not to be confused with preservation: "If we attempt to stand in the way of development our efforts will assuredly be of no avail, either to stop development or to promote conservation. It will not, however, be hard to show that the best and most highly economic development and exploitation in the interests of the people can only take place by having regard to the principles of conservation" (quoted in Thorpe, 1961, p. 4). The latter dealt in particular with the idea of sustained yield, the need for the constant renewal of resources that could, in fact, be renewed—most obviously, forests. The principal concern was not that natural resources were being exploited, but that, in many cases, they were being exploited wastefully. The Conservation Movement was predominantly a crusade against waste and mismanagement in development, not against development itself. Its operational arm in Canada, the Commission of Conservation, was led and staffed by professionals: foresters, soil and water engineers, landscape architects, and planners.

Environmental concern declined in Canada following the demise of the Commission of Conservation in 1921—a decline that was paralleled in the United States. The three decades that followed saw a primary policy emphasis on exploitation and development at almost any cost. During the 1960s, however, there was a re-awakening of interest in conservation. The principles of the Conservation Movement were resurrected in a wider context, and took shape in the form of a new Environmental Movement. The concern was still with waste and mismanagement, but where the conservationists of the 1910s had battled with the quantitative dimensions of waste, those of the 1960s voiced alarm over the deteriorating quality of the environment. In consequence, the debate spilled over from the professional and political domains to the wider public arena. But, because the focus remained primarily on large-scale developments, public involvement was limited principally to organized special interests and pressure groups. Although the new movement gave priority to ecological considerations over economic ones, emphasized aesthetics over science, and advocated a policy of worldwide population control, its influence was most pronounced in the passage of federal and provincial environmental impact legislation. The new environmentalists were passionately devoted to the notion of ecology. One of the most active and vocal of the new environmental organizations, Pollution Probe, argued that we must "cultivate a reverence for nature that will convince us that something is right when it tends to preserve the integrity and beauty of our biotic community, and wrong when it tends to do otherwise" (Chant, 1970, p. 205). Despite this, the movement did not succeed in generating a broadly based environmental ethic in the population at large. It was, for the most part, a movement made up of professionals and lay specialists, with relatively little wider appeal.

Since the late 1980s, a third phase of environmental concern has been gaining strength. Its thrust is the adoption of environmental practices in everyday living. The Report of the World Commission on Environment and Development (The Brundtland Report) in 1987 introduced the concept of sustainable development, which draws from both previous phases of environmental concern. Sustainable development accepts (in fact, it requires) economic growth, but seeks to change its character: "It requires a change in the content of growth, to make it less material- and energy-intensive and more equitable in its impact" (World Commission on Environment and Development, 1987, p. 52). Sustainable development is the kind that meets present needs without compromising the ability of future generations to also meet their needs.

From the concept of sustainable development has emerged the concept of sustainable living, which broadens conservation to include the practices of individuals as well as those of businesses and governments; extends it to connect environmental quality to other aspects of life, including health and wellness; and reaches beyond it to emphasize sound environmental practices as part of the wider societal domain—in the home, at school, in business, and elsewhere.

The concept of sustainable living draws from both the early Conservation Movement (including the work of the Commission of Conservation in the 1910s) and the Environmental Movement of the 1960s. It combines the idea of sustained yield for renewable resources from the former with the concern for ecological balance in the latter to produce the notion of sustainable development. It also extends this notion to encompass the everyday lifestyles of individuals, in addition to the activities of businesses and governments.

ACTIVE LIVING AND SUSTAINABLE LIVING

These brief reviews of the evolution of active living and sustainable living demonstrate the clear kinship between them. The common feature of both is the link to everyday life. Active living embraces the idea that physical activity can and should occur as part of normal, everyday existence. Sustainable living encompasses the same idea. Furthermore, they are not discrete notions, but are parts of a much wider entity called quality of life. There is an inherent assumption that both concepts, if appropriately pursued, will enhance the quality of life of individuals and, by extension, the community. Indeed, in its early manifestations (as the Civilizing Mission to the Poor and Muscular Christianity Movements), active living was simultaneously a reaction to an abysmally poor urban environment and a partial solution to it. Physical fitness and children's play were to be the means of mitigating the worst urban degradation. That these activities would improve the quality of urban life was self-evident to their proponents. The Conservation Movement, too, saw physical activity as a means of enhancing the quality of life. Although its principal thrust was efficient resource management, it included organizations, such as the Sierra Club in the United States and the Alpine Club of Canada, with a particular interest in the use of natural resources for open-air recreation as a healthy and spiritually uplifting part of life. Again, there was no doubt that this kind of recreation was environmentally benign.

In recent years, however, there has been an increasing awareness of the possible detrimental relationships between physical activity and the natural environment. The traditional assumption that physical recreation activities are invariably environmentally benevolent can no longer be sustained. While many of these activities are fully compatible with the maintenance of environmental quality, some are clearly not, and others may be benign or malignant depending upon such things as the numbers of people engaged in them at particular times. In his Fourteenth Annual Report, in 1925, the first Director of Canada's Dominion Parks Branch, J.B. Harkin, remarked: "It is a well established fact that most motorists spend their holidays in their cars. Many facilities already exist which bring the motorists to the foot of the Rockies. What motorist will be able to resist the call of the Canadian Rockies when it is known that he can go through them on first class roads? And what a revenue this country will obtain when thousands of automobiles are traversing the parks" (quoted in Bella, 1987, p. 42). It is a moot point whether he would hold the same sentiment today—when there are millions, not thousands, of cars traveling through the Canadian Rocky Mountain national parks, with their associated impact on campgrounds, hiking trails, alpine vegetation, and wildlife. Furthermore, hikers, climbers, mountain bikers, and other physically active recreationists are, at times, creating serious problems for the maintenance and management of national parks (see, for example, Swinnerton, 1989). Even the seemingly innocuous activity of bird watching has damaged the vegetation and wildlife of Point Pelee National Park (Butler & Fenton, 1987). And hikers, seemingly the least offensive intruders in the environment, have caused severe environmental problems in parks. In West Vancouver, Canada, for example, hiking on trails through ancient stands of western red cedar and hemlock trees adjacent to Cypress Provincial Park was banned in 1991 because it caused soil erosion!

Nor is the consideration of the relationships between physical activity and the environment restricted solely to the natural environment, although the vast majority of the research has focused upon this. Physical recreation activity and the built environment share significant interrelationships, not all of which are entirely positive. The paving over of park trails for jogging, bicycling, and cross-country skiing has been shown to have a detrimental impact upon small wildlife populations and adjacent natural vegetation (Dustin & McAvoy, 1980, 1982). Large-scale "fun runs" and "'birkbeiners" have left nonbiodegradable litter, not all of which has been collected and disposed of properly.

Another point about both active living and sustainable living is that many Canadians currently do not practice these concepts. (Although national data are unavailable for the United States, it is likely that the same pattern holds.) The 1988 *Campbell's Survey on the Well-Being of Canadians* showed that more than two-fifths of the population are physically inactive, with a further one-quarter being only moderately active (Stephens & Craig, 1990). In a similar vein, a Decima national opinion poll in 1989 found that only slightly more than one-half of the Canadian population actually engage in various aspects of sustainable living: approximately half recycle bottles and cans, while about two-fifths have stopped buying products from identified polluters (Gregg & Posner, 1990). In fact, many Canadians and Americans do not practice active living and sustainable living at all, or do so only in an incidental, limited way.

ENVIRONMENT AND SOCIETY

If one is to adequately comprehend the relationships between physical activity and the environment, one must first address the meaning of the term "environment" and attempt to understand society's attitudes toward it. Wall (1989) has suggested that the word encompasses the entire world in which we live, the sum of the conditions that infuse and shape our lives. As such, it is an extraordinarily complex notion. Sonnenfeld (1968) identifies the construct of a nested set of environments. The widest conception of the environment is the *geographical environment*, made up of the entire universe that is external to the individual. Nested within this is the *operational environment*, consisting of those parts of the geographical environment that actually impinge on the individual, whether the individual is conscious of them or not. Nested within this operational environment is the *perceptual environment*, the component of the operational environment of which the individual is aware. And, finally, within the perceptual environment is the *behavioral environment*, the portion of the perceptual environment that influences the individual's behavior. As Wall states: "One can conclude from this not only that the environment is extremely complex, but that individuals are aware of, and respond to, only a portion of all environmental stimuli, and that the process is mediated by selective perception" (Wall, 1989, p. 455).

Wall also demonstrated how the idea of the environment has been compartmentalized in order to reduce its complexity to levels that can at least be defined, if not fully understood. Terms such as *natural* or *physical* environment are employed to identify those portions of the environment relatively free of human modification. Examples of natural environments employed for physical recreation are forests, national and provincial parks, rivers and lakes, wilderness areas, and wildlife refuges. In contrast, *urban* or *built* environments are those elements of the environment that have been entirely or very largely constructed or modified by humans. Examples of built environments used for physical recreation are sports centers and similar facilities, urban playgrounds, ski resorts, golf courses, and even shopping malls.

As suggested earlier, societal attitudes toward both natural and built environments can be best understood in light of two basic paradigms. Authors such as Boulding (1970), Burton (1972), O'Riordan (1981), and Russell (1979) have referred to two divergent societal views of the world, the first of which is dominated by a consumption ethic. Typically, this implies a set of values that reflects a particular view of Sonnenfeld's geographical environment, one in which the biosphere is unlimited in its ability to meet human needs and wants, which possesses a technology that makes possible continuous economic growth and increasing human prosperity, and which measures human progress primarily in material and quantitative terms. The four principal assumptions underlying this worldview were identified by Catton and Dunlap (1978), and are labeled the Dominant Western Worldview (DWW). They have to do with the nature of human beings, social causation, human society, and societal constraints.

1. Human beings are fundamentally different from all other species on earth, over which they have domination.
2. People are masters of their own destiny, who can choose their own goals and learn to do whatever is necessary to achieve them.
3. The world provides unlimited opportunities for human activity.
4. Since every problem has a solution that is simply waiting to be found, the story of humanity is one of continual progress.

The DWW is closely related to the Human Exemptionalist Paradigm (HEP) in sociology, which holds that:

1. Humans have cultural heritage in addition to, and distinct from, their genetic inheritance and, consequently, are different from all other animal species.
2. Social and cultural factors, including technological change, are the principal determinants of human affairs.
3. The social and cultural environments are the pivotal factors influencing the evolution of human society, with the biophysical environment being of lesser significance.
4. Human culture is cumulative and, as a result, technological and social progress can continue indefinitely, eventually solving all social problems.

The core values of this Consumer Society in an environmental context were postulated by Dunlap and Van Liere (1978), who labeled them the Dominant Social Paradigm, (DSP). Jackson has summarized the most significant of these DSP values: "faith in science and technology; support for individual rights; support for economic growth; faith in material abundance; and faith in future prosperity" (Jackson, 1989, p. 360). Essentially, the DSP centers upon a belief in levels of personal consumption which (in principle, if not for any particular individual) are unconstrained by environmental, social, economic, political, and technological limits.

In contrast to this is the Conserver Society, which views Sonnenfeld's geographical environment as severely limited in its ability to sustain human consumption. It sees the biosphere as imposing constraints upon the workings of technology, continuous economic growth is perceived to be impractical, and human progress is measured principally in nonquantitative dimensions. Catton and Dunlap (1978) identified four principal assumptions underlying this worldview, which they called the New Ecological Paradigm (NEP). These are in contrast to the DWW and, therefore, deal with the same items: the nature of human beings, social causation, human society, and societal constraints. They are:

1. While humans are indeed different from other species, they remain one among many that are interdependent parts of the global ecosystem.
2. Human affairs are influenced not only by social and cultural variables, but also by the linkages of cause-effect-feedback in the natural system.
3. Humans live in, and depend on, a finite biophysical environment, which places constraints upon human actions.
4. While technological advances can extend environmental carrying capacity, they cannot rescind the laws of nature.

The core values of this Conserver Society were also identified by Dunlap and Van Liere (1978), who labeled them the New Environmental Paradigm (NEP). They are founded on ecological principles that stress a harmony between human activity and natural processes and include a belief that the fruits of science and technology are limited by the constraints of the ecosystem, support for community rights (which will inevitably constrain some individual rights), and recognition of a limit to economic growth in solely material terms. In sum, the NEP reflects a belief in significant ecological limitations upon human activity.

No studies specifically examine the relationships between the broader concept of active living and the environment. However, many address the relationships between various types of physical recreation activity and the environment, although these have focused almost entirely on the relationships between outdoor recreation activities and the natural and nonurban environments. These studies can be organized into three principal groups: those which have examined the environmental attitudes and behavior of particular kinds of recreationists; studies of the impact of recreation activities on the natural environment; and studies of the management of particular kinds of natural environments for recreational use.

ENVIRONMENTAL ATTITUDES

Before examining the state of knowledge about the environmental attitudes and behaviors of recreationists, it is necessary to consider environmental attitudes generally. In a wide-ranging review, Buttell (1987) suggested that one of the major new directions in environmental sociology during the 1970s and 1980s dealt with environmental attitudes, values, and behaviors. He categorized this literature into three broad groups: studies of the sociostructural aspects of environmental attitudes; the development and testing of sociopsychological theories; and empirical studies of environmental attitudes and behaviors. To this can be added a fourth category—studies of the relationships between environmental attitudes and behaviors and the alternative worldviews or paradigms noted earlier.

Sociostructural studies are those that "examine a sociostructural [problem] such as whether there are differences in the environmental attitudes and beliefs of different segments of the public" (Buttell, 1987, p. 472). A prevalent belief during the Environmental Movement of the 1960s was that positive environmental attitudes were held primarily by elite segments of the population, a view which derived principally from observations of the sociodemographic characteristics of environmental activists, such as members of the Sierra Club and the (then) National and Provincial Parks Association of Canada. Subsequent research focused upon the correlates of environmental concern among the general public, not on particular groups. This led both Buttell (1987) and Jackson (1989b) to conclude that, whether or not environmental concern and pro-environmental attitudes were initially restricted to an elite, they had been diffused to all socioeconomic groups within the population by the mid-1980s. This does not mean that all population groups are equally concerned about environmental problems; only that such concern is not limited solely to a narrow population segment. This conclusion was reinforced by the findings of studies examining the influences upon environmental concern and orientation of such sociodemographic factors as age, level of education, level of income, occupation, and political affiliation. Buttell concluded from his review of these studies that, in general, "while age, education, and, to a lesser extent, residence consistently predict environmental concern, these and other sociodemographic variables explain only modest levels of variance (seldom over 10 percent) in measures of environmental concern" (Buttell, 1987, p. 473). The overwhelming conclusion from the sociostructural studies is, first, that positive environmental attitudes have risen among the population at large over the past two decades or so and, second, that while environmental concern and pro-environmental attitudes are correlated positively with such sociodemographic variables as age and level of education, the strength of this correlation is small.

Research aimed at the development of social-psychological theories of environmental attitude and behavior focuses primarily on the relationships between environmental attitudes and behavior and the cognitive structure of environmental orientations. Two important trends in this research have addressed norm activation and urban-rural differences. Norm activation theory suggests that environmental behaviors and attitudes toward conservation are activated by moral norms concerned with preventing harm to people (Stern, Dietz, & Black, 1986). Moral norms come into play when an individual recognizes that negative consequences can arise for other people as a result of his or her actions and when that individual then accepts personal responsibility for these consequences. This theory has found considerable support in studies of "littering, energy conservation, behavior in wildland settings, and response to natural hazards" (Buttell, 1987, p. 475). Urban-rural studies have postulated that urban dwellers typically hold more pro-environmental attitudes than those who live in rural areas. Graf (1976) noted that urban residents have traditionally provided the base of popular support for the preservation of wilderness and the maintenance and enhancement of environmental quality. Studies over the past two decades or so have supported this contention.

Many empirical studies of environmental attitudes and behavior attempt to determine case-specific factors influencing attitudes toward, and behavior in, the environment and discover what kinds of incentives, appeals, and media messages appear to induce pro-environmental behavior. Not surprisingly, the results of this class of research have been wide and varied. Perdue and Warder (1981) found, for example, that student participation in a wilderness survival course led to the later development of favorable attitudes toward the environment. Walsh, Bjonback, Aiken, and Rosenthal (1990) concluded that householders in Colorado were willing to pay for a program to protect a minimum level of forest quality, but that, as forest quality (density) increases, the willingness to pay for further improvement decreases. Perhaps the only general conclusion to emerge from these empirical studies, however, is that pro-environmental behavior is most often motivated by non-economic incentives, including the level of effectiveness of communication and information and the perceived trustworthiness of the purveyors of this information (Black, Stern, & Elworth, 1985; Heberlein & Warriner, 1983; Stern, 1986).

Relatively few studies exist of the relationships between environmental attitudes and alternative societal paradigms, other than the landmark studies discussed earlier, which helped to formulate the paradigms themselves. Moreover, these studies tend to use data that are now a couple of decades old. Although they offer useful insights, they must be cited with caution. Dunlap and Van Liere (1978), who were primarily responsible for the development of the NEP and DSP measures, carried out an empirical study of two groups of Washington State residents, a general public sample, and an environmental organization sample. They hypothesized that the members of the environmental organization sample would be more likely than the general population sample to endorse the premises of the New Environmental Paradigm. Consequently, a comparison of the two groups would offer a measure of the validity of the NEP as an indicator of environmental attitudes. The results showed a high level of acceptance of the principles of the NEP from both groups, although the environmental organization sample did indeed endorse these principles more strongly than the members of the general population. In a follow-up study examining the linkage between the Dominant Social Paradigm and concern for environmental quality, covering a general sample of residents of Washington State, Dunlap and Van Liere (1984) found that commitment to the DSP was negatively correlated with environmental concern, while commitment to the NEP appeared to be a major factor influencing levels of environmental concern.

ENVIRONMENTAL ATTITUDES AND RECREATION PARTICIPATION

Several empirical studies have attempted to test the relationships between environmental attitudes and participation in physical recreation activities. A chronology of the most important of these studies would begin with the work of Knopp and Tyger (1973), who examined the environmental attitudes of snowmobilers and cross-country skiers in Minnesota. They hypothesized that self-propelled recreationists (such as cross-country skiers) would have stronger environmental attitudes than motorized recreationists (such as snowmobilers). While their hypothesis was generally supported, they noted that snowmobilers came primarily from lower-income occupations than cross-country skiers and that lower-income occupations included a higher proportion of jobs that exploit the environment, thereby fostering a utilitarian view of natural resources and the environment generally.

Dunlap and Heffernan (1975) differentiated between consumptive and appreciative outdoor recreation activities: "consumptive activities, typified by hunting and fishing, involve taking something from the environment and thus reflect a utilitarian orientation toward it. . . . In contrast, appreciative activities (e.g., hiking, camping, and photography) involve attempts to enjoy the natural environment without altering it . . . " (p. 19). Employing a sample of more than 3,000 residents of

Washington State, they hypothesized that (1) there would be a positive association between levels of participation in outdoor recreation activities and levels of environmental concern; (2) the association would be stronger for participation in appreciative recreation activities and environmental concern than for participation in consumptive recreation activities and environmental concern; and (3) there would be a stronger association between levels of participation in outdoor recreation and concern for the protection of aspects of the environment related to that participation (e.g., maintaining trails) than between levels of outdoor recreation participation and general environmental issues (e.g., water quality). The results indicated strong support for the second and third hypotheses, but only weak support for the first.

Recognizing problems with the measurements used by Dunlap and Heffernan, which focused simply upon attitudes toward public policies and actions, Geisler, Martinson, and Wilkening (1977) developed measures that stressed awareness of environmental problems and consequent support for public action. Addressing the same three hypotheses, they found only some support for the first hypothesis and weak support for the second. Most significantly, they found that environmental concern appeared to be affected more by the sociodemographic characteristics of the respondents than by the type of recreation activity they chose. They also suggested that the distinction between appreciative and consumptive activities was insufficiently delineated.

Pinhey and Grimes (1979), continuing the search for refined measures of environmental attitudes, reexamined the thesis underlying the Dunlap and Heffernan study using a regionally specific measure of environmental concern on a (smaller) sample of residents of Louisiana. They hypothesized that (1) persons who participated in outdoor recreation activities would be more environmentally concerned than persons who were inactive; and (2) persons who participated in appreciative recreation activities would be more environmentally concerned than those who favored consumptive activities. The first hypothesis was supported, but not the second. Furthermore, the analysis showed that participation in recreation, by itself, explained less than 1 percent of the total variation in environmental concern. Unfortunately, problems inherent in the design of the study require that these findings be accepted with caution.

Although Dunlap and Van Liere (1978, 1984) did not examine the relationships between environmental attitudes and recreation participation, their development of the NEP and DSP scales facilitated improved measurement of environmental attitudes in studies by others. Van Liere and Noe (1981) used the NEP scale to measure environmental attitudes in a study of visitors to Cape Hatteras National Seashore in the

United States. They then tested the Dunlap and Heffernan hypotheses and found no support for the first of them. There was some support, however, for the hypothesis that participants in appreciative outdoor recreation activities were more pro-environmental than participants in consumptive or abusive activities. They suggested three possible reasons for the weak levels of correlation between environmental attitudes and participation in different kinds of recreation activities. First, there might be a need for better study designs. Second, it may be that outdoor recreation participation is not, in fact, significantly related to environmental concern. And, third, it may be that a relationship does exist, which is far more complex than originally thought.

Jackson (1986) examined how patterns of recreation participation might change with a paradigm shift from a Consumer Society to a Conserver Society. It was expected that participation changes would reflect the greater pro-environmental attitudes inherent in the latter society. A sample of 662 residents of the cities of Calgary and Edmonton in Alberta, Canada, was used to address two hypotheses: (1) that participants in appreciative activities would have stronger pro-environmental attitudes than those who engaged in mechanized and consumptive activities; and (2) that there would be a stronger association between levels of participation in outdoor recreation activities and attitudes toward specific aspects of the environment needed to pursue these activities than toward general environmental issues. An important difference between this study and its predecessors was the use of a multi-item scale and factorial analysis. Jackson labeled the four environmental attitude groups that emerged from the factor analyses ecocentrists, moderate ecocentrists, moderate technocentrists, and technocentrists. The results supported both hypotheses.

Employing the same data set, Jackson (1987) continued his work with a study that added the dimension of attitudes toward resource development and preservation. The sample of urban residents of Alberta was employed to test three hypotheses: (1) that participants in the same groups of recreation activities (whether mechanized, consumptive, or appreciative) would not differ in their views about the development versus the preservation of natural resources; (2) that participants in mechanized and consumptive recreation activities would not differ from each other in their views about the development versus the preservation of natural resources; and (3) that participants in appreciative recreation activities would have stronger pro-preservation views and weaker pro-development views than participants in both mechanized and consumptive activities. The results showed that the preservationist view was endorsed by a majority of all urban Albertans, but that participants in appreciative recreation activities were indeed more favorably inclined to preservation than were participants in mechanized and consumptive activities—with the significant exception of hunters!

A further study by Jackson (1989b) examined the prevalent view among earlier authors that support for the preservation of the environment was found only among elite groups in society. Also, he examined the extent to which views about the development or preservation of resources specifically for recreation and related purposes reflected more deep-seated views toward the environment. Employing data from the same province-wide study of Albertans, he found that (1) for most urban Albertans, wilderness preservation was more important than its development; (2) a majority of the sample held pro-environmental attitudes and favored land use restrictions to decrease conflicts between recreation activities and to limit the impact on the environment; (3) there was a significant correlation between the preservationist view and pro-environmental attitudes; and (4) there was a weak relationship between pro-environmental attitudes and views about preservation and development when controlling for specific sociodemographic variables, such as age, gender, education, and income. Jackson concluded from the latter that Albertans who hold preservationist views were not an elite but were found among all sociodemographic groups.

In summary, research on this topic to date has not demonstrated a consistent, positive association between participation in outdoor recreation generally, as well as specific types of outdoor recreation activities, and environmental attitudes. Earlier studies, which employed single-item scales, generally found that very little (typically less than 5 percent) of the variation in concern for the environment could be accounted for by differences in levels and types of outdoor recreation participation. The later studies by Jackson, which employed multi-item scales based upon the NEP, DSP, and factor analysis, found stronger support for the existence of a relationship. It is worth noting, however, that the data employed in all of these studies were obtained prior to the evolution of the third phase in environmental concern, which was characterized earlier as sustainable living. The 1989 Decima national opinion poll in Canada, noted earlier, found that popular concern about the environment had risen dramatically during the late 1980s. In a previous poll conducted in June 1986, three-fifths of Canadians had described the quality of the environment in their own communities as either excellent or good. Three years later, this figure had dropped to about one-half. Moreover, whereas about one-sixth of respondents in 1986 had indicated that individuals rather than governments were primarily responsible for protecting the environment, by 1989 this figure had risen to one-third. In light of this significant shift in the environmental attitudes of the general population, it would be salient to consider how the attitudes held by specific groups of recreationists have changed. In particular, it would be valuable to examine whether the attitudes of those who participate frequently in mechanized and consumptive recreation activities have become more environmentally sensitive, or whether the general population change noted in the Decima poll reflects stronger pro-environmental views only among those who participate primarily in appreciative activities.

ENVIRONMENTAL IMPACT OF RECREATION

Wall (1989) has pointed out that the term *impact* often has negative associations and is linked in many people's minds with undesirable change. Yet, not all change is bad. Impacts are also both purposive and accidental. Many modifications to the environment occur as a result of deliberate attempts to provide positive recreation experiences. Nevertheless, when consideration is given to environmental impacts, the typical focus is upon the accidental and negative effects of an activity on the environment. Moreover, while there has been some research into the evolution, form, and structure of built recreation environments, such as tourist resorts and ski areas (e.g., Barker, 1982; Butler, 1973; Farrell & McLellan, 1987), the great bulk of the literature has dealt with impacts on the natural environment. In particular, there is a large and growing body of literature concerned with the detrimental side effects of outdoor physical recreation activities on the natural environment.

Wall (1989) has also noted that those who have attempted to study the impacts of recreation activity on the environment face many of the same problems as those concerned with other kinds of environmental impacts. "These include the problems of defining a base level against which change can be measured, of distinguishing between human-induced and natural change, of spatial and temporal discontinuities of cause and effect, and of incorporating the full complexities of direct and indirect effects" (Wall, 1989, p. 461). And some problems are peculiar to recreation, notably the difficulty of drawing generalizations about particular recreation activities (such as skiing and hiking) whose impacts are especially site-specific.

Yet, these problems notwithstanding, a great deal of research has been done, most of which falls into one of three broad categories: ex post facto descriptive studies, site monitoring, or attempts to simulate change. The great majority of studies fall into the first category, which compares recreational sites to similar sites that have not been used for recreation; the differences between the two then being ascribed to the existence of recreation activity at the former sites. Kuss and Graefe (1985), employing this approach, studied the effects of recreation trampling on natural area vegetation. Alternatively, a site previously used for recreation has been studied after recreation activities there ceased. The changes to the environment that then occur are deemed to be "natural," and the extent to which the prior condition of the site deviated from this natural state can be attributed to the recreation activity that previously occurred. Willard and Marr (1971) carried out a study of the recovery of alpine tundra at sites in Colorado's Rocky Mountains following the cessation of recreation activities. The rate and form of the recovery then became a presumed measure of the impact of the previous recreation activity.

These studies are particularly useful for identifying sites that require remedial actions. They are also relatively simple and inexpensive. Their primary limitation, however, is precisely that they are only useful after detrimental impacts have occurred: They cannot anticipate impacts or prescribe actions to avoid or alleviate them. Furthermore, these studies tend to focus principally on the environmental changes caused by particular levels of a given recreation activity; they rarely provide information about the impacts of varying types and levels of activity. Yet, as Wall aptly notes, a manager "needs both types of information if wise decisions are to be made, for both the environment and visitors are open to manipulation" (Wall, 1989, p. 463).

Monitoring studies have attempted to track the impacts of recreation activities on specific natural environments over long periods of time. Such studies can be especially useful if a site can be monitored from the day that it is first used for recreation activity. This, however, explains why such studies are very rare: They are time consuming and invariably expensive.

Simulation studies are experimental in nature. Typically, experimental and control plots are subjected to use in particular volumes and frequencies. Makhdoun and Khorasani (1988), for example, compared the relative resultant changes to understorey vegetation and soil properties from two compatible forms of land use—logging and outdoor recreation—in the Caspian forests of Northern Iran. Differences from the two land uses were measured for 36 sample plots. The degree of resistance of plants to impacts from both uses was ranked by the absence or presence of species in plots with varying intensities of use. They found, among other things, that plant cover was more seriously affected by recreation use than by logging, although different kinds of plant species were more resistant than others to both forms of use. These kinds of studies benefit considerably from measuring use and impact simultaneously. They also have the advantage that they are relatively inexpensive—at least compared to monitoring studies—and can be widened to examine recovery rates in instances where the recreation activity ceases. They are limited, however, in that they can only be applied to areas and activities that are easily controlled and where the numbers and kinds of variables involved are relatively few.

A final, important environmental impact is that of one group of recreationists on another. A great deal of research has been done on this topic. The conflicts reported are invariably the result of differences in the experiences sought by different recreationists. Groups such as snowmobilers and cross-country skiers (Jackson & Wong, 1982); sailors, motor boaters, water skiers, and fishermen (Gramman & Burdge, 1981; Owens, 1977); and hikers, trail bikers, and campers (Clark, Hendee, & Campbell, 1971) have been the subjects of major studies. The results have shown that, in general, the conflict is asymmetrical. While recreationists who have expectations of solitude and quiet, such as canoeists, resent the presence of those participating in activities that generate noise and social contact, such as motor boaters, the reverse is not the case: The motor boaters do not resent the presence of the canoeists. There have been occasions, however, where the conflicts were indeed symmetrical: The resentment of one type of recreationist for the other is reciprocated—sailors and power boaters often dislike each other (Devall & Harry, 1981).

Closely associated with the issue of conflicts between different types of recreationists is the question of crowding. Early research into crowding focused on its objective measurement. It was linked directly to the notion of carrying capacity, the idea that there is a limit to the amount of recreational use an area can sustain without adverse and irreversible effects. Social carrying capacity derived directly from biological carrying capacity. The latter is a concept employed in wildlife management to determine the numbers of a species that can populate a particular habitat on a sustained basis, given available supplies of food, water, and shelter (Dasmann, 1964). When applied to outdoor recreation management, the concept was broadened to include a social or perceptual component (Wagar, 1964). The attraction of the concept lay in its potential to indicate "how much use an area could receive before controls and limitations on use would need to be introduced" (Stankey & McCool, 1989, p. 497). At the biological level this may be relatively easy to determine, but when perceptions are included, it becomes much more difficult to determine how much is too much! The idea of social carrying capacity therefore evolved, with its emphasis not on the objective measurement of excessive use but on the subjective measurement of crowding.

Research on the topic of crowding in outdoor recreation continues. It has been recognized that an individual might perceive a certain number of people in a particular area as crowded, but not in another area (Owens, 1985). In outdoor recreation, then, crowding is defined as perceived crowding. Westover and Collins (1987) studied the factors affecting perceived crowding in an urban park in Lansing, Michigan. They found that the more familiar a person was with the park, the more perceived crowding was experienced. They also concluded that, in particular instances, crowding can have a positive connotation: "it may be that visitors who perceived the park to be generally unsafe only visited during high use times because they felt safer with many others around" (Westover & Collins, 1987, p. 95). Another study, by Shelby, Vaske, and Heberlein (1989), examined data from 35 studies previously conducted in North America and New Zealand. Fifty-nine crowding ratings were obtained from the studies. The researchers tested five hypotheses relating perceptions of crowding to (1) time and season, (2) resource abundance, or availability, (3) resource accessibility, or convenience, (4) type of use, and (5) management practices. They concluded that "as anticipated, crowding varies across settings and by time or season of use, resource abundance or availability, resource accessibility or convenience, and management actions. The type of use hypothesis (consumptive or nonconsumptive activity) was not supported by the comparative analysis" (Shelby, Vaske, & Heberlein, 1989, p. 276).

ENVIRONMENTAL MANAGEMENT FOR RECREATION

McCool (1988) has suggested that there are four alternative strategies that can be employed in the management of natural environments that are under recreation use pressures of one kind or another:

1. Do Nothing strategy.
2. Ad Hoc strategy.
3. Use-Limit strategy.
4. Decision-Making Framework.

The Do Nothing strategy is usually employed when managers wish to avoid stress and the professional or personal risks associated with more interventionist approaches. It is a strategy which may even be beneficial in the short run, but which inevitably leads to long-term problems.

The Ad Hoc strategy involves incremental decisions but with the absence of long-term goals. Again, this may be beneficial in the short term, since immediate problems are resolved, but will assuredly lead to longer-term difficulties because it fails to address underlying causal problems.

The Use-Limit approach assumes that the quality of a recreation experience has a direct and linear relationship to the numbers of recreationists in an area. For all of the reasons discussed earlier, this approach has been found wanting. The central problem, of course, lies in the perceptual component of the method. If the quality of the recreation experience at a given site is a function of the biophysical characteristics of the site and visitor perceptions, how are perceptions to be measured and operationalized as part of a management tool?

Finally, McCool's Decision-Making Framework consists of a rational strategy that provides a manager with "the route to get to a specific destination, a destination that is well described in goal statements" (McCool, 1988, p.4). The attributes of these decision-making frameworks have been described by McCool, Cole, Lucas, and Stankey (1988) as rational and systematic, explicit and defendable, adaptable, focused more on process than output, and politically viable. It is McCool's contention that recreation site managers today have little choice but to pursue these rational strategies. He notes that "all major organic legislation concerning national parks, wildernesses, and wild and scenic rivers require administering agencies to protect the values which led to designation of the unit" (McCool, 1988, p. 4). Certainly this condition would rule out the Do Nothing and Ad Hoc strategies, but it does not, per se, imply the rejection of the Use-Limit strategy. The following review will concentrate, therefore, on selected current approaches that fall within both the Use-Limit strategy and Decision-Making Framework.

Use-Limit Strategies

Two approaches in the Use-Limit category are worthy of discussion: the carrying capacity approach and the participant containment and dispersal approach.

Carrying capacity approach. The carrying capacity approach, the oldest in the Use-Limit category, was described briefly earlier in connection with the problem of perceived crowding in recreation. There are three components to the approach:

1. *Management objectives,* which serve to define what is acceptable in terms of the numbers of recreationists in an area and the levels of impact on the environment.

2. *Participant attitudes,* which seek to determine the ways in which recreationists measure the quality of their recreational experiences.

3. *Impacts on the natural environment,* which serve to show what happens to flora and fauna as a result of differing levels of recreational use.

The carrying capacity approach requires that these three components be employed iteratively and interactively: For example, "objectives founded without any knowledge of visitor attitudes probably stand little chance of being met" (Stankey & McCool, 1989, p. 499).

The principal disadvantages of the carrying capacity approach to recreation area management are threefold. First, it assumes that the biological capacity of an area is discrete and singular. But, since carrying capacity changes considerably with a wide range of variables (such as slope and climate), the idea that an area will have a single biological carrying capacity is untenable. Second, the approach focuses on physical and biological capacities rather than social-psychological ones, even though it seeks to incorporate participant attitudes. Third, it tends to submerge technical and scientific issues within normative and value questions. The issue of "how much is too much" is ultimately a value judgment, and "while managers play a key role in resolving it, their technical expertise is no greater credential for settling what is fundamentally a value judgment than are the values, preferences, and expectations of their clients" (Stankey & McCool, 1989, p. 502).

Participant containment and dispersal approach. The second approach in the Use-Limit category is the participant containment and dispersal approach. Marion and Sober (1987), discussing the Boundary Waters Canoe Area wilderness, noted many adverse impacts of recreational use on the environment localized on trails and at campsites. They suggested that many of these localized areas could be rehabilitated, and future adverse effects limited, by the use of participant containment and dispersal strategies. Participant containment reduces the numbers of trails and campsites available and controls their location. Participant dispersal, on the other hand, requires that recreationists be directed to sites that have little or no evidence of previous use. Marion and Sober suggest that either approach can be effective, depending on the nature of the area to be managed. Heavily used areas would most likely be better managed through containment, while remote or low-use areas would likely be best served by a dispersal scheme. The Boundary Waters Canoe Area wilderness was one of the first in which a containment strategy was attempted. It was found that success is heavily dependent upon "adequate information being given to the visitor before the trip, solidly marked campsites, a reliable travel mode, campsite impact monitoring, and a rehabilitation program to assure that the effects of use on campsites do not exceed acceptable limits" (Marion & Sober, 1987, p. 8). There are, of course, unanswered questions. How much resource manipulation, for example, is justified to restore natural conditions? And what techniques are appropriate? Does participant dispersal serve only to distribute impacts throughout a greater proportion of the area, as has been claimed by critics? There is also the fundamental problem of determining what constitutes an unacceptable level of impact on a trail or campsite. The same issues of measurement that pertain to the carrying capacity approach are also pertinent. In particular, one must ask how important the biological and physical measures of impacts are relative to social-psychological ones.

Decision-Making Frameworks

As recreation planning developed in the 1960s and 1970s, it was generally assumed that a recreation opportunity could be defined simply as the provision of the facilities and services that would make it possible for an individual to participate in a given recreation activity. As a result, land classification systems, such as the Canada Land Inventory, classified land areas in terms of their potential to support particular recreation activities or classes of recreation activities. Later research, however, led to the development of a behavioral definition of recreation opportunity that sees an opportunity as a product of both the management of resources and facilities and the desired services of recreationists. This definition has three dimensions—behavior, setting, and experience. Specifically, a recreation opportunity is defined as "an opportunity to engage in a preferred activity, such as hiking; in a preferred setting, such as a remote area; to realize desired experiences, such as physical exercise, isolation, and nature appreciation" (Driver & Brown, 1987). This led, in time, to the development of the Recreation Opportunity Spectrum (ROS) approach to the management of recreation sites, as well as multiple-use areas which include recreation (Driver, Brown, Stankey, & Gregoire, 1987; Manning, 1986; U.S. Department of Agriculture, 1982). This approach has been adopted by two major federal land management agencies in the United States—the Forest Service and the Bureau of Land Management.

ROS framework. The ROS framework is concerned only with those kinds of recreation experiences that are directly dependent upon a specific kind of relationship between activity and setting (e.g., hiking in the wilderness). It does not address aspects of experience that are not interdependent in this way (e.g., watching television at home). The resources in the areas controlled by the U.S. Forest Service and the U.S. Bureau of Land Management have been considered in the context of the ROS system and subsequently organized into a continuum of six classes, ranging from the primitive to the urban: primitive; semi-primitive non-motorized; semi-primitive motorized; roaded natural; rural; and urban. Each of these resource classifications provides an array of recreation opportunities (Virden & Knopf, 1988). A primitive area might, for example, provide a hiker with an opportunity to experience physical exercise in isolation, a canoeist with an opportunity to experience communion with nature, and a painter with an opportunity to experience a sense of supreme creativity.

Since the Forest Service and the Bureau of Land Management oversee a majority of the public lands in the United States, their use of the ROS system has enormous practical implications. The validity of the tenets that underlie the ROS system is, therefore, a matter of great concern to researchers and managers alike. These are receiving increasing scrutiny. At the heart of the system is its assumption about the relationships between environmental settings, recreation activities, and psychological experiences. Yuan and McEwen (1989) have examined the validity of the assumption that recreationists "in different types of settings have a high probability of realizing different types of experiences," while Virden and Knopf (1988) tested the validity of the relationships between measures of desired experience, measures of preferred recreation activity, and measures of relative preference for six ROS-defined environmental settings. The former study concluded that the validity of the assumption is unclear. The latter showed that recreation activity preference is not independent of environmental setting and that, while there is a link between desired experience and environmental setting, the nature of the relationship is not simple. Manning (1985) addressed a different aspect of the system, suggesting ways in which it could be extended to include unconventional opportunities (what he calls "outliers"), such as a Grand Hotel in a national park or a Wilderness Fort in an urban resort.

By its nature, the ROS system is an unfinished product. Its central proposition—that a recreation opportunity must be defined by reference to preferred activities in preferred settings that lead to desired experiences—has changed considerably the nature and focus of environmental management for recreation. The particular assumptions that have sprung from this proposition will no doubt be tested, rejected, refined, and amended as research efforts expand. In the meantime, its application in areas owned and managed by the Forest Service and the

Bureau of Land Management provides exceptional opportunities to study its practical effectiveness.

Limits of acceptable change system. Whereas the carrying capacity approach noted earlier is concerned with the question "how much is too much?" the Limits of Acceptable Change (LAC) system aims at determining overall desired conditions, including both the state of the resource base and the nature of the recreation experience. The basic premise underlying the system is that change is a natural and inevitable consequence of recreation activity. The level of acceptable change then becomes a matter for judgment. The system employs technical, quantitative information, but as an aid to decision making, not as the determinant of decisions.

The Limits of Acceptable Change planning system is exactly what it purports to be—a process for planning a recreation area or site. The process consists of nine steps, including the identification of issues and concerns by both managers and users, a statement of indicators of desired, general well-being, an inventory of existing resources to determine the extent to which current conditions deviate from the desired ones, the derivation of standards, the specification of alternative, appropriate management actions, evaluation of alternatives, and the implementation of chosen alternatives. The system is currently being applied to recreation area management in the United States, but it is too early to judge its success.

Even though one cannot yet assess the overall utility of the Limits of Acceptable Change system, McCool (1988) has made some observations about the system based upon its early application to the Bob Marshall Wilderness Complex in the United States. He stated, first, that because planning occurs in a political context, it is essential that users and the general public become involved in the process in an interactive rather than a reactive manner. Second, managers must be convinced that they will likely be better off with the process than without it; otherwise, they will have no incentive to commit themselves to its successful application. Third, while the different types and large amounts of technical information required for the application of the process may appear daunting, it is important to present this information in a nonthreatening manner which is easily understood by lay managers and the public.

CONCLUSION

Active living describes the integration of physical activity into everyday life. It seeks to include not only activities traditionally associated with exercise and fitness, but also unstructured, unregulated activities, such as walking the dog. It emphasizes the place of physical activity in the things that people do almost as a matter of routine as well as those that are specifically chosen for their exercise value. It encompasses physical activities done at home, in the workplace, at school, and in a wide variety of recreation sites as well as those that take place in gymnasiums and sports facilities. Not surprisingly, then, active living has strong associations with physical recreation. But while various kinds of physical recreation activity have always been linked to fitness, far more are connected with active living. It is, in fact, through physical recreation that one can examine the relationships between active living and the environment.

The term *environment* embraces a wide array of ideas. It cries out for a qualifying adjective! Perceived as the sum of the conditions which infuse and shape our lives, it has physical, biological, social, political, economic, religious, technological, architectural, and many other dimensions. To consider the relationships between physical recreation and all of these dimensions of the environment would be an impossible task. However, the overwhelming majority of research that has considered the relationships between physical recreation and the environment has focused upon the natural, nonurban environment. We have reviewed this research under three broad headings: environmental attitudes and, in particular, the ways in which these are expressed through participation in different kinds of physical recreation activities; the impacts of different kinds of physical recreation activities on the natural environment; and the nature and characteristics of alternative approaches to the management of the natural environment for physical recreation.

Considering the empirical literature simply as a set of research studies undifferentiated as to time, concepts, and methodological quality leads to the conclusion that research has been unable to demonstrate a consistent positive association between participation in physical (outdoor) recreation activities and favorable environmental attitudes. Many studies have found that recreationists who participate in appreciative and self-propelled activities, such as hiking, photography, and cross-country skiing, have a greater concern for the natural environment than those who participate in motorized and consumptive activities, such as hunting, snowmobiling, and downhill skiing. But these findings account for only very small variations in environmental attitudes. If, on the other hand, one views the literature as evidence of an increasing sophistication in conceptualization, operationalization, and research design, then it can be argued that research has demonstrated a closer relationship than is apparent from the body of literature as a whole.

While, in most instances, very little (typically, less than 5 percent) of the variation between the two groups in levels of concern for the environment can be explained by differences in levels and types of outdoor recreation participation, it is evident that Jackson's ecocentrists, moderate ecocentrists, moderate technocentrists, and technocentrists do, indeed, exist—even if differences in their respective attitudes toward the natural environment are only partially linked to their choice of physical recreation activities.

It has become increasingly evident during the past two decades or so that physical recreation activities can and do have detrimental impacts on the natural environment. While many recreation activities are fully compatible with the maintenance of environmental quality, others are clearly not, and still others may be benign or malignant depending upon such things as the numbers of people participating at particular times in specific places. Studies of the impacts of physical recreation activities on the natural environment blossomed during the 1970s and 1980s. Yet, there is much that remains unknown. The term *impact* begs the question "on what?" While some research has attempted to consider impacts upon ecosystems as a whole, most has examined impacts on particular components of an ecosystem, such as soils and vegetation, air quality, water quality, and wildlife populations. Descriptive and simulation studies have both demonstrated that hiking can have deleterious effects upon natural area vegetation, while large-scale developments for recreation, such as downhill ski resorts, can dramatically change the numbers and "lifestyles" of wildlife populations. It is clear that while, in most instances, the impacts of recreation activity on the environment are individually small, taken cumulatively they can result in relatively large environmental changes. Most recreationists are sociable; even in the wilderness, they are usually concentrated in a relatively small area. As a result, their impacts, too, are concentrated. These impacts modify the environment. Recreationists clearly accept—perhaps sometimes even welcome—environmental modification. What is not yet clear is the point at which the modification of an environment as a result of recreation activity becomes perceived as the deterioration of that environment.

Environmental attitudes and impacts are the bases for the development of environmental management processes and tools. For many years, research into environmental management for physical recreation derived almost exclusively from the impacts side. Approaches such as social carrying capacity were based upon the assumption that the biological capacity of a recreation area is discrete and singular. In practice, the approach was employed by defining a physical and biological capacity and setting limits on the types and levels of recreation activity that would not contravene these limits. The containment and dispersal approach, too, was based, in the final instance, on biological measures of impacts. Only with the advent of the Recreation Opportunity Spectrum approach was a serious attempt made to give equal consideration to both the biological resources (setting and characteristics) and the recreation activity (behavior and experience). The Limits of Acceptable Change approach then took this notion further by setting out to determine, by means of judgment rather than measurement, the acceptable levels of environmental change resulting from recreation activity. In so doing, it was really addressing the earlier question: How much can an environment be modified through recreation activity before the level of modification is perceived as an unacceptable deterioration of that environment?

Some glaring omissions occur in the research on the relationships between physical recreation activity and the environment. For one thing, research has very largely ignored built recreation environments: sports halls, multipurpose fitness centers, domed stadiums, indoor ice arenas, downhill ski resorts, and more. There is a substantial volume of work on spas (e.g., Lawrence, 1983; Patmore, 1968; Wightman & Wall, 1985), tourist areas (e.g., Butler, 1987; Hovinen, 1981; Meyer-Arendt, 1985), and ski resorts (e.g., Barker, 1982), but it focuses more on the cycle of development of such places than on the interactions between participants and their environments.

A more significant omission is the failure to look closely at both sides of the relationship between recreation participation and the environment. When considering impacts, the focus has always been upon the effects of physical recreation activities on natural environments. Reverse effects—the impacts of particular natural environments on recreation activities—have been conspicuously absent from the research. Yet, there clearly are such impacts. In fact, this is one area where studies of built environments have progressed further. Shields (1992), for example, has studied the effects of large-scale shopping malls—now known as megamalls—on social spatialization. These privately owned "public" spaces are hybrid creations, incorporating shops, restaurants, offices, and a wide array of recreation facilities and services. The largest of these malls, West Edmonton Mall in Edmonton, Canada, houses 825 stores, a 15-acre indoor fairground, a 2.5-acre indoor lake, an 18-hole minigolf course, a 10-acre water park complete with water slides and 6-foot-high artificial waves, a full-size ice arena, and more. The success of the mall flies in the face of all accepted marketing wisdom. Shields argues that the sheer scale of the mall (4.5 million square feet covering about 20 square city blocks), together with the dazzling array of facilities, services, and streetscapes, encourages users to leave behind the "real world" of order and structure in favor of a fantasy world. Indeed, the indoor fairground is called Fantasyland (although this will change as a result of a successful court action by the Walt Disney Company in 1994, which claimed that the choice of name infringed its copyright). Postmodernists argue that the mall offers fantasy and carnival as a break from the repetitive routines of everyday life. In sum, the mall creates a condition that Shields calls carnivalesque, "the inversion of social norms and codes within the spaces of everyday life" (Shields, 1992, p. 8). Like Disneyland, West Edmonton Mall offers illusion and fantasy through recreation and shopping. The built environment dramatically influences not only the form of recreation activity, but also its meaning and spirit.

Given the lessons beginning to emerge from built environments such as Disneyland and West Edmonton Mall (see, for example, the special edition of the *Canadian Geographer* edited by Jackson and Johnson in 1991), it would be instructive to consider the effects of other kinds of both built and natural environments on the forms and experiences of physical recreation. For example, how is the nature of the physical recreation experience different for the activity of swimming in a waterpark, a wave-pool, a conventional public pool, at a beach, and in a private pool at home? How does the experience of hiking change from an urban river valley trail to an improved trail in a national park to a wilderness track? What effects do these different environments have on the nature of the participants' experiences?

In the end, the most significant point that can be made about the relationships between physical recreation and the natural environment lies in the connection of each to the wider concepts of active living and sustainable living. The latter are not separate and discrete notions, but part of something much larger called quality of life. Human well-being and the welfare of the natural environment are inextricably linked; research into both areas should be similarly integrated.

ACKNOWLEDGMENTS

The author is indebted to Drs. E.L. Jackson and G. Wall for their published reviews of research on "Environmental Attitudes, Values, and Recreation" and "Perspectives on Recreation and the Environment," previously referenced. While several research reviews have been cited here, these two were especially valuable to the present work. As well, the author would like to thank E.L. Jackson, D. Whitson, and C. Coburn for their comments on an earlier draft of the chapter.

REFERENCES

Barker, M.L. (1982). Beach pollution in the Toronto region. In W.R.D. Sewell & I. Burton (Eds.), *Perceptions and attitudes in resources management* (pp. 37-47). Ottawa: Department of Energy, Mines and Resources.

Bella, L. (1987). *Parks for profit*. Montreal: Harvest House.

Black, J.S., Stern, P., & Elworth, J.T. (1985). Personal and contextual influences on household energy adaptations. *Journal of Applied Psychology, 70*, 3-21.

Boulding, K.E. (1970). The economics of the coming spaceship Earth. In G. De Bell (Ed.), *The environmental handbook*. New York: Ballantine.

Burton, T.L. (1972). *Natural resource policy in Canada*. Toronto: McClelland & Stewart.

Butler, J.R. & Fenton, G.D. (1987). Bird watchers of Point Pelee National Park, Canada: Their characteristics and activities, with special reference to social and resource considerations. *Alberta Naturalist, 17*, 135-146.

Butler, R.W. (1973). The social impact of tourism. *Proceedings of the 6th International Congress of Speleology VII*, Fc, 139-146.

Butler, R.W. (1987). Tourism and heritage use and conservation. In R.C. Scace & J.G. Nelson (Eds.), *Heritage for tomorrow* (Vol. 5). Ottawa: Supply and Services Canada.

Buttell, F.H. (1987). New directions in environmental sociology. *Annual Review of Sociology, 13*, 465-488.

Catton, W.R., Jr. & Dunlap, R.E. (1978). Environmental sociology: A new paradigm. *American Sociology, 13*, 41-49.

Chant, D.A. (Ed.). (1970). *Pollution probe*. Toronto: New Press.

Clark, R.N., Hendee, J.C., & Campbell, F.L. (1971). Values, behavior, and conflict in modern camping culture. *Journal of Leisure Research, 3*, 143-159.

Dasmann, R.F. (1964). *Wildlife biology*. New York: Wiley.

Devall, B. & Harry, J. (1981). Who hates whom in the great outdoors: The impact of recreation specialization and technologies of play. *Leisure Sciences, 4*, 399-418.

Driver, B.L. & Brown, P.J. (1987). Probable personal benefits of outdoor recreation. *President's Commission on Americans Outdoors: A literature review* (pp. 63-70). Washington, DC: U.S. Government Printing Office.

Driver, B.L., Brown, P.J., Stankey, G.H., & Gregoire, T.G. (1987). The ROS planning system: Evolution, basic concepts, and research needed. *Leisure Sciences, 9*, 201-212.

Dunlap, R.E. & Heffernan, R.B. (1975). Outdoor recreation and environmental concern: An empirical examination. *Rural Sociology, 40*, 18-30.

Dunlap, R.E. & Van Liere, K.D. (1978). The "new environmental paradigm." *Journal of Environmental Education, 9*, 10-19.

Dunlap, R.E. & Van Liere, K.D. (1984). Commitment to the dominant social paradigm and concern for environmental quality. *Social Science Quarterly, 65*, 1013-1028.

Dustin, D.L. & McAvoy, L.H. (1980). Hardening national parks. *Environmental Ethics, 2*, 39-44.

Dustin, D.L. & McAvoy, L.H. (1982). The decline and fall of quality recreation opportunities and environments? *Environmental Ethics, 4*, 49-57.

Farrell, B. & McLellan, R.W. (1987). Tourism and physical environment research. *Annals of Tourism Research, 14*, 1-16.

Fitness Canada. (1988). *Fitness . . . the future.* Ottawa: Fitness and Amateur Sport Canada.

Fitness and Amateur Sport Canada. (1992). *Active living: A conceptual overview.* Ottawa: Government of Canada.

Geisler, C.C., Martinson, O.B., & Wilkening, E.A. (1977). Outdoor recreation and environmental concern: Are-study. *Rural Sociology, 42*, 241-249.

Graf, W.L. (1976). Resources, the environment, and the American experience. *Journal of Geography, 1*, 28-41.

Gramman, J.H. & Burdge, R.J. (1981). The effect of recreational goals on conflict perception: The case of water skiers and fishermen. *Journal of Leisure Research, 13*, 15-27.

Gregg, A. & Posner, M. (1990). *The big picture.* Toronto: MacFarlane, Walter and Ross.

Heberlein, T.A. & Warriner, G.K. (1983). The influence of price and attitude on shifting residential electricity consumption from on- to off-peak periods. *Journal of Economic Psychology, 4*, 107-130.

Hovinen, G. (1981). A tourist cycle in Lancaster County, Pennsylvania. *Canadian Geographer, 25*, 283-285.

Jackson, E.L. (1986). Outdoor recreation participation and attitudes to the environment. *Leisure Sciences, 8*, 1-23.

Jackson, E.L. (1987). Outdoor recreation participation and views on resource development and preservation. *Leisure Sciences, 9*, 235-250.

Jackson, E.L. (1989a). Environmental attitudes, values, and recreation. In E.L. Jackson & T.L. Burton (Eds.), *Understanding leisure and recreation: Mapping the past, charting the future* (pp. 357-383). State College, PA: Venture Publishing.

Jackson, E.L. (1989b). Public views about resource development and preservation: Results from an Alberta study. *Canadian Geographer, 32*, 163-168.

Jackson, E.L. & Johnson, D.B. (Eds.). (1991). The West Edmonton Mall and mega-malls (Feature issue). *Canadian Geographer, 35*, 3.

Jackson, E.L. & Wong, R. (1982). Perceived conflict between urban cross-country skiers and snowmobilers in Alberta. *Journal of Leisure Research, 14*, 47-62.

Knopp, T.B. & Tyger, J.D. (1973). A study of conflict in recreational land use: Snowmobiling versus ski-touring. *Journal of Leisure Research, 5*, 6-17.

Kuss, F.R. & Graefe, A.R. (1985). Effects of recreation trampling on natural area vegetation. *Journal of Leisure Research, 17*, 165-183.

Lawrence, H.W. (1983). Southern spas: Source of the American resort tradition. *Landscape, 27*, 1-12.

Makhdoun, M.F. & Khorasani, N. (1988). Differences between environmental impacts of logging and recreation in mature forest ecosystems. *Environmental Conservation, 15*, 137-144.

Manning, R.E. (1986). Diversity in a democracy: Expanding the recreation opportunity spectrum. *Leisure Sciences, 7*, 377-399.

Marion, J.L. & Sober, T. (1987). Environmental impact management in the Boundary Waters Canoe Area wilderness. *Northern Journal of Applied Forestry, 4*, 7-11.

McCool, S.F. (1988). Experiencing management for quality: Implementing the Limits of Acceptable Change planning system. In S.F. McCool (compiler). *Application of the Limits of Acceptable Change planning system*. Missoula, MT: University of Montana.

McCool, S.F., Cole, D.N., Lucas, R.C., & Stankey, G.H. (1988). Maintaining wilderness quality through the Limits of Acceptable Change planning system. In S.F. McCool (compiler). *Application of the Limits of Acceptable Change planning system*. Missoula, MT: University of Montana.

McFarland, E.M. (1970). *The development of public recreation in Canada*. Ottawa: Canadian Parks/Recreation Association.

Meller, H.E. (1976). *Leisure and the changing city, 1870-1914*. London: Routledge & Kegan Paul.

Meyer-Arendt, K.J. (1985). The Grand Isle, Louisiana resort cycle. *Annals of Tourism Research, 12*, 449-466.

Minister of State for Fitness and Amateur Sport. (1979). *Toward a national policy on fitness and recreation*. Ottawa: Supply and Services Canada.

O'Riordan, T. (1981). *Environmentalism* (2nd ed.). London: Pion.

Owens, P.L. (1977). Recreational conflict: The interaction of Norfolk Broads coarse anglers and boat users. In J. Alabaster (Ed.), *Recreational freshwater fisheries: Their conservation, management and development*. Stevenage: Water Research Centre.

Owens, P.L. (1985). Conflict as social interaction process in environmental and behaviour research: The example of leisure and recreation research. *Journal of Environmental Psychology, 5*, 243-259.

Patmore, J.A. (1968). Spa towns in Britain. In R.P. Beckinsale & J.M. Houston (Eds.), *Urbanization and its problems* (pp. 47-69). Oxford: Blackwell.

Perdue, R.P. & Warder, D.S. (1981). Environmental education and attitude change. *Journal of Environmental Education, 12*, 25-29.

Pinhey, T.K. & Grimes, M.D. (1979). Outdoor recreation and environmental concern: A re-examination of the Dunlap-Heffernan thesis. *Leisure Sciences, 2*, 1-11.

Russell, M. (1979). Conflicting perceptions of energy's future role. In S.H. Schurr, J. Darmstadter, W. Ramsay, H. Perry, & M. Russell (Eds.), *Energy in America's future: The choices before us* (pp. 401-408). Baltimore: Johns Hopkins Press.

Schreyer, R. & Driver, B.L. (1989). The benefits of leisure. In E.L. Jackson & T.L. Burton (Eds.), *Understanding leisure and recreation: Mapping the past, charting the future* (pp. 385-419). State College, PA: Venture Publishing.

Shelby, B., Vaske, J.J., & Heberlein, T.A. (1989). Comparative analysis of crowding in multiple locations: Results from fifteen years of research. *Leisure Sciences, 11*, 269-291.

Shields, R. (1992). Spaces for the subject of consumption. In R. Shields (Ed.), *Lifestyle shopping: The subject of consumption* (pp. 1-20). London: Routledge & Kegan Paul.

Sonnenfeld, J. (1968). *Geography, perception, and the behavioral environment*. Paper presented to the American Association for the Advancement of Science, Dallas.

Stankey, G.H. & McCool, S.F. (1989). Beyond social carrying capacity. In E.L. Jackson & T.L. Burton (Eds.), *Understanding leisure and recreation: Mapping the past, charting the future* (pp. 497-516). State College, PA: Venture Publishing.

Stephens, T. & Craig, C.L. (1990). *The well-being of Canadians*. Ottawa: Canadian Fitness and Lifestyle Research Institute.

Stern, P.C. (1986). Blind spots in policy analysis: What economics doesn't say about energy use. *Journal of Political Analysis Management, 5*, 200-227.

Stern, P.C., Dietz, T., & Black, J.S. (1986). *Public support for environmental protection: The role of moral norms*. Washington, DC: National Research Council.

Swinnerton, G.S. (1989). Recreation and conservation. In E.L. Jackson & T.L. Burton (Eds.), *Understanding leisure and recreation: Mapping the past, charting the future* (pp. 517-566). State College, PA: Venture Publishing.

Thorpe, F.J. (1961). Historical perspective on the Resources for Tomorrow Conference. *Resources for Tomorrow Conference background papers* (vol. 1). Ottawa: Queen's Printer.

United States Department of Agriculture. (1982). *ROS users guide*. Washington, DC: United States Department of Agriculture, Forest Service.

Van Liere, K.D. & Noe, F.P. (1981). Outdoor recreation and environmental attitudes: Further examination of the Dunlap-Heffernan thesis. *Rural Sociology, 46*, 505-513.

Virden, R.J. & Knopf, R.C. (1988). Activities, experiences, and environmental settings: A case study of the recreation opportunity spectrum. *Leisure Sciences, 11*, 159-176.

Wagar, J.A. (1964). The carrying capacity of wildlands for recreation. *Forest Science Monograph, 7*. Washington, DC: Society of American Foresters.

Wall, G. (1989). Perspectives on recreation and the environment. In E.L. Jackson & T.L. Burton (Eds.), *Understanding leisure and recreation: Mapping the past, charting the future* (pp. 453-480). State College, PA: Venture Publishing.

Walsh, R.G., Bjonback, R.D., Aiken, R.A., & Rosenthal, D.H. (1990). Estimating the public benefits of protecting forest quality. *Journal of Environmental Management, 30*, 175-189.

Westover, T.N. & Collins, J.R., Jr. (1987). Perceived crowding in recreation settings: An urban case study. *Leisure Sciences, 9*, 87-99.

Wightman, D. & Wall, G. (1985). The spa experience at Radium Hot Springs. *Annals of Tourism Research, 12*, 393-416.

Willard, D.E. & Marr, J.W. (1971). Recovery of alpine tundra under protection after damage by human activities in the Rocky Mountains of Colorado. *Biological Conservation, 3*, 181-190.

World Commission on Environment and Development. (1987). *Our common future*. Oxford: Oxford University Press.

Yuan, M.S. & McEwen, D. (1989). Test for camper's experience preference differences among three ROS setting classes. *Leisure Sciences, 11*, 177-185.

CLOSING REMARKS: PROGRESS, POTENTIAL, AND PROBLEMS IN THE HOLISTIC STUDY OF PHYSICAL ACTIVITY

James E. Curtis
and Barry D. McPherson

It would be presumptuous to conclude this volume by attempting to summarize in a few pages the very rich contribution of the seven foregoing chapters. The authors have been generous in providing information and insights on physical activity drawn from each of seven research perspectives. Their contributions stand on their own, and we won't oversimplify them here. However, we would like to conclude with some general observations on the progress, prospects, and potential problems of multidisciplinary (i.e., multifield) and interdisciplinary (interfield) studies of physical activity.

A HOLISTIC APPROACH

This book makes it abundantly clear that the study of human physical activity is most instructive from a *multidisciplinary* approach. To say that much would be lost if we used any sort of narrower perspective for our readings would be an understatement. We can readily see that much valuable knowledge would be left out if a strictly biological or physiological account of physical activity were adopted. The same holds true for one that is strictly psychological, social psychological, sociological, cultural, environmental, or economic. Nothing short of a fully multidisciplinary approach can convey a clear understanding of physical activity.

The importance of an *interdisciplinary* approach is demonstrated by the fact that, in seeking explanations for physical activity phenomena, none of the contributors limits his or her discussion to the central subject matter and disciplinary boundaries typically observed within a given field. For example, the sociologist Nancy Theberge looks to cultural studies for much of her interpretive material; the physical scientist Claude Bouchard looks to social psychology and sociobiology for some explanations; and the psychologist Mihaly Csikszentmihalyi emphasizes sociological and social psychological processes and the physical environment, while explaining the psychology of activity.

The value the contributors place on interdisciplinary work is apparent from their chapters. Each chapter clearly demonstrates that a good deal of important interdisciplinary work exists related to the authors' respective areas of study; each presents material that "links" physical phenomena on the one hand and psychological, social, cultural, or environmental phenomena on the other. The chapters show that individual levels of physical activity, and thinking processes concerning activity, are shaped by physical, social, cultural, and environmental processes. At the same time, individuals create group life and culture and shape environments. All of these phenomena are part of a *whole cloth of human movement in sociocultural and environmental context.*

The linking processes specified in the chapters may be said to be the essence of interdisciplinary studies. It is here that the phenomena of the different fields of study come together or influence each other. It is this that makes it impossible for people in one field of study to ignore the work of those in other fields for very long. If such linking processes could not be shown to occur, and thereby did not improve our understanding of physical activity phenomena, then all we need to have available to us is multidisciplinary research. That is, we would have reason to be content with a situation where studies are done from the narrower point of view of one specific discipline or the other and then set side by side for us to read and contemplate. Of course, our contributors have done this to some degree as a result of their seven specific sets of tasks, but they also go beyond this to describe linking analyses.

POTENTIALS OF A HOLISTIC APPROACH

We believe that these linking processes, and further research on them, represent one of the major future potentials of a holistic study of physical activity. By "potentials" we do not mean to imply that the future of holistic studies is in doubt. This kind of approach has already led to the insights described in this volume, and further similar yields are sure to follow because of the extensive development and acceptance of a holistic approach and its organizational base in various multidiscipline university departments, multidiscipline journals, and multidiscipline literature data bases (Glassford, 1992; Landry, 1992).

To describe the linking mechanisms suggested by the authors, we must briefly discuss the alternative levels of analysis included in the chapters. The materials make it clear that physical activity (indeed, human life in general) can be analyzed from a number of different research perspectives. Because of the extreme complexity of human life, we normally try to describe or understand it from a particular perspective, as our chapter authors have done; in other words, we "cut into" the complexity from some angle of observation. While there are many disciplines and angles of observation represented in the book, they can be reduced to five distinct perspectives: physical, psychological, social, cultural, and environmental (Bouchard, 1992; Gauvin, Wall, & Quinney, 1994). At the same time, physical activity—indeed all of human existence—must be conceptualized as a single, unified whole, because all aspects of the ongoing process of human life are to some extent interrelated.

• A *physical perspective* focuses on the biological features of human life and views individuals primarily as organisms. Medical practice provides a good example of this perspective. Much of a physician's training involves studying the body as a biological and physical organism, and not as something belonging to a particular set of social relationships or a social group, and with culture definitions to it. Other examples may be found in the research work of physiologists and biologists. Bouchard's chapter describes such research, although his own analyses in the chapter range beyond purely biological and physiological considerations.

• A *psychological perspective* focuses on thoughts, perceptions, cognition, and human behavior. Individuals are studied as minds or personalities. This perspective predominates, for example, in research on attitudes towards physical activity, where one set of attitudes or beliefs might be correlated with certain behaviors and/or another set of attitudes and beliefs, and in the study of psychological aspects of adherence to physical activity, as described in Wankel's chapter. *Social psychological* research typically moves beyond the focus on individuals' minds or personalities, as in studies of relationships between aspects of the group or cultural environment and people's thinking about physical activity.

The chapters by Professors Csikszentmihalyi and Wankel report on both types of research.

- A *social relationships perspective* focuses on the interpersonal aspects of human life and studies individuals primarily as members of social relationships or social groups. Also, the object of study can be the relationships or groups themselves. Examples of this include studies of power structures in sport and physical activity which show that men—more so than women—have been involved in organizing, and in benefiting from, the community's opportunities for recreational or elite sport involvement. The chapters by Theberge and Russell, on the sociology and economics of physical activity, provide examples of the application of this perspective. Russell focuses on those social relationships that may be said to have an "economic" component of costs and benefits, whereas Theberge deals with issues of power and inequality in social relations.

- A *cultural perspective* focuses on the symbolic meanings in human life and regards individuals primarily as creators and carriers of shared cultural ideas. The meanings themselves, and their consequences, often become the focus of study. This perspective informs the study of the meanings we attach to physical activity, the body, or fitness, and how these meanings change over time and differ across subcultures. The chapter by Gruneau exemplifies this approach. The material on the sociology of the body presented by Theberge is also representative of this approach.

- An *environmental perspective* focuses on the physical environment and the way it constrains and shapes individuals' activities, and, at the same time, is altered by that activity. Burton's chapter gives myriad examples of this research approach, and Russell's describes others.

All five of these perspectives on human life are constructed, in the sense that they are intellectual abstractions imposed upon ongoing processes of human life by the researcher or observer. Nonetheless, the distinctions among them are not arbitrary. These perspectives on human life have been used by scholars throughout much of intellectual history, and provide the foundation for different analyses of human experience. Each perspective suggests a different set of questions to be asked, problems to be investigated, and theoretical explanations to be formulated.

The five types of analysis—physical, psychological, social, cultural, and environmental—may be said to represent increasing degrees of separation or independence from the physical body and physical activity in the biological sense. The social psychological, social, cultural, and environmental perspectives are not necessarily more conceptually abstract, or complex, than the physical perspective. Rather, the social psychological, social, and cultural life are somewhat less directly related to the physical/biological body than are physical phenomena. At the same time, social psychological, social, and cultural phenomena presuppose the existence of physical beings.

The order in which the levels of analysis are discussed does not imply that one level of analysis or type of study is more basic or more important for learning about physical activity; rather, each level of phenomena is dependent upon the existence of the others. Neither does the ordering mean that the levels increase in abstraction in a particular direction. All the levels involve abstraction.

On the issue of links or relationships between the levels of analysis, we can see that they are interrelated in at least three ways: by emergence, independence, and constraint. These relationships are suggested by the preceding chapters and in the general literature as well.

• *Emergence* refers to the observation that each successively higher level of analysis develops out of the level immediately preceding it and is always dependent to some extent on all lower levels. That is to say, (a) personalities develop only in conjunction with organic life and cannot survive if the organism dies, (b) social relationships occur only when two or more personalities interact and cease to exist when all of their members withdraw either psychologically or physically, (c) cultures are outgrowths of social activities and become mere relics when the people and groups that created them or the individuals who carry them disappear, and (d) environments for physical activities are shaped by social activity and the culture they generate.

• *Independence* refers to the observation that each level of phenomena, although emergent from those below it, nevertheless possesses some degree of autonomy. Phenomena at each level have characteristics uniquely their own, which are not fully determined by the lower levels. It is impossible to explain any given level solely in terms of those below it; the properties of the prior phenomena do not sufficiently explain the emergent phenomena. A person doing physical activity is something more than just an acting organism; a sport or exercise group is something more than just several interacting personalities; and shared ideas about activity, health, and exercise (i.e., culture) or a physical environment are more than just reflections of society.

• The concept of *constraint* refers to the observation that each successively higher level of analysis, by virtue of its partial independence, can and frequently does influence the lower levels from which it emerged, even though it could not exist alone. In other words, influences between levels of analysis seem to be interactive and reciprocal. For example, people's self-efficacy for exercise and their exercise intentions affect their physical activity levels and, in turn, their increased involvement in physical activity affects their self-efficacy for exercise and their exercise intentions. Subcultures or communities both impose many constraints upon the actions of their members and provide for their psychological and material needs. At the same time, the sustenance needs and personality characteristics of individuals continually affect the nature and scope of community activities. At the cultural level, beliefs and ideas can shape societies, change personalities, and affect people's beliefs while concurrently reflecting the social life, personality structures, and organic characteristics of their proponents.

Because relatively little research has been done on the linkages between the levels of analysis, our understanding is necessarily general and somewhat vague (Turner, 1991, chapter 32). It is not yet clear, for example, what *other* patterns of linkage occur. Consequently, there is enormous potential for important contributions to be made, both in physical activity studies and in disciplinary and interdisciplinary research more generally. In this regard, few interdisciplinary areas of study offer the breadth of perspectives and the extent of development of interdisciplinary research that one finds in physical activity studies. Thus, the area is well-positioned to produce conceptual refinements around the linkages of levels of analysis. We must expect to see major contributions to the linkage question from the physical activity sciences in the future.

The relationships between levels of analyses that we have just listed do not, of course, constitute a systematic *theory* of physical activity, encompassing biological, social, and cultural phenomena. Indeed, a general theory for the physical activity sciences has not yet been developed, as has been noted by each of the seven chapters in this volume. Whether more effort should be directed toward developing a *general* theory of physical activity that addresses its many aspects and all levels of analyses simultaneously is debatable. It can be argued that the more abstract, general, or all-encompassing a given theoretical approach, the greater the risk that important details of another discipline's research findings will be overlooked. Thus, we suggest that while more work is needed on linkages, and on interdisciplinary research more generally, priority be given to establishing how specific phenomena at one analytic level are related to specific phenomena at other levels. Accumulated study of this sort may lead to the development of a general theory. However, because such a theory would likely be formulated at a high level of abstraction, it may well have limited utility for understanding physical activity in its many manifestations, or for providing specific direction for further research and practice. A more useful approach may be to recognize the great sweep and complexity of physical activity in human experience, and then extract some reasonably specific aspects for close study. In this way, hopefully, much of this work will range across the analytic levels described earlier, thereby contributing to inter-disciplinarity.

In discussing potential problems that may arise with the use of broad abstract theories, Bouchard (1992) has warned that holistic approaches may lead researchers and practitioners to overlook more focused, yet important issues. One such issue is that of exercise prescription and the need to identify the correct "dose" of physical activity necessary to elicit certain physical or psychological health outcomes, or "responses." Many health researchers argue, for example, that in order to derive measurable protection from cardiovascular disease, physical activity must be regular, reasonably frequent (three or more times per week), and of sufficient intensity to bring about a cardiovascular "training effect." Bouchard has concerns that broad concepts such as active living, which emphasize personal choice and encourage involvement in all forms of physical activity, including low- through high-intensity, may be overly encompassing. Such an approach, he argues, may divert researchers' and practitioners' attention from important questions relating to the "dose-response" issue by focusing on forms of physical activity that may not have any discernible physical health benefits.

Given current research trends, however, it seems likely that researchers will continue to investigate the various types and levels of exercise needed to bring about specific physical health benefits, even while recommending a holistic understanding of physical activity. A holistic perspective may even contribute to an expansion of the whole dose-response question, so that a much broader range of potential health and social benefits is examined. These could include physical and psychological benefits to the individual as well as the broader social, environmental, and economic consequences of a physically active population. In this view, a holistic approach and more specific research foci can be both compatible and mutually beneficial. Research that is narrow and specific can and should be pursued by the researcher, with the understanding that it constitutes a smaller piece in the much larger puzzle of physical activity phenomena. This approach would seem to make the most sense for scientists, practitioners, and policy makers alike, and will yield valuable insights into human physical activity.

Furthermore, the task of bringing together research findings from various disciplines and interdisciplinary research for stock-taking and possible synthesis should be pursued regularly and vigorously. Publications such as those included in the present volume have an important contribution to make to the field, and should be strongly encouraged.

PROBLEMS OF A HOLISTIC APPROACH

As a field of study, the physical activity sciences have made genuine contributions to our understanding, and will play an important role in the future. At the same time, the field will also face some challenges that are more political than intellectual. We will consider these before we conclude.

One political problem pertains to nomenclature and identity. University departments responsible for training and research in this field are known by a wide variety of names, including "kinesiology," "human movement studies," "human development," "applied health sciences," "physical education," and many others. This lack of a common nomenclature reflects a historical lack of a common identity among the many disciplines that make up the broader field of study. In discussing this problem, Bouchard (1992) has proposed the use of the term "physical activity sciences." This he defines as "the field of study devoted to the understanding of all aspects of human physical activity (biological, physical, behavioral, and social) and the application of this understanding to meet the needs of the entire population" (p. 5). It is hoped that the adoption and use of this term will bring greater coherence and integrity to the field and encourage a more holistic study of physical activity phenomena.

Another political challenge the field will likely face in coming years is that of increased competition for funds associated with shrinking financial resources of governments, universities, and colleges in North America and abroad. Universities and colleges will likely embark on a painful but necessary restructuring phase. Some faculties, departments, and programs may close as a result, others may be downsized. A small few may be expanded and their budgets increased. How will physical activity studies fare in this restructuring?

The answers to these questions are unclear. Multidisciplinary university departments may choose depth over breadth in particular subfields, resulting in an increasing specialization and an accompanying loss of an interdisciplinary perspective. These dynamics will have consequences both for research and for the training of graduates who will form the next generation of researchers in this field.

The importance of opportunities for interdisciplinary training in the development of holistic research is highlighted by the contributors' biographical accounts of their work contained in the "In Perspective" pieces at the beginning of each chapter. Training in more than one discipline, and work in multidisciplinary academic settings, is common in the authors' backgrounds. Most of them indicate how these experiences have influenced their interdisciplinary approach in the study of activity.

Moreover, the case for a multidisciplinary, interdisciplinary understanding of physical activity has been made so compelling by the research literature to date that any return to narrower, less adequate faculty complements may put departments at a competitive disadvantage in recruiting students and research grant dollars. Hopefully, this will provide a valuable disincentive against retrenchment of interdisciplinary programs. Continued funding for interdisciplinary and multidisciplinary work from government and other funding agencies will also be important for maintaining the strength of such programs although it is not yet clear how current cutbacks in funding might affect holistic research.

In closing, we will address a misperception of interdisciplinary work that can interfere with recruitment of students and new scholars to holistic studies. It is sometimes argued that interdisciplinary research is difficult because one must cover more ground than is reasonable in interdisciplinary training. In other words, one must learn all of two or more disciplines (say, sociology and psychology) or that one needs to acquire two PhDs. This is a false view, as Campbell (1969) has shown in a marvelous article on what he calls "omniscience." By this he means various types of interdisciplinary studies such as physical activity studies.

Campbell emphasizes that no scholar in any particular field or discipline knows all there is to learn within that field; scholars must quickly specialize when they pursue research in order to assimilate the myriad details and problems related to their specific research topics. The problem is not one of specialization, however. All scholars specialize. It is a question of whether one specializes largely *within* one discipline or *across* disciplines in studying some particular topics. Scholars interested in interfield studies, such as physical activity research, must specialize across disciplines, and they easily do so.

According to Campbell, what hinders most people from choosing interfield studies is that the scholars in various fields in traditional, more narrowly defined university programs are often ethnocentric—they believe that what is known and being taught in their own field or department is more important than what is being studied in other fields or departments. To the extent that this message is taught to, and accepted by, undergraduate and graduate students who are majoring in studies in these departments, these young scholars are less likely to acquire an interdisciplinary perspective or a preference for holistic approaches to research. Of course, many university programs take a broader perspective toward physical activity training, and it is in these programs where future interdisciplinary researchers are more likely to develop.

The ethnocentrism of people in different fields of study, along with individuals' perceptions of their own best interests, will influence patterns of decision making. It may be that faculty members who are trained in interdisciplinary programs (as opposed to narrow or disciplinary programs) and involved in interdisciplinary research will argue against any narrowing of the breadth of disciplines and resist any changes to a less heterogeneous department, or university, during difficult financial times. The same hypothesis can be applied to university administrators outside the interdisciplinary departments. The more interdisciplinary their own work and training, the more supportive they likely will be of interdisciplinary programs.

It will be important to monitor university restructuring and hiring dynamics during the next few years. We hope that the pressures of increased financial restraint do not result in major dismantling or truncating of important, successful, interdisciplinary programs.

On a more optimistic note, the abundant evidence of the importance of the holistic approach in the scholarly work of previous decades will continue to counterbalance potential opposition to interdisciplinary research.

CONCLUSION

This volume has presented systematic reviews of scholarly knowledge about physical activity from the perspective of seven fields of study. Research has been carried out both within the conceptual domains of the specific fields and in the areas between the fields; that is, on the linkages of the conceptual domains of the fields. There has been much more intense and sustained research of the first type (intrafield) than the second (interfield). Some important questions of the linkages between the domains of the fields need to be addressed, and they will continue to be studied. There is much more research, both intrafield and interfield, remaining to be done, as the chapters and our preceding arguments make clear. Taken together, the two types of research constitute a holistic study of physical activity. A holistic research approach may face some organizational and political problems in the future. However, physical activity is clearly many processes occurring simultaneously—physical, biological, psychological, sociological, cultural, and environmental—and thus the multifaceted nature of human physical activity will continue to create a strong demand for multidisciplinary and interdisciplinary studies.

REFERENCES

Bouchard, C. (1992). The field of the physical activity sciences. In C. Bouchard, B.D. McPherson, & A.W. Taylor (Eds.), *Physical activity sciences* (pp. 1-8). Champaign, IL: Human Kinetics.

Campbell, D.T. (1969). Ethnocentrism of disciplines and the fish-scale model of omniscience. In M. Sherif & C.W. Sherif (Eds.), *Interdisciplinary relationships in the social sciences* (pp. 328-348). Chicago: Aldine.

Fitness Canada. (1991). *Active living: A conceptual overview.* Ottawa: Government of Canada.

Gauvin, L., Wall, A.E.T., & Quinney, H.A. (1994). Physical activity, fitness, and health: Research and practice. In H.A. Quinney, L. Gauvin, & A.E.T. Wall (Eds.), *Toward active living: Proceedings of the international conference on physical activity, fitness, and health.* (pp. 1-5). Champaign, IL: Human Kinetics.

Glassford, R.G. (1992). History of the physical activity sciences. In C. Bouchard, B.D. McPherson, & A.W. Taylor (Eds.), *Physical activity sciences* (pp. 9-12). Champaign, IL: Human Kinetics.

Landry, F. (1992). Science and physical activity. In C. Bouchard, B.D. McPherson, & A.W. Taylor (Eds.), *Physical activity sciences* (pp. 21-29). Champaign, IL: Human Kinetics.

Turner, J. (1991). *The structure of sociological theory.* Belmont, LA: Wadsworth.

INDEX

ABOUT THE CONTRIBUTORS

Claude Bouchard is a professor of exercise physiology and founder of the Laboratoire des Sciences de L'activité Physique at the Université Laval in Québec, Canada. His research deals with the role of genes in adaptation to exercise training, and in obesity and various nutritional stresses.

Thomas L. (Tim) Burton specializes in the study of leisure policy and planning. Dr. Burton studied political economy at the University of London, England. He is currently a professor of leisure studies at the University of Alberta, Canada.

Mihaly Csikszentmihalyi is well-known for his extensive work on the psychology of flow and optimal experience. Dr. Csikszentmihalyi is currently a professor of psychology and education in the Department of Psychology at the University of Chicago.

Richard Gruneau is a professor of communication in the School of Communication at Simon Fraser University, British Columbia, Canada. Dr. Gruneau's current research examines informal mechanisms of selection and "censorship" in news production in Canada.

Barry D. McPherson is Dean of Graduate Studies and Research at Wilfred Laurier University in Canada. Dr. McPherson's research focuses on sociocultural aspects of aging, leisure, physical activity, and public policy.

Louise B. Russell is a professor in the Department of Economics and Research at Rutgers University. She also chairs the health care policy division in the Institute of Health, Health Care Policy, and Aging Research at Rutgers. Her major area of research is the economics of medical care.

Nancy Theberge is a professor at the University of Waterloo, Canada, where she holds a joint appointment in the departments of kinesiology and sociology. Dr. Theberge's main areas of research are gender relations, the sociology of sport, and the sociology of the body.

Leonard M. Wankel is a professor with the faculty of education and recreation at the University of Alberta, Canada. His recent research focuses on factors influencing regular physical activity involvement, with particular emphasis on the nature and importance of enjoyment.

ABOUT THE EDITORS

James E. Curtis, PhD, is a professor of sociology and faculty member of the applied health sciences and health studies and the gerontology departments at the University of Waterloo in Ontario. Dr. Curtis has more than 20 years' experience as a teacher and researcher in the field of sociology of physical activity and sport. His other principal research interests include voluntary association activity, social inequality, comparative sociology, and the sociology of knowledge.

In addition to his teaching and research duties, Dr. Curtis has been the editor of various scholarly journals and consulted widely for governmental organizations and journals. A prolific contributor to the professional literature, he has coauthored several books, most notably *The Social Significance of Sport, Social Inequality in Canada,* and *The Sociology of Knowledge*. He also was editor of the *Canadian Review of Sociology and Anthropology* from 1989 to 1992.

Dr. Curtis is a member of the North American Society for Sociology of Sport and the North American Society for the Psychology of Sport and Physical Activity (NASPSPA).

Storm J. Russell, PhD, is a senior researcher with the Canadian Fitness and Lifestyle Research Institute, where she conducts research in health and physical activity behavior, theories and models of behavioral change, and physical activity and lifestyles in Canada.

Dr. Russell received her PhD in psychology from the University of Queensland in Australia in 1990. Her work on the structure of expert knowledge in sport, quantitative and qualitative research methodologies, and health and physical activity behavior has been published in the *Journal of Applied Sport Psychology, Pediatric Exercise Science,* the *International Journal of Sport and Exercise Psychology,* the *Sport Psychologist,* the *International Journal of Sport Psychology,* and in edited volumes, such as the *Handbook on Research in Sport Psychology* (1993) and *Movement and Sport: Psychological Foundations and Effects (1994).* She is a member of the Editorial Board of the *International Journal of Sport Psychology* and a reviewer for a variety of scholarly journals and boards. Dr. Russell and her colleagues at the Institute also provide ongoing direction and data to the Canadian government in the form of position papers, scientific reports, and research expertise for the development of national physical activity and health policy.

Dr. Russell is a member of the International Council for Physical Activity and Fitness Research, International Society of Sport Psychology, the Association for the Advancement of Applied Sport Psychology, and the NASPSPA.